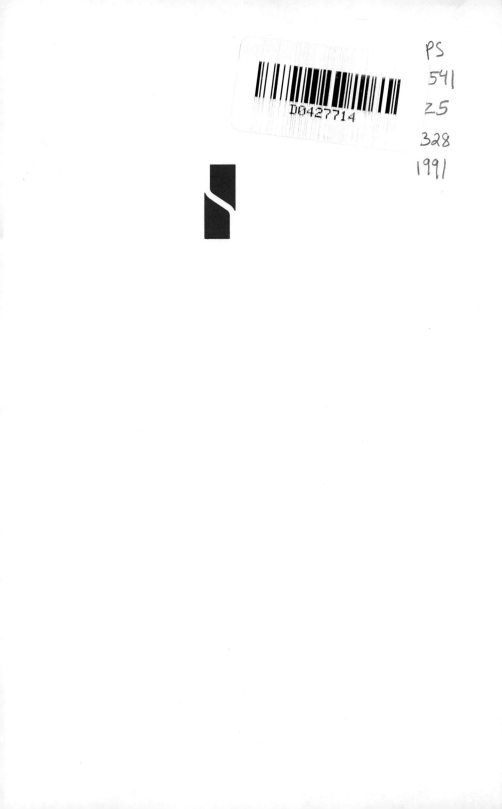

Ad Feminam: Women and Literature
Edited by Sandra M. Gilbert

Christina Rosetti
The Poetry of Endurance
By Dolores Rosenblum

The Literary Existence of Germaine de Staël
By Charlotte Hogsett

Margaret Atwood
Vision and Forms
Edited by Kathryn VanSpanckeren and Jan Garden Castro

He Knew She Was Right
The Independent Woman in the Novels of Anthony Trollope
By Jane Nardin

The Woman and the Lyre
Women Writers in Classical Greece and Rome
By Jane McIntosh Snyder

Refiguring the Father
New Feminist Readings of Patriarchy
Edited by Patricia Yaeger and Beth Kowaleski-Wallace

Writing in the Feminine
Feminism and Experimental Writing in Quebec
By Karen Gould

Lunacy of Light
Emily Dickinson and the Experience of Metaphor
Wendy Barker

Southern Illinois University Press
Carbondale and Edwardsville

To Larry

Library of Congress Cataloging-in-Publication Data

Barker, Wendy.
    Lunacy of light: Emily Dickinson and the experience of metaphor /
Wendy Barker.
      p. cm.—(Ad feminam)
    Includes bibliographical references and indexes.
    1. Dickinson, Emily. 1830–1886—Criticism and interpretation.
    2. Feminism and literature—United States—History—19th century.
    3. Light and darkness in literature. 4. Metaphor. I. Title.
    II. Series.
PS1541.Z5B28 1991
811'.4—dc20   90-40929
                                                CIP
ISBN 0-8093-1707-9 (pbk.)

Contents

Ad Feminam: Women and Literature

Ad Hominem: to the man; appealing to personal interests, prejudices, or emotions rather than to reason; *an argument ad hominem.*
—*American Heritage Dictionary*

Until quite recently, much literary criticism, like most humanistic studies, has been in some sense constituted out of arguments *ad hominem*. Not only have examinations of literary history tended to address themselves "to the man"—that is, to the identity of what was presumed to be the *man* of letters who created our culture's monuments of unaging intellect—but many aesthetic analyses and evaluations have consciously or unconsciously appealed to the "personal interests, prejudices, or emotions" of male critics and readers. As the title of this series is meant to indicate, the intellectual project called "feminist criticism" has sought to counter the limitations of *ad hominem* thinking about literature by asking a series of questions addressed *ad feminam:* to the woman as both writer and reader of texts.

First, and most crucially, feminist critics ask, what is the relationship between gender and genre, between sexuality and textuality? But in mediating on these issues they raise a number of more specific questions. Does a woman of letters have a literature—a language, a history, a tradition—of her own? Have conventional methods of canon-formation tended to exclude or marginalize female achievements? More generally, do men and women have different modes of literary representation, different definitions of literary production? Do such differences mean that distinctive male- (or female-)

authored images of women (or men), as well as distinctly male and female genres, are part of our intellectual heritage? Perhaps most important, are literary differences between men and women essential or accidental, biologically determined or culturally constructed?

Feminist critics have addressed themselves to these problems with increasing sophistication during the last two decades, as they sought to revise, or at times replace, *ad hominem* arguments with *ad feminam* speculations. Whether explicating individual texts, studying the oeuvre of a single author, examining the permutations of a major theme, or charting the contours of a tradition, these theorists and scholars have consistently sought to define literary manifestations of difference and to understand the dynamics that have shaped the accomplishments of literary women.

As a consequence of such work, feminist critics, often employing new modes of analysis, have begun to uncover a neglected female tradition along with a heretofore hidden history of the literary dialogue between men and women. This series is dedicated to publishing books that will use innovative as well as traditional interpretive methods in order to help readers of both sexes achieve a clearer consciousness of that neglected but powerful tradition and a better understanding of that hidden history. Reason tells us, after all, that if, transcending prejudice and special pleading, we speak to, and focus on, the woman as well as the man—if we think *ad feminam* as well as *ad hominem*—we will have a better chance of understanding what constitutes the human.

Sandra M. Gilbert

Acknowledgments

Ten years ago I discovered the body of Emily Dickinson's poetry to be radically different from the isolated poems of Emily Dickinson I had previously read, and energized by the burgeoning number of excellent feminist critical studies, I began to build this book.

Since that time many people have aided in the growth and completion of this manuscript. I am grateful to James Woodress for his kind, sustained encouragement and to Joanne Feit Deihl for her thoughtful, pertinent suggestions. I also wish to thank Nicolas J. Perella for his interest in the project at a crucial point in the early planning stages and Susan Gubar for her clear insights and wise advice. Others have provided helpful references and suggestions: among them, Elyse Blankley, Alan E. Craven, Nancy Gutierrez, Andrea Hammer, Theresa M. Kelley, Arthur Orman, and Denise Rankin. In particular, I owe thanks to Barbara Clarke Mossberg, for offering not only warm encouragement but also incisive criticism in the last stages of revision. I am grateful, in addition, to the University of Texas at San Antonio for a Faculty Research Grant to help with manuscript preparation. And to Teresa White at Southern Illinois University Press I am especially grateful; she has been an ideal editor.

Others have helped in more intangible, and yet invaluable, ways: Mark Allen, Helen Aristar-Dry, Margaret Bedrosian, Judy Fisher, Elliot Gilbert, and Martha Smith have offered the best sort of "Society" for the stoniest "Soul." Finally, the energy, expertise, wit, patience, and understanding that Sandra M. Gilbert has unstintingly provided can never be adequately acknowledged. Similarly, my debt to family members will be difficult to repay; I am keenly aware of the patience it has taken to live with this project. My son, David, has demonstrated an understanding uncanny for someone of his years and shares with his father, Larry, in the dedication of this book. On the most obvious level, my gratitude is due to Larry for entering several early drafts of the manuscript on a word processor and for patiently teaching me, later, to use the word processor myself. But on less obvious levels, I must say that without him, none of it would ever have happened at all—there would never have been any comfortable shade, any quiet private space, to begin with.

Quotations from the poems of Emily Dickinson are reprinted by the publishers and the Trustees of Amherst College from *The Poems of Emily Dickinson*, edited by Thomas H. Johnson, Cambridge, Mass.: The Belknap Press of Harvard University Press, Copyright 1951, © 1955, 1979, 1983 by the President and Fellows of Harvard College, and from *The Complete Poems of Emily Dickinson* edited by Thomas H. Johnson, Copyright 1914, 1929, 1935, 1942 by Martha Dickinson Bianchi; Copyright © renewed 1957, 1963 by Mary L. Hampson. By permission of Little, Brown and Company. Poem 1455, "Opinion is a flitting thing," is reprinted from *Life and Letters of Emily Dickinson* by Martha Dickinson Bianchi. Copyright 1924 by Martha Dickinson Bianchi. Copyright renewed 1952 by Alfred Leete Hampson. Reprinted by permission of Houghton Mifflin Company.

Lines from "For Archeologists" by Margaret Atwood are reprinted from *Procedures for Underground: Poems by Margaret Atwood*, Copyright © 1970 by Oxford University Press (Canadian Branch); first appeared in *Poetry*. By permission of Little, Brown and Company, in association with The Atlantic Monthly Press, and by permission of Oxford University Press (Canadian Branch). Lines from "Eating Fire" and "Song of the Worms" from *You Are Happy*, Copyright © 1974 by Margaret Atwood, are reprinted by permission of Harper & Row, Publishers, Inc., and Phoebe Larmore. "Heat" and lines from "The Moon in Your Hands" from *H. D., Collected Poems*, Copyright© by the Estate of Hilda Doolittle, are reprinted by permission of New Directions Publishing Corporation and Carcanet New Press, Ltd. "Noon of the Sunbather" is reprinted from *Breaking Camp*, Copyright © 1968 by Marge Piercy, by permission of Wesleyan University Press. Lines from "Mother-Right" from *The Dream of a Common Language, Poems 1974–1977*, by Adrienne Rich, are reprinted by permission of the author and W. W. Norton & Company, Inc., Copyright © 1978 by W. W. Norton & Company, Inc.

Lunacy of Light

Introduction

Gender, Hierarchy, and the Great Principle of Light

                              What
One believes is what matters. Ecstatic identities
Between one's self and the weather and the things
Of the weather are the belief in one's element.
Wallace Stevens[1]

Activity/passivity,
Sun/Moon,
Culture/Nature,
Day/Night,

Father/Mother,
Head/heart,
Intelligible/sensitive,
Logos/Pathos.

Form, convex, step, advance, seed, progress.
Matter, concave, ground—which supports the step,
   receptacle.
Man
——————
Woman   *Hélène Cixous[2]*

    When in 1859 Emily Dickinson casually asked a friend "Are you afraid of the sun?"[3] she poses a question that metaphorically reverberates throughout the canon of her seventeen hundred-odd poems. Sounding rather like an encoded test for entrance to a private club, Dickinson's question in fact reveals a major theme of

I

her poetry. Repeatedly in Dickinson's writing, images of sun dazzle only to abandon, beckon only to burn, while images of darkness—although at times suggesting the awful finality of death—frequently provide quiet refuge from the often-frightening and obliterating rays of the sun. In many instances Dickinson associates the sun and daylight with her Calvinist God, with the expectations of the fathers, with housework and daily duty, and with male sexuality: in short, the sun's light comes to represent male energy, male power. In making these associations, moreover, she shares in a countertradition formed by women writers ranging from Anne Finch to Anne Sexton, a tradition in which the normative cultural associations of sun and of darkness are radically revised. But although Dickinson's light/dark imagery compares to that of many other women, no other female writer has used such imagery so spectacularly or so consistently. A metaphoric pattern of light and dark assumes obsessive proportions in this poet's work: single-word references to sun or to light, for instance, occur in the poems almost a thousand times.[4]

Perhaps the preponderance of sun imagery in Dickinson's poems can be explained by a suggestion of Martin Wand and Richard B. Sewall, that Dickinson may have suffered from the genetic optic condition exotropia, a misalignment of the pupils that might have caused eye strain and sensitivity to light.[5] These theories could certainly account for Dickinson's often painfully intense images of light, and they could also explain why such imagery dominates in many of the poems. As her male contemporary Walt Whitman demonstrated extreme sensitivity to touch, Dickinson exhibits extreme sensitivity to light. And just as the branches of Whitman's enormous *oeuvre* grew from the metaphoric seeds suggested by his title *Leaves of Grass*, so is the fabric of Dickinson's 1775 poems in large part woven, warp and woof, with metaphoric threads of light and dark.

Whereas David Porter, for instance, has complained that a "sure sense of coherence in Emily Dickinson's poetry evades readers of her piecemeal canon," I shall argue that *The Poems of Emily Dickinson* can be read as a life work with far more unity than many readers have recognized.[6] I shall show, moreover, that her poetry is shaped by metaphoric clusters as significant—and as essential to an under-standing of her work—as such clusters are in the poetry of someone like Yeats. Along with Thomas Johnson, I believe that this poet "thought in poetry." And to think in poetry is to think in images, in metaphors.

First glimmerings of light/dark metaphors actually begin in Dickinson's writings about fifteen years before any mention of her optical difficulties; letters written between 1846 and 1851 show the youthful poet already developing imagery that expresses her sense of opposition to the sun. In fact, even this early, she is not only describing the light of day with painful ambivalence, but she is also associating the sun's light with constraints upon her ability to communicate, with constraints upon her own use of language, her intellectual freedom.[7] These early associations develop into a pat-tern of metaphor that reveals her most central conflicts as a woman and as a poet, and, in addition, her artistic strategy for transcending these conflicts.

But although Dickinson's poems have often been described as linguistically private, the metaphors I shall examine are hardly unique to the Amherst Poet. And whereas many have tended to view this poet's writings as isolate phenomena, as comprising a closed, internally linked circuit, as if her own word "circumference" described a tight circle surrounding her writings like a wall with no door, more and more recent critics are pointing to her correspon-dence with the world, to her soul's relation to her society. Barbara Mossberg analyzes her relation to her family, Barton Levi St. Armand discusses her relation to cultural practices and popular literature of the mid-nineteenth century, Shira Wolosky examines her relation to the Civil War, Sandra Gilbert and Susan Gubar study her relation to the nineteenth-century literary imagination and in particular to other female texts, and Jack Capps has shown the extent of her reading. Richard Sewall, of course, in his thorough biography, has examined her relations to family members, friends, social and artistic community, and to literature.[8] Dickinson did not write in a cultural vacuum. She would have been keenly aware, for instance, of Emerson's dictum that "Every natural fact is a symbol of some spiritual fact. . . . Every appearance in nature corresponds to some state of the mind."[9] Although, to be sure, physiological difficulties may have provided the impetus for her frequent association of light with pain, nevertheless, to rely solely upon a medical rationale for the profusion of these images throughout the poems would be to ignore the pervasiveness and complexity of Dickinson's metaphorical associations and their correspondences to similar metaphors occurring in the works of other writers. It would also be to deny the enormous power of these images as metaphors throughout history, throughout the culture which Emily Dickinson inhabited.

If, as Jonathan Culler has clearly stated, "a culture is composed of a set of symbolic systems," then one of our most dominant sets of symbols revolves around images of sunlight, just as the literal earth revolves around the literal sun. Culler has also, however, warned that "In the case of nonlinguistic signs there is always a danger that their meanings will seem natural; one must view them with a certain detachment to see that their meanings are in fact the products of a culture, the result of shared assumptions and conventions."[10]

The star we depend upon for life and health has long been invested with numerous meanings, many of them, of course, naturally linked to its literal functions. Traditionally, the sun has represented vitality, the life force itself, whereas darkness, or absence of sun, has represented loss of that life, death. Darkness is chaos, light is order; darkness is evil, light is good; darkness is Satan, light is God. And the sun has also traditionally been considered masculine. According to Plato's explanation of the sexes' origins, for instance, the male sex sprang from the sun and the female sex from the earth; a third sex, he imagined, originated from the moon, composed of both sun and earth.[11] In addition, sun gods have normally been male; one thinks of the Egyptian Ra, and especially of Apollo, who for the Greeks governed not only light but also music and poetry. For Nietzsche, Apollo was "the god of all shaping energies," the "shining one" who rules "over the fair appearance of the inner world of fantasies." Whereas "Apollonian" light creates orderly and harmonious artistic expressions, "Dionysian" darkness consists of chaotic, unexamined, and uncontrolled primitive urges.[12]

Of even more significance for Emily Dickinson are the metaphoric valuings of the Judeo-Christian tradition which, as such writers as Joseph Campbell have explained, accelerated what he has labeled the victory of the "solar view."[13] Judith Ochshorn more recently has argued that until the flowering of Western monotheism, "divine power was not seen as the exclusive prerogative of either sex, and the ascription of power to deities of one sex was rarely associated with the inferiority of the other." Ochshorn insists that only since the development of Judeo-Christian monotheistic culture has deity been regarded as essentially masculine and as all-powerful, a view that has deeply affected both women and men throughout the history of Western culture.[14] That the Judeo-Christian divinity has also been associated with the sun has had enormous ramifications for women. Not only does the Old Testament God create light and call it good, thereby immediately associating light with language, but the New Testament God also creates light in the form of Christ as the "sun of righteousness," the light of the world. The extent to which Christian culture has insisted upon a strictly solar view of divinity is evidenced especially by the Nicene Creed, which does not even mention the "feminine" darkness: "We believe in one God, the Father all-Sovereign, maker of all things, both visible and invisible: And in one Lord Jesus Christ, the Son of God, begotten of the Father, God from God, *Light from Light*" (emphasis mine).[15] Here even Mary the mother, any suggestion of the dark womb, any aspect of a female goddess of earth or darkness, has been supplanted by a completely solar and masculine view of divinity.

Such hierarchical valuations of light and dark—and by implication, masculine and feminine—have dominated our culture as philosophical dualism; Hélène Cixous argues in her suggestions for deconstructing classical philosophical and psychoanalytic thought that throughout literature and philosophy, thought has worked by "Dual, *hierarchized* oppositions." "Male," she argues, has always been identified with activity, the sun, and the day, and "female" has always been identified with passivity, the moon, and the night.[16] It follows that according to this binary, hierarchical pattern that Cixous proposes as the essence of patriarchy, women are excluded from the world of light, which is, also, after all, the world of life, thought, and language. An exceptionally striking analysis of the influence of this hierarchical pattern is Luce Irigaray's demonstration that Plato's parable of the cave, with its contrast between a dark maternal womb and a divine paternal *logos*, represents just one in a series of philosophical categories that have relegated the feminine to a position of subordination.[17]

Such culturally-embedded polarities cause acute difficulties for a woman writer. Indeed, although our culture revolves around a universally-shared assumption about the generative and divine aspects of the sun, one can readily see from legend and literature that the sun as image has not always engendered health—indeed, it has not always been available—in the same way for women as it has for men.

A short story by D. H. Lawrence, for instance, graphically depicts the effects of the metaphoric pattern I have been describing. In "The Woman Who Rode Away," a young Indian man tells a white woman, "our men are the fire and the day-time, and our women are spaces between the stars at night." When she asks, "Aren't the women even stars?" he answers, "No"; when she asks, "Have I got to die and be given to the sun?" he laughs and answers, "Some time." This woman is in fact eventually quite literally "yielded up" to the sun, to use Dickinson's words. Lawrence's female character is "given to the sun" by being killed: deep in the back of a cave, legs outstretched, she is figuratively raped and literally knifed to death at the precise moment that the setting sun's rays hit her body.

Lawrence's story is of a woman who, in losing her life, supposedly saves a race of people, thereby righting a universal imbalance: white men have misused the sun, or power, and now with the sacrifice of one white woman, the ancient tribe will supposedly be able to use the sun and its forces wisely.[18] In this sense, the sacrificed woman becomes a savior of a people, a kind of goddess, for the suggestion of sexual union with the sun is in itself a suggestion of divinity, impregnation by the sun causing one to bear the divine light within one's own womb, so that one in a sense becomes the divine mother oneself.

This idea of the sun's impregnating women is a common one in legend: in Greek myth, Danae is impregnated by a shower of gold. A Siberian legend also uses similar imagery to tell a similar story:

A Certain Khan had a fair daughter, whom he kept in a dark iron house, that no man might see her. An old woman tended her; and when the girl was grown to maidenhood she asked the old woman, "Where do you go so often?" "My child," said the old dame, "there is a bright world. In that bright world your father and mother live, and all sorts of people live there. That is where I go." The maiden said, "Good mother, I will tell nobody, but show me that bright world." So the old woman took the girl out of the iron house. But when she saw the bright world, the girl tottered and fainted; and the eye of God fell upon her, and she conceived. Her angry father put her in a golden chest and sent her floating away.[19]

The messages implicit in a tale such as this one are many, but the correlation between the bright world of the sun, divinity, and masculine sexuality is very clear. On the one hand, in the light, the maiden is not strong enough even to stand on her own feet: she stumbles and loses consciousness. But on the other hand, after receiving the rays of the sun, the eye of God, she carries divinity within her own body and, containing a power of her own, becomes a threat to her father's authority. If we extend the metaphor in Lawrence's story that women are the spaces between stars, it would follow, then, that any light directed at those dark spaces would eradicate them *as dark spaces*, or as traditionally thought-of female beings. Lighting up these areas of darkness would cause them to contain light themselves, to contain the qualities associated with light: energy, power, divinity.

Sir James Frazer has shown that in many primitive cultures girls were ritually kept away from the sun, sometimes for months, sometimes even for years. According to Frazer, a Cambodian girl at puberty was said to "enter into the shade," was secluded from the rest of the community, and was kept from the light. In a British Columbian tribe, a girl attaining puberty was forced to sit motionless indoors for four days. If for some reason she had to leave the house in which she had been isolated, she was required to wear a large hat which would protect her face from the sun, for "if the sun were to shine on her face her eyes would suffer." (The nineteenth-century European and American use of parasols seems amazingly close to such "primitive" customs.) In some of the cultures described by Frazer, girls menstruating for the first time were isolated, sewn into closed hammocks, and kept away from both ground and light for extended periods of time. On being freed, these girls would walk blinking and exhausted into the sun—to meet a bridegroom and be married.[20] The implications of such customs are far reaching. One fear quite obviously expressed by these rites is that of a girl's too-early sexual initiation, causing social difficulties for family and community. Removing her both from the community and from the sun as symbol of masculine sexual power will keep her "safe" until marriage. But it is also clear that in keeping the girl away from the sun, community members symbolically deny power of any kind to the maturing girl herself. Just as she is developing her adult sexuality, she is removed from the source of energy and power, the sun, for a period long enough to ensure her emergence as one of the spaces between stars, with no expectation of ever becoming a star—a sun—herself.

The customs outlined by Frazer may seem remote and farfetched, but this metaphoric pattern with its sexual and social implications pervades even the popular literature of Dickinson's own time. The "fairy" stories of the enormously popular nineteenth-century Christian moralist George MacDonald, for instance, which frequently consist of thinly veiled metaphoric lessons for young men and women, draw upon traditional hierarchized oppositions associated with images of light and dark. MacDonald was well known in America during Dickinson's lifetime, receiving unprecedented receptions from American audiences in 1872–73. His short stories have been collected by Glenn Edward Sadler, who remarks that Macdonald's fantasies are especially interesting for their "subverbal aspects, or natural symbols."[21] Natural symbols of light and dark figure particularly in "The History of Photogen and Nycteris," a "little" fairy story that represents one more instance in a long line of "stories" that retell the victory of the solar view and reemphasize the implicit misogyny in Judeo-Christian thought, reminding readers of their prescribed sexual/social roles.

MacDonald's story involves two children who are raised by a wicked witch, Watho. The boy of the pair, Photogen, is brought up entirely in the daytime, never allowed to see the night, but encouraged to bask "in the full splendour of the sun," to grow like a "live thunderbolt." However, the female child, Nycteris, is forced to sleep during the day, confined to a tomblike room lit only by one lamp, which does not even provide reading light. Taught very little, and vaguely but urgently wanting "more room," she follows a firefly outside to the breeze and the moonlight. Photogen, however, displays no such curiosity about the darkness. In fact, when he accidentally remains outside one evening, terror of the night overwhelms him. Coincidentally meeting Nycteris, he describes the sun as "the soul, the life, the heart, the glory of the universe." As the sun begins finally to rise again, so does his confidence. In contrast, however, at the sun's approach the girl Nycteris fears that she will be blinded—or killed. She cries out to the arrogant Photogen, "Don't leave me: oh, don't leave me. . . . I am dying! I am dying! I cannot move. The light sucks all the strength out of me." Photogen responds by bounding up a hill like Apollo himself, while Nycteris is left below, her mind "pierced" by the arrows of the sun.

Finally, of course, in good fairy-tale fashion, the pair marry. We are told, moreover, that before a year has passed "Nycteris had come to love the day best, because it was the clothing and crown of Photogen, and she saw that the day was greater than the night, and the sun more lordly than the moon." The last sentence of the story provides the turn of the screw for any "resisting reader," to borrow Judith Fetterley's phrase:[22] "But who knows," Nycteris asks her young husband, "that, when we go out, we shall not go into a day as much greater than your day is greater than my night?"[23] Nycteris could well have added what Milton's Eve pledges to Adam: "My Author and Disposer, what thou bidd'st / Unargu'd I obey; so God ordains, / God is thy Law, thou mine: to know no more / Is woman's happiest knowledge and her praise."[24] After reading such a tale, a young female reader in England or America would have a clear reminder of her place in the sociosexual pecking order.

MacDonald's Chistian moral, moreover, that God and his Light are as much greater than man and his sunlight as these are greater than woman and her moonlight or lamplight, is also closely related to the pagan customs described by Frazer. Like the tribal girls, Nycteris is kept away from the sun until her optic nerves grow so sensitive she is almost blinded when she finally does come into the light. In addition, at the same time she begins to experience the light of day, she experiences what MacDonald would probably have called "the joys of marriage," or sex. Indeed, Photogen's role of guide into the light suggests the traditional custom of the sexually experienced husband guiding his innocent wife, who until now has been "kept in the dark" about such matters, into sexual awakening. That sexual enlightenment is so closely equated with divine enlightenment further underscores the difficulties this traditional pattern of light/dark imagery poses for women.[25]

We have no actual evidence that Dickinson had even dabbled in the writings of her contemporary George MacDonald, but she could not have escaped total immersion in the pervading Judeo-Christian hierarchical pattern of light/dark metaphors. Indeed, the dominance of these images in her own writing indicates that this poet was in fact responding through her writing, through her art, to the cultural dictates implicit in the dominant solar view of Western culture. In one well-known example of such a response, part of a letter that is so crucial to an understanding of Dickinson's metaphors that I shall discuss it at length in Chapter 2, the poet meditates on the entire subject of marriage in terms of a too-bright sun. Writing to her intimate friend Susan Gilbert who in 1852 is about to marry the poet's brother, Dickinson observes that both young women have avoided speaking of marriage and its realities: "You and I have been strangely silent upon this subject, Susie, we often touched upon it, and as quickly fled away, as children shut their eyes when the sun is too bright for them." And although the twenty-two-year-old Dickinson is also in a state of great excitement that Sue is about to become her own sister-in-law, she goes on in this letter to describe young wives, who, like "sweet flowers," will at noon bow their heads "in anguish before the mighty sun." This powerful sun "scorches them, scathes them"; the poet worries that "they have got through with peace—they know that the man of noon, is *mightier* than the morning and their life is henceforth to him." Dickinson's "man of noon" is a figure of intense crisis, one associated with problems such a masterful "mighty sun" would cause as husband to a "sweet" flower. Yet Dickinson's passage also shows this man of noon as seductively attractive: "think you these

thirsty blossoms will *now* need nought but—*dew*? No, they will cry
for sunlight, and pine for the burning noon," she goes on to say (*L*
I, 93). Of course the time of day of most intense light, noon, has
long been associated with a sense of crisis, often of an erotic
nature.[26] But as this key passage suggests, Dickinson's crises of light
are characterized by her uniquely female position in relation to a decidedly male solar power. For a woman, a crisis of light that involved both suggestions of divinity and eroticism involves a quali-
tatively different response from that of a male writer.

Of course, one's individual response to the physical source of life
on our planet reveals much about one's attitudes toward one's own
life and toward the universe in general. In his study of noon as
archetype throughout Italian literature, Nicolas Perella observes
that "in the choice of metaphors and images that a poet makes in
expressing the human experience and awareness of nature (i.e.,
landscapes and the weather) there is surely a clue to the poet's temperament, and one can agree with Gaston Bachelard who says that
the imagination is nothing other than the subject transported into
things."[27] The manner in which images of light occur in the works
of nineteenth-century American male writers, Dickinson's immediate literary contemporaries, suggests a very different temperament,
a very different attitude toward one's position in relation to the surrounding universe than those we shall find at work in the metaphors of Dickinson. Although images of sunlight do not appear to
dominate in the works of these writers as they do in the poems of
Dickinson, they do appear frequently, and they do in fact reveal
much about the artists' temperaments. Furthermore, it is of enormous significance to my argument that in the writings of many
nineteenth-century male poets and novelists, the sun is imaged traditionally, which is to say that it is usually seen positively, healthfully. Although an exhaustive study of light and dark imagery in
nineteenth-century literature as it reveals personal and artistic
temperaments is obviously far beyond the possible scope of this
study, nevertheless, I do want to indicate briefly how images of sunlight generally function in the normative masculine tradition of
literature that surrounded Emily Dickinson, who, as we know,
avidly read and reread many of her male contemporaries.

America's mid-nineteenth-century transcendentalists, for instance, often portray their optimism about possibilities for human growth and perfectability through imagery of light. Ralph Waldo Emerson writes of a sun that brings a tiny blackberry to full fruition: "Look at the summer blackberry lifting its polished surface a few inches from the ground. How did that little chemist extract from the sandbank the spices and sweetness it has concocted in its cells? Not so; but the whole creation has been at the cost of its birth and nurture. A globe of fire near a hundred millions of miles distant in the great space, has been flooding it with light and heat as if it shone for no other."[28] Emerson's imagery suggests that the gemlike berry's nurturing has derived entirely from the sun itself—"Light from Light"—rather than from the dark and female earth. The berry has developed its polish and sweetness (and one wonders if, for Emerson as for Dickinson, berries are metaphors for poems) because of a fructifying fatherly light. Similarly associating light with growth, he rejoices, "I expand and live in the warm day like corn and melons."[29] Furthermore, in keeping with traditional light/dark imagery, he also equates light with knowledge and darkness with ignorance; indeed, to Emerson, human knowledge—by the exercise of reason and the act of reflection, or en-lightenment—can in turn actually light the sun itself. Thus the sun and human thought are mutually sustaining, existing in a comfortable state of reciprocity and equilibrium.[30]

In a poem with which we know Dickinson was familiar (*L* III, 1004), he states his feeling that his own access to power and divinity lay in becoming a "lover of the sun":

> Burly, dozing humble-bee,
> Where thou art is clime for me.
> . . . .
> I will follow thee alone,
> Thou animated torrid-zone!
> . . . .
> Insect lover of the sun,
> Joy of thy dominion!
> Sailor of the atmosphere;
> Swimmer through the waves of air;
> Voyager of light and noon. . . .[31]

By steering toward the source of light, the humble-bee achieves superhuman wisdom and freedom from "fate and care." The sun's light and heat provide the energy to think and act, and by thinking and acting, he in turn has the power to refuel the sun—becoming as powerful or as divine as the sun itself.

Similarly, Henry David Thoreau writes of a sun that supports him in his physical and mental endeavors; in *Walden* sunlight straightens warped boards, heats the house, ripens beans, and melts winter vegetation into spring brilliance. Furthermore, the sun allows the narrator vistas of the pond's expanse and flashes of natural beauty that serve as what William Wordsworth called spiritually regenerative "spots of time." Like Emerson, Thoreau imagined his own thought and mental expansion in terms of sun imagery: "To him whose elastic and vigorous thought keeps pace with the sun, the day is a perpetual morning." Even the conclusion of *Walden* is dependent upon such imagery, for the writer joyfully affirms: "There is more day to dawn. The sun is but a morning star." Unlike Dickinson, Thoreau seems able to move in and out of sunlight as he chooses; if noon becomes too bright and hot, he simply makes his own "pleasant harbor" in the shade.[32]

According to a recollection published by Mrs. Ellen F. Dickinson, "Thoreau was naturally one of [Dickinson's] favorite authors from his love of nature and power of description."[33] But of that other major American transcendentalist, Walt Whitman, Dickinson apparently knew nothing except that "he was disgraceful" (*L* II, 261). It is significant, however, to observe that Whitman's writing, like Thoreau's, is also characterized by mobility in the sun. His light images suggest a vital connection between his own ebullience and the energy of the sun that allows him to transcend practically any situation. In "Song of Myself" he associates a "feeling of health" with "the full-noon trill, the song of me rising from bed and meeting the sun," promising the reader that "You shall possess the good of the earth and sun, (there are millions of suns left)." As he moves through physical and psychic space, he affirms, "The bright suns I see and the dark suns I cannot see are in their place." Even when he affirms the value and beauty of darkness, as in "The Sleepers," for instance, wandering "all night" through his own vision, an immense energy and mobility predominate: he steps, stops, bends, wanders, gazes, even "pierces" the darkness itself, knowing that he can return to "gallivant with the light and air" at will, unlike Dickinson, who felt herself to be, like Nycteris, pierced by the sun, and imprisoned by the dark—even as she felt herself to be, paradoxically, nurtured by the dark.[34]

In his vibrant ability to say "Yes" to both day and night, light and dark, good and evil, male and female, human and animal, Whitman is of course a writer of a very different color from Nathaniel Hawthorne, who as Melville phrased it, so grandly said "No! in thunder." But even Hawthorne says "yes" to sunlight, associating it with movement and vitality—and, as he does in *The House of the Seven Gables*, with feminine and nurturing energy. Whereas for Dickinson it is sunlight that serves as metaphor for patriarchal demands and constraints, for Hawthorne it is darkness that images the curse of the patriarchal past. In this novel, the character Phoebe represents health and vigor to the gloomy old pair of Pyncheons who have lived too long under the "shadow" of interiority. Phoebe brings life from the outside world of health, and is clearly described as an agent of sunlight itself. She is associated variously with the sunlit garden, yellow cornbread, butter, and gold; her sympathy is "sunny," and her grace is like a "gleam of sunshine falling on the floor." She is as hostile to mystery "as the sunshine to a dark corner." While brightening the corners of the Pyncheons' dark house, moreover, she acts as a protecting light over the old, dreary couple of Hepzibah and Clifford. Phoebe is also connected in the novel with the simple yet venerable Uncle Venner, who, again in contrast to the gloomy, withered old pair of Pyncheons, likes nothing better than to spend his time chatting with friends "on the sunny side of a barn." The novel concludes with Phoebe's opening the house wide to the sun, to life, and to freedom from the dark, guilt-ridden Puritan past.[35]

Sunny Phoebe is not, however, intellectual or artistic. And, like Dickinson, Hawthorne has difficulties reconciling the bright world of common sunlit dailiness with the shadowy world of uncommon imagination and art. As he gently complains in his Preface of 1859 to *The Marble Faun*, America was unfortunately still too young a country to have developed any fascinating shadows: "No author, without a trial, can conceive of the difficulty of writing a Romance about a country where there is no shadow, no antiquity, no mystery, no picturesque and gloomy wrong, nor anything but a common-place prosperity, in broad and simple daylight, as is happily the case with my dear native land. . . . Romance and poetry, like ivy, lichens, and wall-flowers, need Ruin to make them grow."[36] Such a statement comes very close to expressing the kind of poetic difficulty Dickinson often faced; simple daylight was all very well, but it did not feed the muse. However, to Dickinson, daylight was not associated with the kind of health and purity Hawthorne gives to such redeeming characters as Phoebe, or Hilda of *The Marble Faun*. As I shall show, sunlight for the Amherst poet is often as enervating as it is energizing for Hawthorne. Indeed, even with his predilection for the shadows and for art, one could argue that throughout Hawthorne's work, he continually advocates the practice of "coming clean" in the sunlight, of emerging into community and open air in order to escape the dark, destructive consequences of solopsism.

If in his introduction to *The Scarlet Letter*, "The Custom House," Hawthorne describes the combination of moonlight and coal-fire in a dark room as the perfect climate for the imagination (unlike Emerson, for instance), he also equates darkness with knowledge distorted, grown monstrous and destructive.[37] His scientific characters who probe too far into "the secrets of the human heart," such as Aylmer in "The Birthmark," are associated with a world that has shut out the sun. Similarly, in *The Scarlet Letter* both Chillingworth and Dimmesdale, whose names suggest darkness, are associated with the evil that results when truth is kept away from the light. As Dimmesdale hides his guilt from the light of day (in contrast to Hester, who carries her inner self on her breast, the gold thread of her embroidered "A" glistening in the sun's light), Chillingworth grows increasingly influential over his patient, Dimmesdale. It is Chillingworth's "dark" influence that almost destroys Dimmesdale; only at the final scene of the novel, when Dimmesdale bares his breast to the light of day in the marketplace, is the minister saved spiritually. Although Hawthorne often wrote of the artist as a shadowy character who preferred the filtered light of a windowsill to the open light of day,[38] his concern is still nevertheless that an alliance between the artist and "dark" forces results in an unhealthy and destructive alienation from the healthful, normal world of the sun—and, of course, from God.

Herman Melville is also obsessed with the results of such alienation from the normal, "pleasant sun," for his character Ahab in *Moby Dick* is consumed by an unnatural light, the "hot fire of his purpose" seeming closer to the dark fires of hell than to the "great principle of light" which he pursues. It is the artificial fire that consumes, the narrator warns: "Tomorrow, in the natural sun, the skies will be bright; those who glared like devils in the forking flames, the morn will show in far other, at least gentler, relief; the glorious, golden, glad sun, the only true lamp—all others but liars!"[39] As I shall show, such associations are very different from Dickinson's, for she often finds the sun untrustworthy, glaring, and destructive, while she defines internal fires as redemptive. In Melville's novel, however, the natural sun illuminates, whereas light kindled in the blackness of a man like Ahab, who is shut in the "caved trunk" of his body, destroys. Furthermore, although one could argue that "the great principle of light," the whale, does destroy Ahab, it is nevertheless always clear that Ahab is going after the light himself, is bent upon destroying the light, and moves freely about the earth with a crew of other men in order to try to accomplish his aim. As I shall show, in the writings of women and in particular of Emily Dickinson, the light of day seems in fact to cause immobility and powerlessness, rather than allowing one a mobility, or a power, of one's own.

Even the images of the British Romantics, whose rebelliousness against the rational order Dickinson certainly shares, do not evidence the painful ambivalence that characterizes the light/dark images of Dickinson. As Joanne Feit Diehl has demonstrated, Dickinson represents "an alternative line to the dominant male canon, the beginning of a countertradition of post-Romantic women poets. Unlike the male Romantics, Diehl argues, Dickinson cannot read the natural world as a reliable text—she "is more absorbed by what she cannot see."[40]

Thus although Wordsworth in *The Prelude*,[41] for instance, values darkness as a "blind cavern," the birthplace of the imagination, which moves "to light / And open day" (p. 520)—as I shall show, a view in many ways similar to Dickinson's notion of "Races—nurtured in the Dark"—his affirmation of the reciprocity of World and Mind is described as "A simple produce of the common day," a statement of easy confidence completely alien in character to the poems of Dickinson. And although Wordsworth is moved by a night vision of an enormous (and female) moon over Mount Snowdon, he has actively moved *to* this sublime phenomenon, and so is then also able to reflect upon this external vision, to "see, hear, perceive," the power of Nature (p. 517). Wordsworth's observations of Nature, of light and dark, are, like Whitman's, characterized by mobility—he wanders, hikes, and climbs, "Communing" with "every form of creature." Furthermore, his "holy calm," his own "auxiliar light" had originated in his early love of "visible things." As a boy, the poet tells the reader, he had loved the sun, a love that led to his ecstatic experiences of union with the natural landscape (p. 83). As I shall show, Dickinson in contrast feels herself relegated to the darkness, imprisoned there as a result of having, as she phrases it, "No Station in the Day," no place in the world of the sun. That she does in the end find imaginative and creative strength—as Karl Keller says, "the magic within the prison"[42]—from darkness requires a decidedly different metaphoric strategy from that of Wordsworth. For a woman writer, a Paradise reached by uniting with a nature revealed by the sun was, at best, a highly ambiguous kind of heaven.

Although to find Paradise in "the common day" was a common Romantic notion, for a woman to find Paradise or even simple peace in any actual common day was very difficult. As Diehl perceptively observes, Dickinson's relation to God and nature is characterized by discord, by wrestling, by a feisty determination not to be overpowered. As Diehl phrases it, "Not for her the wedding between the poet's ego and nature as bride."[43] For if she were to be the bride, and the sun—and nature—were bridegroom, such a union would be fraught with complications of social and sexual expections—that she remain passive receptacle, for instance—that would hinder the creation of poetry.[44]

In her discussion of Keats and Dickinson, Diehl posits that, in her "vision of the analogue between the origins of creativity and the paradigms of romantic (and Romantic) love, Dickinson most closely resembles Keats," one of the nineteenth-century poets we know she did read (*L* II, 261). In contrast to Dickinson, however, when Keats imagines a sexual drama free from anxiety, he expresses such an ideal love in terms of a beneficent sunlight:[45] "The flower I doubt not receives a fair guerdon from the Bee— its leaves blush deeper in the next spring—and who shall say between Man and Woman which is the most delighted? . . . but let us open our leaves like a flower and be passive and receptive—budding patiently under the eye of Apollo."[46] No scathed daisies here; the sun as "eye of Apollo" seen from Keats' perspective is not only benign but, as Walter Evert proposes, serves as symbol for the source and inspirer of song and poetry. In "Ode to Apollo," for instance, which Evert calls Keats' "clearest statement of his mythological aesthetic," poets are inspired to seize their lyres "Whose chords are solid rays and twinkle radiant fires" as Apollo sits in his "western halls of gold." Evert argues that Keats conveys sheer delight in the sun's pouring its own power lavishly into the earth to make it fruitful, "beneficently providing a golden harvest for men, that instilled in the poet a sense of some divine agency operating actively in nature." Keats often uses the color gold to suggest this entire association with Apollo, who, as classical charioteer of the golden sun, brings many of the growing things of earth to golden ripeness, and as inspirer of poetry, brings forth the richness of human thought.[47] Contrast the following passage from "I stood tip-toe upon a little hill" with Dickinson's "man of noon" letter:

> Open afresh your round of starry folds,
> Ye ardent marigolds!
> Dry up the moisture from your golden lids,
> For great Apollo bids
> That in these days your praises should be sung
> On many harps, which he has lately strung.

And when again your dewiness he kisses,
Tell him I have you in my world of blisses,
So haply when I rove in some far vale,
His mighty voice may come upon the gale.

Here the sight of sun-colored marigolds sets off a chain of associations which includes gold, poetry, and Apollo as god of both sun and song. The marigolds are even a bit like small earthly suns themselves, as golden as Apollo's lyre.

Later in this poem, Keats speaks to the moon as "Maker of sweet poets, dear delight / Of this fair world and all its gentle livers, / Spangler of clouds, halo of crystal rivers," adding "For what has made the sage or poet write / But the fair paradise of Nature's light?"[48] As Evert asserts, this adoration of the moon is for Keats simply part of the poet's adoration of the sun: just as Apollo and Artemis were classically twins of a single birth, sharing the task of illuminating the earth, for Keats "there was no time when the world was without that visible enlightenment [of] which . . . the intellectual corollary was poetic inspiration."[49] "Nature's light," then, includes the light of both sun and moon; as the moon is literally illuminated by the sun, so in Keats' thinking, the two orbs and their mythological deities are both agents of the same inspiration for poets.

Similarly, in "Endymion," the narrator is drawn to the moon-goddess through a chain of encounters: first, he is led to a spot where he can see the sun-god in full power, and by the sun's rays, sees a "magic bed" of poppies (flowers sacred to the moon-goddess Diana), whose fragrance lulls him to sleep so that he encounters the moon-goddess herself. As a lover of the sun, Endymion has been made subject to the influence of the moon. Later in the poem, in the second book, a golden butterfly guides Endymion through the evening sunset to the cave he must enter. What he sees after descending to the underworld are such visions as only the "light-bringing poets" can describe, "The mighty ones who made eternal day."[50] The light of day, symbolized by Apollo and his powers of fruition, healing, and song, coupled with the night's light represented by the moon, as a reflection of the sun, provide the inspiration for poets, who in turn also make light, providing mankind with a never-ending day of their own creating. Like Emerson, Keats finds power from the sun which enables him to add his own power to the workings of the universe.

Of course, brilliant imaginative power for the British Romantics could often stem, as well, from darkness as nurturer of the imagination, whether as Keats' "embalmed darkness," Coleridge's "deep romantic chasm," or Shelley's "awful shadow of some unseen Power" that remains "dearer for its mystery."[51] But for these nineteenth-century male writers, sunlight hardly ever impedes creativity. Light/dark images are not complicated for these writers by ramifications of gender as they are for women novelists and poets. For if to a male writer a descent into darkness represented a union of the masculine with the feminine Other, the light was familiar, home territory, an image of masculine energy. For a woman writer, however, as I shall show, darkness is no "dear mystery"; rather, it is home, a familiar place of truth, dream, and nightmare, and the daylight world is governed by a powerful, dazzling, and masculine sun.

In heeding Jonathan Culler's warning to remember that the meanings of nonlinguistic signs are products of shared cultural assumptions, we must also remember that everything we now know about Emily Dickinson tells us that this was a writer who refused to share in many of her culture's assumptions. Dickinson's rebelliousness is perhaps most significantly manifested in her refusal to accept even the basic shared human assumption that the sun's light causes growth, life, health, that the sun's light is good. In writing with such painful ambivalence about light, moreover, Dickinson reveals a great deal about her sense of her own place under the sun, about her sense of restrictions upon her own health and possibilities for growth, particularly as a woman poet striving for her own place among the immortals of her art. She was acutely aware of her place within literary tradition; she had eaten "the precious Words" of literature from girlhood.[52] A voracious reader, Dickinson was also an observant and perceptive reader. She could not have escaped noticing that the women writers she read and reread, Eliot, the Brontës, Barrett Browning, for instance, used the sun and images of light very differently from Emerson and Keats, that these nineteenth-century women wrote of the sun as a force which constrained their energies rather than freeing them.

Indeed, Emily Dickinson's intense preoccupation with gender-related artistic conflicts as imaged by sun and light, shadow and darkness, represents a female metaphoric tradition in which women writers have covertly expressed their views of societal and sexual realities in terms of light and dark. Over and over, women novelists and poets of the nineteenth century wrote from the perspective of dark spaces between stars—from an awareness that, in the dominant imaginative outlets of their culture, the sun, God, masculine vigor, sexuality, and language are all representative of each other. Such a train of associations caused great difficulty to a woman poet who—for whatever reasons— wanted to appropriate language and energy for herself. By yoking sun imagery with the repression of female energies, such writers as Charlotte Brontë, Emily Brontë, George Eliot, Elizabeth Gaskell, and Elizabeth Barrett Browning imply that the very light of their culture was hostile to intelligent women. That so many women writers demonstrate similar concerns through similar imagery is to realize a pattern that, like the warp threads on a loom, helps shape the designs of the series of complex and related tapestries we now identify as comprising a tradition of literature by women.[53] Furthermore, identifying such a pattern as the background upon which Dickinson plied her own metaphoric threads enables us to see her poems in even brighter and higher relief—perhaps, I might say, in a new light.

Charlotte Brontë, whom Dickinson admired so much that she once said it would be a great day for heaven "When 'Brontë' entered there" (*P* 148), uses light in several novels to dramatize the cultural limitations on women. In *Villette*, for instance, while visiting a gallery, Lucy Snow angrily rejects the image of a fleshy Cleopatra, wryly described as a mindless, sensual "commodity of bulk" with "broad daylight" blazing around her. Reacting with aversion to this image of woman as purely physical, Lucy calls the entire view that produces such paintings (and images of women) "clap-trap." This notion of womanhood that Lucy so furiously rejects reminds us of an observation made by another Brontë character, Shirley, when she comments that even the "cleverest, the acutest men are often under an illusion about women: they do not read them in a *true light*: they misapprehend them, both for good and evil: their good woman is a queer thing, half doll, half angel; their bad woman is almost always a fiend."[54] Somehow, Brontë implies, the light of day actually hides and distorts, rather than reveals, a woman's true nature and potential.

Similarly in Brontë's *Jane Eyre*, sunlight becomes image for expectations that hinder female development, expectations that are rejected by the main character. For example, in imagining her fate if she were to join St. John Rivers as his wife in India, Jane thinks in terms of too much sun. She instinctively fears that she would be "grilled alive" by Rivers' energy and piety, by his view of her as automatic advocate of his own principles. Becoming submissive agent of an active and overbearing master would be like being broiled in the sun, Brontë's imagery suggests.[55]

In Brontë's *Shirley*, a novel far more broadly and overtly political in its scope than either *Villette* or *Jane Eyre*, female characters continuously shrink from a daylight of tedious and exhausting tasks, visits, and sermons. Daylight means a woman must sew until her head aches all the while enduring silly, unimaginative visitors who stay too long. Even the dreary, misogynist speeches of the vicar are associated with sun, for while Shirley and Caroline wander at leisure in the pleasantly warm evening, they dread entering the stifling church, since it will have retained the day's heat. Emphatically linking the language and dicta of patriarchal deity with the heat of the day, Brontë's character Shirley sounds much like her trans-Atlantic literary sister Dickinson, when she announces: "I would rather not enter" (pp. 314–18).

Another passage from *Shirley* (p. 590), which depends upon a yoking of sunlight and male violence, offers a sweeping criticism of the tenor of nineteenth-century society:

The winter is over and gone: spring has followed with beamy and shadowy, with flowery and showery flight: we are now in the heart of summer—in mid-June,—the June of 1812.

It is burning weather: the air is deep azure and red gold: it fits the time; it fits the age; it fits the present spirit of the nations. The nineteenth century wantons in its giant adolescence: the Titan-boy uproots mountains in his game, and hurls rocks in his wild sport.

Often in women's writing mountains have served as female images;[56] with this association in mind, Brontë's tone is indeed ominous. Her imagery suggests that the era of nineteenth-century "progress" must be borne in the same way one patiently bears the violent games of unthinking twelve-year-old boys. Like a mountain, one will be uprooted, parts of oneself will be hurled about by giant boys in this "burning weather." Brontë's imagery suggests further that women will be fractured, used in fact as the equipment for this "wild" adolescent masculine sport.

George Eliot also uses images of light to show a female character's awareness of restrictions upon her energies. In the same way that, as I shall show, Dickinson writes of disappointment and loss in terms of sunlight, Eliot in *Middlemarch* expresses Dorothea Brooke's disillusionmment over her hideous marriage in terms of too-strong light (a rather paradoxical image, since her husband's house is also described as a dark tomb): "The light had changed, and you cannot find the pearly dawn at noonday."[57] In *Daniel Deronda*, the virtuous but destitute Mirah tells of abuse by her father in terms of light: "What could I do? This life seemed to be closing in upon me with a wall of fire—everywhere there was scorching that made me shrink. The high sunlight made me shrink."[58] One of Emily Brontë's most striking poems is interesting in this context for its similarities to Mirah's speech; to Emily Brontë, the sun's rising to an apex of power is compared with— even seems to cause—a woman's sinking to a nadir of hopelessness:

> Blood-red he rose, and arrow straight
> His fierce beams struck my brow:
> the soul on Nature sprang elate,
> But mine sank sad and low![59]

Furthermore, as with the Brontës, the light for George Eliot seems neither to nourish comfortably nor to illuminate truthfully. Eliot's character Dorothea despairs over her husband's refusal to acknowledge her intelligence and curiosity— his inability to see her in a "true light"—by describing the interior of St. Peter's, historical seat of Christian patriarchal power, as illuminated by the "monotonous light of an alien world." The cathedral's decorations, she deplores, spread "everywhere like a disease of the retina."[60]

As Jack Capps notes, Dickinson not only regarded Eliot's fiction as "glorious," but she also identified characters from the novels with certain friends and family members.[61] The characters of another major nineteenth-century English woman novelist, Elizabeth Gaskell, may have been unknown to the Amherst Poet, although Gaskell's biography of Charlotte Brontë was a work she highly regarded. Whether or not Dickinson knew any of Gaskell's fiction, it is still significant that, in at least one of her novels, light/dark imagery closely parallels that of Eliot's. In Gaskell's *North and South*, the main character is also trying to see life and its possibilities in a true light, and she seems to find that the brighter the sunlight, the fewer the choices for a woman. Although the sunny commons of the south of England are warm and scented, the air seems "too soft and relaxing," conducive only to mindless and purposeless activities. The one library to which Margaret has access proves hopelessly limited, and her only future seems one of loveless years in marriage or fruitless labors in village charity. However, she finds the darker, cloudier, even dirtier North conducive to her own intelligent, active participation in society. And when she returns to her old village in the South, Helstone seems truly to fit its name, for by this time she sees through the sunny pastoral mist to the grim reality that this seemingly idyllic country landscape is inhabited by primitive, superstitious people who roast cats alive and strew cottage gardens with the disordered clutter of too many unruly, untidy, uneducated children. Such a life "flooded in the sunlight" requires living with no mind at all.[62]

Another long work by a woman writer of the nineteenth century also deals with a contrast between two places in geography that represent two different, even opposing mental states; we know that Dickinson not only read Elizabeth Barrett Browning's verse novel *Aurora Leigh* but also thought it akin to glory.[63] And like Gaskell's novel, Barrett Browning's poem concerns itself with the importance for a bright woman of finding real work. Aurora is ambitious, determined to succeed as a dedicated writer. But again, the forces that, from earliest in her life, work against her are described in terms of light. As she leaves her mother's country of Italy and approaches

her father's country, England, she feels starved "into a blind fero-
city / And glare unnatural," an exceedingly paradoxical image in
that most readers would associate the more southerly Italy with
light and glare. And even though she also complains that England is
frosty and cold, as if Shakespeare "and his mates" had absorbed "the
light here," the eyes of her aunt are described the way Dickinson, as
I shall show, describes the proscriptive eye of God—for her aunt,
who represents all the cultural demands upon Aurora to learn sewing, the decorative arts, and especially "keeping quiet by the fire,"
stabs through Aurora's young face with eyes like naked "gray-steel
blades." This same aunt is later described "With smile distorted by
the sun" as she tries to persuade Aurora to capitulate to a marriage
of traditional role assignments and expectations that would be
disastrous to this female poet's literary ambitions.[64]

For many of these women, as for George Eliot's character
Gwendolen in *Daniel Deronda*, the light of day brings "into more
dreary clearness the absence of interest from . . . life."[65] Rather than
serving as agent of growth and rather than allowing possibilities for
development, the light of day for all these women writers seems to
order prescriptions: sew, bend your head, bear children, be chaste,
be quiet, be humble, be married, be good. A light whose rays
carried such constraining admonitions seemed, especially for Dickinson, to cast a stain over one's possibilities, infecting everything
like Eliot's "disease of the retina."

With the sun so often seeming to stain—or constrain—hopes and
ambitions, described so frequently as "an alien light" that restricts
rather than encourages possibilities, it is no wonder that in the
imagery of many women writers we find the darkness paradoxically
offering relief. Following the metaphoric logic of traditional light/
dark polarities, if sun is male and absence of sun is female, then as a
woman, one really belongs, after all, in the dark. And if the sun is
absent from the night, then it would follow that male presence and
male dominance are also absent. For a number of women writers,
night allows a time of one's own. As I shall show, Dickinson in particular found that under the cover of night, she could assume her
full dimensions, very much like her eighteenth-century precursor

Anne Finch, whose "A Nocturnal Reverie" is a poem of delight in

> a night, when every louder wind
> Is to its distant cavern safe confin'd
> And only gentle Zephyr fans his wings,
> And lonely Philomel, still waking, sings.

In Finch's peaceful nocturnal landscape, "trembling leaves" and "freshen'd grass" rise and play uninterrupted; cattle and partridges eat and call to each other freely in a "short-lived jubilee" that lasts only "whilst tyrant-man do's sleep," while "no fierce light disturbs." Finch concludes the poem by pleading:

> In such a night let me abroad remain,
> Till morning breaks, and all's confus'd again;
> Our cares, our toils, our clamours are renew'd,
> Or pleasures, seldom reach'd, again pursu'd.

Until the sun interrupts such peaceful activity, the poet has been free for "silent musings" that urge the mind to seek / something, too high for syllables to speak."[66] We shall find that Dickinson too rejoices in a night associated with an ability to muse, to think, to seek the something higher that she called "fine philosophy."

Night as nourishing wellspring for female vigor is a common image among nineteenth-century women writers. The late-Victorian poet Mary Coleridge, for instance, uses imagery of sun, flowers, dew, and night with precisely the same kinds of associations as her American precursor in Amherst:

> I asked of Night, that she would take me
>   Where I could not go by day.
> I asked of Day, he should not wake me
>   Ere the sun was on his way;
> For as the sun steals from the flowers
>   The crystal dew by which they live,
> He kills the memory of those hours
>   Which Night, for my delight, will give.[67]

In "Winged Words," moreover, Coleridge associates darkness not only with delight but, in addition, with a silence that enables her to speak: against the backdrop of a dark, tranquil, and silent lake, she writes, "Our winged words dart playfully."[68]

Such imagery showing *absence* of sunlight as nurturing climate for feminine energies occurs frequently in nineteenth-century women's fiction, as it does in Charlotte Brontë's *Jane Eyre*. At night Jane hears Rochester's voice, a mystical moonlight call that strengthens her so that she can refuse St. John Rivers' manipulative proposal and return to the man she really loves.[69] Night also becomes a congenial time for female bonding. In *Shirley*, the seriously ill Caroline begins to recover after hearing Mrs. Pryor's moonlight confession that she is the girl's actual mother and that they need no longer be separated. Again in *Shirley*, both Shirley and Caroline manage to witness a violent workers' rebellion under cover (or, to use Dickinson's word, "vail")[70] of the dark; alone in the vicarage, they furtively arm themselves with pistols and tramp out to the fields in order to see "what transpires with our own eyes." All but invisible in "the friendly night, its mute stars," together they are able to break loose from the confines of gentility that would keep them immobile and ignorant of reality.

But this same sheltering darkness can also entomb—and lead to despair, blindness, or even death. And, of course, by aligning oneself with forces of darkness, one may also be aligning with forces of evil. Mary Coleridge identifies with such forces in her revision of the creation story according to Genesis in which she complains that instead of light springing from light, the light has paradoxically destroyed light for her, leaving her with only "Two forms of darkness":

> Two forms of darkness are there. One is Night,
> When I have been an animal, and feared
> I knew not what, and lost my soul, nor dared
> Feel aught save hungry longing for the light.
> And one is Blindness. Absolute and bright,
> The Sun's rays smote me till they masked the sun;
> The Light itself was by the light undone;
> The day was filled with terrors and affright.
> Then did I weep, compassionate of those
> Who see no friend in God—in Satan's host no foes.[71]

As paradoxical as any of Dickinson's poems, Coleridge's "Doubt" suggests that the sun is somehow responsible for relegating the poet to a universe in which she has, rather than a choice between the two polarities of light and dark, a choice only between two varieties of darkness. The first of these is one in which Coleridge feels herself to be subhuman, just as we shall find Dickinson often identifying with snakes, rats, and goblins. The second, however, is a darkness that the light actually causes and that results in the poet's eyes being "put out," as Dickinson phrased it. Coleridge's conclusion that she now understands those who find "no friend in God" is similar to Dickinson's blunt statement that "Jehovah's Watch is wrong."

Such critical statements of deity could of course cause enormous fear. Dickinson in particular found that at the heart of her own darkness lurked a monster at times as terrifying as the sun itself: her own energy, of necessity often suppressed, loomed like a powerful force that seemed more akin to Satan than to God. Dickinson's sense of her energy as monstrous compares with that of Elizabeth Barrett Browning's in "A True Dream," a poem of nightmare in which the poet finds herself unintentionally practicing "the magic art" and treading "the evil way." In this poem, Barrett Browning releases wreaths of smoke that solidify into frightening snakes, incessantly warning the dreamer of their absolute strength.[72]

As terrifying as these fears of identification with satanic powers of darkness could be, however, I shall show that such monstrous madness could also ultimately redeem; just as Dickinson connects madness with "divinest Sense," she also finds strength from what she calls Barrett Browning's "Lunacy of light" which made "The Dark—[feel] beautiful." Through such a "Conversion of the Mind," I shall argue, Dickinson affirms her membership in a race of women writers "nurtured in the Dark," thereby enlarging her soul's society and affirming her own literary power. Deeply influenced by her literary sisters across the Atlantic, she found a countertradition of metaphor that expressed "slant" similar conflicts to those she too felt compelled to express. Indeed, Dickinson found that the Brontë's, Eliot, and Barrett Browning served as nurturing older sisters—as foremothers—in the enterprise of creation, of literature. If these glorious writers, women like Dickinson, were "Queens" also residing in darkness, then how could the dark be completely lonely?

Finally, I shall show that, from early in her writing, Dickinson imagines that there must be *another kind* of light, just as Charlotte Brontë writes in *Shirley* that there must be "another sort of sky" where one will not be "buried in marble" or paralyzed under "a black trance like the toad's" (p. 384). Other places, other countries, perhaps, may be illuminated and governed by kindlier lights for intellectual women. For when Shirley is "joyous," her rapture is described as if her heart housed "all the light and azure of Italy" with all its "fervour" (p. 465). Brontë's imaging of Italy as *another place* illuminated by a friendlier light is also a major characteristic of Barrett Browning's verse novel *Aurora Leigh*. When the blinded Romney comes to Aurora, it is in her mother's country Italy, during a night "softer than an English day." On her own terms in her mother's country, now that the "sun is silent," Aurora can finally, safely, return Romney's love. As Jane Eyre in Charlotte Brontë's novel can only marry Rochester after he has been blinded, (the assumption being that he can now learn to see through *her* eyes, from her perspective), so can Aurora now plan with Romney to lay the "first foundations of that new, dear day" that will lead to a "perfect noon" in which they both shall share equally.[73] Similarly, in the beginning of *Shirley*, Brontë writes of evading the present "sun burnt" years by dreaming of dawn, very much like Dickinson, who dreams of—and also poetically constructs—"a different dawn" (page 39).

Such images of kindlier lights possible for women occur extensively in Dickinson's poems of artistic triumph. In the same way that Jane and Aurora can love only after Rochester's and Romney's patriarchal vision and constraining power are replaced by gentler understanding, Dickinson can experience harmony and transcendence only when the male sun's destructive power is reduced, replaced by a quality of light different from that of the normal, overwhelming, judgmental sun—a light that she, in effect, creates herself, from long nurturing in the dark.

A space between stars. What does it mean to a woman writer to be metaphorically linked with the dark? The same year Dickinson asked Catherine Scott Turner if she feared the sun, she would certainly have read an article published in the *Atlantic* by Thomas Wentworth Higginson, who later became her "preceptor." Higginson's article "Women and the Alphabet" may very well have provided the twenty-nine-year-old poet with more literary determination than anything else published within the pages of that popular literary journal, which members of the Dickinson family read assiduously. For Higginson's essay is as feminist a piece as Wollstonecraft's *A Vindication of the Rights of Women*: not only does he scathingly criticize traditional "contempt for the supposed intellectual inferiority of woman," but he also suggests that such contempt both causes and perpetuates failure. "Soul before sex," he argues; "Give an equal chance, and let genius and industry do the rest."[74] If Dickinson indeed knew her genius, as Adrienne Rich has argued she did, such encouragement from a contemporary literary figure of Higginson's stature must have greatly reassured and further inspired the young poet.[75] But such encouragement was the exception rather than the rule. Higginson's attitude toward educating and encouraging intelligent women was a controversial one, and even he in time proved a disappointment, for his advice that Dickinson regularize her verse showed how little he actually understood the poet's genius. Experiencing on the one hand such inspiration as Higginson offered women in 1859, and on the other hand such restrictions as her own family, culture, and religion provided, Dickinson expresses her awareness of what Suzanne Juhasz has called the "double bind of the woman poet"[76] as a major theme throughout her work. This poet wrote keenly aware of her individual talent in relation to the normative tradition preceding and surrounding her, and, through her metaphors, repeatedly and consistently defined herself in opposition to this tradition. Whether writing directly and obviously about herself or indirectly and coyly about a "supposed person" (*L* II, 268),[77] Dickinson's extensive pattern of light/dark imagery comprises an encoded statement of a female poetics: by "decoding" her metaphors, we shall find that her canon of nearly eighteen hundred poems is neither piecemeal nor contradictory.

I Broad Daylight, Cooking Stoves, and the Eye of God

The Formation of a Common Metaphor

> laid under the burning-glass
> in the sun's eye   *Adrienne Rich*[1]

> The pattern of the sun
> Can fit but him alone
> For sheen must have a Disk
> To be a sun—   *Emily Dickinson (P 1550)*

> The world said with a guffaw, Write?
> What's the good of your writing?   *Virginia Woolf*[2]

For Emily Dickinson daylight itself was heavily burdened by familial and household demands, demands that chafed. Although this poet's obsessive determination to remain within the bounds of her family's house has resulted in at least one critic's labeling her a "little home-keeping person," such a label points directly to the central conflict underlying Dickinson's position.[3] As Barbara Mossberg in particular has shown, the role of daytime daughter Emily Dickinson was expected to fill was anathema to the life of poetry she yearned to live.[4] Even though throughout her life she carried out the domestic and familial duties expected of her, her writing contains hundreds of statements (many cryptic and covert)[5] about her realization that the round peg of her literary genius could not fit the square hole of nineteenth-century American womanhood. What other critics have not demonstrated, however, is that Dickinson expresses these statements through sun imagery. The forces that she felt conspired against her "real life," her private life of writing, become linked with the sun; in particular, the light of day comes to be associated—at first in letters, then in poems— with the realities of her household responsibilities, the demands of her parents, the condescension of her brother Austin, and the prescriptions of her Calvinist religion.[6]

Like her near contemporary, Alice James, who was surrounded by male brilliants, Dickinson was part of a family in which males were leading lights, suns (and sons) around whom her world revolved.[7] Although not a semiprofessional intellectual like Henry James, Sr., Edward Dickinson was not only a successful lawyer and politician but also an instrumental figure in Amherst College's early development; without question he was the most influential man in Amherst. Brother Austin followed his father's lead, also becoming a dominant community figure. Such social prominence necessitated social obligations: the Dickinsons frequently hosted teas, receptions, and dinners. Just as often, they hosted houseguests— sometimes for weeks. And although contemporary readers might argue, "Yes, but they had a maid," certainly the one Irish maid who helped the family with the daily and seasonal chores could not have done everything. The amount of housework would still have been prodigious, as George Whicher has sympathetically observed.[8] We know, for instance, that Emily was roused long before daylight by her father to light the kitchen fire and make breakfast for the entire family. We also know that she was responsible for all the bread and dessert making for the family and its guests, a task which, no matter how much one might enjoy kneading or stirring flour and butter, cinnamon and eggs, must have been prodigious indeed. One can either "make bread or verses," *Aurora Leigh* observes in Barrett Browning's verse novel; Emily Dickinson was required to make bread.

The earliest statements in which Dickinson links the sun's light with constraints upon her writing appear in the letters. At age twenty-three she complains, for instance, to close friends Dr. and Mrs. Holland: "If it wasn't for broad daylight, and cooking stoves,

and roosters, I'm afraid you would have occasion to smile at my letters often, but so sure as 'this mortal' essays immortality, a crow
from a neighboring farm-yard dissipates the illusion, and I am here
again. And what I mean is this—that I thought of you all last week,
until the world grew rounder than it sometimes is, and I broke several dishes" (*L* I, 133). Dickinson's letters are usually crafted as carefully as her poems; variants of many poems are included in many of
the letters. In writing to the Hollands, friends she regarded as
kindred spirits, she did feel she was going beyond the round of
mortality, reaching beyond the tightly restricted circle of dailiness.
Writing was a way to immortality, but it is "broad daylight," with
its demands associated with cooking stoves and roosters, that keeps
her from trying for such transcendence. Certainly when reading
anything Dickinson wrote, we must account for her playfulness and
penchant for exaggeration, and must remind ourselves that nobody
likes doing dishes. However, we must also take into account how
often this strain of tiresome bustle in broad daylight is repeated.

As I have mentioned, the Dickinson household was not only
characterized by the normal chores required to keep a normal middle class family up and doing, but it was also continuously invaded
by visitors. In reading the letters, one can see that the young Dickinson did not easily adjust to the responsibilities—as well as the lack
of privacy—required of a hosting family. Often the letters complain
of company. In one letter she describes their household as "belea-
guered" by the "usual rush of callers" (*L* I, 145). When she was
twenty-four she wrote her brother Austin, complaining that "We
are almost beside ourselves with business, and company" (*L* I, 158).
Later that year she wrote her friend Abiah that "the summer has
been warm, that we have not had a girl, that at this pleasant season,
we have much company" (*L* I, 166). Over and over she complains of
being too busy with company to write: to Austin, she explains, "We
hav'nt written you oftener, because we've had so much company,
and so many things to do (*L* I, 131). And in another letter to Austin
she conveys a sense of just how *crowded* she felt her world to be:

> I expect all our Grandfathers and all their country cousins will come here
> to pass Commencement, and dont doubt the stock will rise several percent
> that week. If we children and Sue could obtain board for the week in some

"vast wilderness," I think we should have good times. Our house is crowded daily with members of this world, the high and the low, the bond and the free, the "poor in this world's goods," and the "almighty dollar,["] and "what in the world are they after" continues to be unknown—But I hope they will pass away, as insects on vegetation. (*L* I, 128)

Such bustle in the "business" of visiting might be good for the local economy (her father's notion of success, perhaps), but, Thoreau-like, she suggests that it is antithetical to her private economies: the solitude and discipline, together with the company of selected intellectual equals and kindred spirits, that fed her writing.

Richard Sewall and Jean Mudge in particular have emphasized Edward Dickinson's determination to achieve worldly success, his financial and political ambitions. Certainly much of the company for whom Emily, as one of two daughters, was partially responsible, would have arrived because of Edward Dickinson's position either as lawyer, politician, or treasurer of Amherst College. So that when this young woman poet expresses so humorously her derision about these social and household functions, one senses that her wit is directed very much toward her father's world of social and fiscal respectability and visibility, as well as toward the requirements upon her as a daughter of such a father.

In another complaint, again to Mrs. Holland, Dickinson writes: "'House' is being 'cleaned.' I prefer pestilence. That is more classic and less fell" (*L* II, 318). That housework seems "fell" suggests that Dickinson may be thinking of it in the sense of "fallen," reminding us of Anne Finch's query about women, "How are we fallen, fallen by mistaken rules?"[9] And although Dickinson's preference for pestilence rather than housecleaning is of course another example of her penchant for exaggeration, as Barbara Mossberg has emphasized, Dickinson's foolery is often very serious; when she mockingly prays, for instance, "God keep me from what they call households," she expresses her awareness that household chores only keep her from writing, the only activity that can give her the status she seeks. And of course Dickinson's "household" was governed by a man whose notions of appropriate female behavior coincided directly with nineteenth-century views about women;[10] Edward Dickinson undoubtedly would have agreed, for instance, with the *Mount*

Holyoke Female Seminary Bulletin's definition of woman's role: "Skill and expedition in household duties. Let a young lady despise this branch of the duties of woman and she despises the appointment of the Author of her existence." [11] That her life was indeed regulated—at least until the deaths of both parents (her father died when she was forty-four, her mother when she was fifty-two)—by household duties may indeed have caused her at times "to despise the appointments of the Author of her existence," both on a biological and a theological level—or at least to feel that that Author despised *her*.

Furthermore, the long illnesses of their mother were a frequent concern for both Emily and her sister Vinnie. After 1856, when the Dickinsons moved back into the patriarchal home built originally by Edward's father, Emily Norcross Dickinson was often ill. Shortly after this traumatic move Dickinson wrote to Mrs. Holland in a tone characterized less by playful wit than by witty fear: "Mother has been an invalid since we came *home*, and Vinnie and I 'regulated,' and Vinnie and I 'got settled,' and still we keep our father's house, and mother lies upon the lounge, or sits in her easy chair. I don't know what her sickness is, for I am but a simple child, and frightened at myself. I often wish I was a grass, or a toddling daisy, whom all these problems of the dust might not terrify" (*L* II, 182). Jean Mudge has commented that Emily must have been painfully aware of the consequences of her father's financial ambitions;[12] she suggests that when the poet refers to her "father's house," her own awareness of the grief and greed underlying all the dealings with the Dickinson mansion lay behind her phrase. This move back to the mansion on Main Street from the comfortable, less imposing house on Pleasant Street was associated with two generations of the Dickinsons' financial difficulties and embodied a symbolic repossession of the Father's House for Edward Dickinson, signifying to him that finally, financial ease and status had arrived. After this move, however, the tone of his daughter's letters changes to become less light hearted, while from this time on, his wife was often unwell. This straight-up-and-down Regency house that still rises rigidly above Amherst's Main Street may not have been a sympathetic dwelling for at least one mother and one daughter.

What did not change with the move to Main Street, however, was Emily Dickinson's obligation to the familial enterprise. Together with her sister Vinnie, she continued to wait upon her two parents; indeed, she was at their beck and call all but the last four years of her life. At the age of thirty-nine, the poet wrote Vinnie, who was visiting friends in Boston: "I am so hurried with Parents that I run all Day with my tongue abroad, like a Summer Dog" (*L* II, 333). So much speculation has arisen about why Dickinson never married, about what failed romance sent her reeling into seclusion, that we have overlooked the prosaic but common custom (that still exists, incidentally) of aging parents simply expecting their daughters to care for them.[13] Edward Dickinson apparently wanted his daughter at home, liked her bread best. In those days, if father ordered, what daugher could say no? One reason she never left home may have been that her parents—probably unconsciously, and certainly very subtly—arranged that she shouldn't. Clearly, they needed her. Edward's wife was by all accounts, no matter how much we would like to defend the writer's mother, not particularly bright; and Emily was. Her father may have quite simply felt better with his intelligent, even though rebellious, daughter in the house. However, the needs of these parents must often have drained the poet of her own energies, even while enhancing her sense of her own self-worth. Certainly, catering to a semi-invalid mother and a stern, authoritarian father would deplete one's own creative strength. That Dickinson describes herself as feeling like a dog ordered back and forth in the heat gives us a sense of how much these parents remained her masters. And in describing herself as a summer dog, Dickinson again associates domestic obligation with the force of the sun, with too much heat.

These broad daylights that are shaped by the demands of cooking stoves, visitors, and parents are also influenced by another relation, one in which Dickinson often did behave much like a dog trying desperately to please: her relation to her brother, Austin. Austin was a key member of the family for the poet; brother and sister were intellectual companions, sharing a highly intelligent and often sarcastic sense of humor regarding other family and community members and events. They saw eye to eye on many issues, including their father's disapproval of most popular current literature. Emily teased Austin, obviously adored him, and missed him painfully when he was gone from home. In several letters to him, she shows how deeply she wants his approval as intellectual equal. But as Mossberg insightfully points out, the poet "constantly battles Austin's preconception of women,"[14] an attitude that influences her own writing strategy, so that her style becomes increasingly characterized by circumlocution, posing, and affected childishness.

In 1851, at twenty-one, Emily Dickinson wrote her brother Austin:

> I suppose I am a fool—you always said I was one, and yet I have some feelings that seem sensible to me, and I have desires to see you now that you are gone which are really quite intelligent. Dont take too much encouragement, but really I have the hope of becoming before you come quite an *accountable being*! Why not an "eleventh hour" in the life of the *mind* as well as such an one in the life of the *soul*—greyhaired sinners are saved—simple maids may be *wise*, who knoweth? (*L* I, 44)

Then a week later, Dickinson writes Austin again:

> I feel quite like retiring, in presence of one so grand, and casting my small lot among small birds, and fishes—you say you dont comprehend me, you want a simpler style. *Gratitude* indeed for all my fine philosophy! I strove to be exalted thinking I might reach *you* and while I pant and struggle and climb the nearest cloud, you walk out very leisurely in your slippers from Empyrean, and without the *slightest* notice request me to get down! As *simple* as you please, the *simplest* sort of simple—I'll be a little ninny—a little pussy catty, a little Red Riding Hood, I'll wear a Bee in my Bonnet, and a Rose bud in my hair, and what remains to do you shall be told hereafter. (*L* I, 45)

Dickinson's tone in these letters is both fond and sarcastic. Apparently Austin has teased her in the past for being a fool, an *un*accountable being. In the first letter, Dickinson asks her brother to take her seriously: "simple maids may be *wise*, who knoweth?" She is asking him to look at her afresh, to see her in a new light, and to put aside his old attitude toward her, which seems to have been characterized by the patronizing interest common to older brothers who see themselves as wiser than their younger sisters. After reading the next letter, we can imagine his reply: older brother must have insisted on remaining older brother; rather than taking seriously her intellectual hopes, he apparently condescended only to castigate his younger sister for her stylistic defects.

The tone of Dickinson's response to her brother is complex and significant. Although "cute" and "coy," these passages radiate sarcasm. Whereas she says she feels "quite like retiring, in presence of one so grand," she doesn't retire at all. Instead she rebukes Austin, constructing a metaphor that tells the truth of her feelings, albeit "slant." She has been struggling (and panting again) to rise to a higher level, one she associates with him. But rather than helping her up, he (an already secure resident of this exalted dwelling place) saunters out as if he were God, barely noticing her *except* to note that she is out of place. Immediately, he tells her to "get down," get below him, get back where she belongs. Dickinson's extended metaphor in this passage shows her realization that as a young woman, she is trespassing on male ground in attempting "fine philosophy."

But this passage shows her going far beyond simply accepting her brother's attitude toward her desire for intellectual development. In the last sentence of her response to Austin, her irony increases. If Austin wants her to write in a simpler style, she will, with a vengeance. For in becoming "a little ninny—a little pussy catty" (a domestic animal, like a dog), by ostensibly using a "simple" and childish, *seemingly* less exalted (and certainly less threatening) level of language, she can very cleverly twist meanings beyond even double entendre, and veil her actual thoughts, thoughts of immense complexity and "fine philosophy," behind a mask of disarming childlike simplicity.[15]

Furthermore, this highly playful but deadly serious passage is followed immediately in the letter with a new paragraph that associates Austin's writing and thinking with too much heat: "Your letters are richest treats, send them always just such warm days—they are worth a score of fans, and many refrigerators—the only 'diffikilty' they are so very *queer*, and *laughing* such hot weather is *anything* but *amusing*. A little more of earnest, and little less of jest until we are out of August, and then you may joke as freely as the Father of Rogues himself. . . . It is *very* hot here, now." At first it looks as though Dickinson has stopped her ironic castigation of Austin's male-superior fraternal criticisms. His letters are treats, he must write often. But the request shifts, very cleverly and subtly: the only "diffikilty" (a simpler, more childlike "pussy catty" way of spelling?) is that his letters are so funny they cause the family discomfort, because even though at first they *seem* cooling and refreshing, actually, laughing so hard at Austin's language in the hot weather causes the family to become even hotter, even more uncomfortable in the summer weather. Dickinson has found her own metaphoric way to tell her older brother what she thinks of his patronizing attitude toward her writing. And what she ends up telling him in this passage is that his very language, *although at first it seems delightful*, actually intensifies the heat for her. Her last sentences are told so "slant" that her message is fully understood only within its larger metaphoric context.

Dickinson's reactions to her brother must have also been enormously compounded by her father's open adoration of his son. One can imagine the complex nature of her emotional response in writing Austin "Father says your letters are altogether before Shakespeare, and he will have them published to put in our library" (*L* I, 46). Since it is difficult to imagine Edward Dickinson commenting so effusively on any subject, even that of his son's epistolary talents, no doubt the extreme nature of the praise is of Dickinson's own composing. Her exaggeration gives us additional insight into how intimidated she must have felt by her brother's intellect and the respect it engendered from her father.

Her own determination to write, however, became stronger than her sense of intimidation. On March 27, two years later, in 1853, she wrote Austin, who had just sent her some poems he had written: "Now, Brother Pegasus, I'll tell you what it is—I've been in the habit *myself* of writing some few things, and it rather appears to me that you're getting away my patent, so you'd better be somewhat careful, or I'll call the police!" (*L* I, 110). She lets him know in no uncertain terms that even though two years before he could preach to her from above that she should remain lower than he, should use simpler language since as a woman she of course had a simpler mind, and that even though their father practically classed his letters with the classics, *she* is the poet in this family. She has staked her claim.

However, as we know, Dickinson's determination to develop her genius for writing, to struggle and pant to reach the highest Empyrean clouds of literary accomplishment, was fraught with anxiety. Knowing that her culture expected her to spend her days cheerfully in simple domestic pursuits, knowing that her brother disliked her attempts to compete with him in intellectual and literary matters, she could not make the open artistic commitment that her genius needed. Whereas American male writers such as Hawthorne and Melville also experienced painful difficulties, their anxieties were very different from Dickinson's as she experienced what Suzanne Juhasz has labeled the "double bind" of the woman poet.[16] For her, to write at all seriously was *not* to be dutiful, cheerful, and helpful like sunny Phoebe in Hawthorne's *House of the Seven Gables*. And not to be a cheerful, domestic homebody in Emily Dickinson's culture was to be, quite simply, wicked. There was no way that Dickinson could escape the all-powerful Calvinist God who judged everyone, and who, Dickinson felt, had very definite ideas about what a good girl should be like.

This judgmental God becomes, moreover, even more than the condescending judgments of her brother, associated with the sun's heat. In a letter of 1877 to Mrs. Holland, Dickinson writes: "The Days are very hot and the Weeds pant like the centre of Summer. They say the Corn likes it. I thought there were others besides the Corn. How deeply I was deluded! Vinnie rocks her Garden and moans that God wont help her—I suppose he is too busy, getting 'angry with the Wicked—every Day' " (*L* II, 502). Such a description of too much heat reminds one of the fires of hell. Many critics and biographers have discussed Dickinson's disaffection from the prevailing religious excitement of the mid-nineteenth century; the fervor of Connecticut Valley Christianity during her lifetime served as source for one of the poet's major conflicts. As we know from letters, the pressure on Emily to "give up this world," as she phrased it, was considerable. At Mt. Holyoke she was labeled one of the "no-hopers," even though she herself was apparently saddened by the fact that she could not "cast her burden on Christ" (*L* I, 23). Throughout her life, she retained a suspicion of traditional Christian zeal, especially of the sort that surrounded her as a young woman. To watch her friends give themselves up to Christ and wear blank, beatific expressions pained her, for she felt increasingly that she had little in common with these obedient creatures.[17] Significantly, Dickinson's religious rebellion, like her rebellion against the burden of required female household duties, is often expressed in terms of the sun.

In a letter of 1851, Dickinson writes Austin:

> I am at home from meeting on account of the storm and my *slender constitution*, which I assured the folks, would not permit my accompanying them today.
> It is Communion Sunday, and they will stay a good while—what a nice time pussy and I have to enjoy ourselves! Just now the sun peeped out. I tell you I chased it back again behind the tallest cloud, it has not my permission to show its face again till after all the meeting, *then* it may shine and shine, for all pussy and I care! (*L* I, 54)

One senses again how difficult it must have been for Dickinson to find moments alone, even to write a letter; for in this letter to Austin, as in the one quoted above to Dr. and Mrs. Holland, "broad daylight" interferes with thought and communication. The stormy, sunless weather has provided her both literal excuse and metaphorical inspiration to withdraw from the family excursion to church, with its inevitable small talk and sermonizing—that will undoubtedly draw attention to Dickinson's unregeneracy. Her playful ordering of the sun to remain behind the clouds until the meeting is over and the folks all come home is further evidence of just how much she associated the sun with familial and religious forces that worked against her intellect and her writing.

In another letter written the same year as the preceding passage, Dickinson complains that she has "just come in from church very hot, and faded, having witnessed a couple of Baptisms, three admissions to the church, a Supper of the Lord, and some other minor transactions time fails me to record" (*L* I, 46). The church service itself increases her sense of discomfort in the heat. Sounding much like Shirley in George Eliot's novel, moreover, she has been "faded" by the heat of the ritual; it is as if in the light of orthodox belief, Dickinson feels that her own essence is somehow bleached, or partially erased.

A letter Dickinson wrote at twenty to her close friend Abiah Root reveals, moreover, an association of God and religious expectations with illness as well as with the demands of daylight's duties. Writing Abiah, she first mentions that, as in the letter to Austin, "The folks have all gone away." But if they thought they left her alone, she continues, they were mistaken, for with her—or within her—reside "A curious trio, part earthly and part spiritual two of us—the other all heaven." Immediately she follows this strange statement with the comment that "*God* is sitting here, looking into my very soul to see if I think right tho'ts." She adds that she is not afraid, since she tries "to be right and good." But one wonders. Certainly the youthful Dickinson would want her pious friend Abiah to believe she is trying to be good. What follows in this letter indicates just how divided she felt herself in relation to her culture's expectations for her spirit—and her body.

When she states that God looks so "gloriously" that "everything bright seems dull beside him," that she doesn't "dare to look directly at him for fear I shall die," the God she describes sounds very much like the sun itself. Shortly after this reference to God and his expectations of her, she constructs an elaborate and amazing story of how she caught the cold from which she is, at the moment, suffering. The cold in fact seems like one of the trio— perhaps one of the divisions of self which the poet might like to hide from this bright eye of God. For the cold has traveled, almost like a demon, all the way "from that distant Switzerland"—from the mountains and snow, to attach herself like a "little creature" to the poet. The cold kisses the young poet, hugs her, and now sleeps in her bed, eats from her plate, and "will tag me through life for all I know." Certainly the cold character is comical with its "huge pocket-handkerchief, and a very red nose," but certainly it is also very interesting that immediately after describing herself as divided into three, she goes on to describe herself as two—a healthy person overpowered by a sick one. Furthermore, this cold/incubus is associated with snakebite, with "fictions—vain imaginations," and "flowers of speech," all metaphors that Margaret Homans, for one, has convincingly argued refer to language.[18]

If healthy, religiously upright young women must succumb to the demands of church and sewing society, then Dickinson must struggle against such yielding. But according to the dualistic nature of her culture's thought, if she will not be a healthy little sunshine girl like Hawthorne's Phoebe, and will not be a good little religious girl like her friend Abiah, then it logically follows that she will be dominated by a sick self, a *cold* self (that has come all the way from decadent Europe!) who prefers writing "fictions" (or poetry) to the insistent demands of a too-bright God who allows her no mental privacy. This letter is particularly revealing of the enormity of the conflicts tugging at the youthful poet: day, sun, and God are all opposed to her naughty longing to be "snake bit" and to her equally naughty, perverse delight at having been "caught" by a foreign disease—inhabited by a strange, fictive creature (*L* I, 31).

One week before she wrote this letter to the already converted, pious Abiah, she had written an even longer letter to her adored former teacher Jane Humphrey. She tells Jane that she had written her many letters, although "not the kind of letters that go in post-offices—and ride in mail-bags." Dickinson's letters have been "queer—silent ones—very full of affection—and full of confidence." These she has written at night, "when the rest of the world were at sleep—when only God came between us—and no one else might hear. No need of shutting the door—nor of whispering timidly—nor of fearing the ear of listeners—for night held them fast in his arms that they could not interfere—and his arms are brawny and strong." Even God seems friendly in this night that seems like an agent on Dickinson's side, an agent so strong that he physically keeps bothersome, interruptive "listeners" (perhaps like "Whitman's "Trippers and askers") safely away from her in their sleep. Her *real thoughts*, she states metaphorically, can be expressed safely at night, away from broad daylight.

Furthermore, the letter continues to describe the world of broad daylight as a world of narrowing possibilities. Beginning to realize the expectations upon her as a nineteenth-century female entering adulthood, Dickinson emphasizes to Jane how "perfectly hateful" to her are the "halt—the lame—and the blind—the old—the infirm—the bed-ridden—and the superannuated—the ugly, and disagreeable." She rebels against the prevailing notion that she should see her obligations toward such unfortunates as "an opportunity rare for cultivating meekness—and patience—and submission—and for turning my back to this very sinful, and wicked world." This "path of duty looks very ugly indeed" to twenty-year-old Dickinson. She exaggeratedly fears that she is already "set down as one of those brands almost consumed," her "hardheartedness" providing opportunity for "many prayers" (*L* I, 30).

Rather than expressing a lack of human sympathy, Dickinson on the contrary is reacting against the cultural expectation that it was woman's obligation to care for the poor, aged, and infirm while men actively worked in the healthy, vigorous marketplace—and perhaps published openly under the sun. Already at twenty, Dickinson saw her future as her community saw it, to continue as a dutiful daughter (not only within her family but about the community as well), caring for the less fortunate, thereby cultivating such desirable female characteristics as "meekness—and patience—and submission."

Undoubtedly Dickinson would have seen eye to eye with Thoreau on the worth of "Charity"; one can, in fact, imagine her saying along with the author of *Walden*, "If I knew for a certainty that a man was coming to my house with the conscious design of doing me good, I should run for my life." But Dickinson cannot "run for her life" to escape from such expectations, for she in fact is expected to be one of those who will try to do a man good. She can only withdraw from a broad daylight that seemed, with its very rays, to be reminding her over and over again that if, as she says, bad angels sing songs while good ones weep (presumably over the pathetic charitable cases they are cooped up caring for), then, if she insists upon becoming a singing—or writing—angel, she is aligning herself with Satan.[19]

But she wants to sing. She knows she can sing, that, indeed, she has a "patent" on poetry. And just as she associates in her letter to Abiah the movements of snakes in the grass with "fictions" and "flowers of speech" she also at other times associates her own literary ambitions with movement, in particular, with climbing. About ten years after Dickinson's letter to Austin about her "fine philosophy," and about eleven years after the letter to Jane Humphrey, Dickinson wrote a poem which compresses many of these letters' concerns. In fact, the poem in a sense rephrases the earlier exchange between older brother and younger sister, although in the poem, God himself replaces Austin:

> Over the fence—
> Strawberries—grow—
> Over the fence—
> I could climb—if I tried, I know—
>
> But—if I stained my Apron—
> God would certainly scold!
> Oh, dear,—I guess if He were a Boy—
> He'd—climb—if He could!   (*P* 251)

Whereas in the letter to Austin, Dickinson is climbing toward a heaven of "fine philosophy," here she is trying to reach berries. And here she is even more cryptic than in 1851, for "strawberries" could be words, poems themselves.[20] Of significance in this poem is that Dickinson wants to pick her own berries—but she is blocked from doing so by two obstructions: one, a physical barrier, a fence, but she makes it clear that this is actually not an obstruction at all, for she knows she is capable of climbing over it, to get to the other side where the berries are (or the poetry is). It is the second obstruction that is the real one: the eye of God and culture that tells her she is no longer a good girl if she hikes up her skirts and clambers over to pick her own fruit. God expects her, she knows, to remain passive and clean, unrumpled, on the berryless side, waiting patiently, the poem implies, for someone to bring berries *to* her. Climbing, in fact, would probably result in a stained apron, a metaphor, as Mossberg has insightfully observed, for femininity itself.[21] Wearing the apron, she comments, keeps a little girl from the act of climbing. Because it can be so easily "stained," it serves as a telltale sign of any disobedient or inappropriately ambitious behavior a female child has been up to.

A bit of doggerel from *Little Women* expresses a similar concern with similar imagery. Jo March, tomboy and writer, alone of all the March sisters ambitious, writes for the girls' *Pickwick Portfolio*:

> Poetic fire lights up his eye,
> He struggles 'gainst his lot.
> Behold ambition on his brow,
> And on his nose a blot![22]

The blot on "his" nose is similar to the stain that would mar Dickinson's apron; in both Alcott and Dickinson such struggling against one's lot results in becoming dirty, sullied as a woman. Dickinson's speculation that if God "were a Boy" he'd want to climb is especially interesting here, because Dickinson often did use "boy" the same way she used "daisy" or "child," as a metaphor for herself, just as Alcott has Jo write of herself "Poetic fire lights up *his* eye." In Dickinson's poem there is also a strong implication that since God is (or was, at one time) a boy, instead of a girl like Emily Dickinson, he naturally would be allowed to climb, that nobody worries about boys dirtying their clothes, that they are not expected to remain charming visual objects while accomplishing household chores or sitting demurely at needlework. In this short poem, Dickinson succinctly expresses the truth of life for nineteenth-century British and American middle-class women. Although domestic chores may dominate one's day, struggling to climb higher to develop intellectually, to reach "berries" or read books or write poems was not the thing to do; one was expected to remain passive, dressed in spotless apron, waiting for someone else, preferably male, to bring berries—or poems—*to* one. As a woman one could not be like the sun itself, then, climbing up over the fences of earth's horizons, reaching for new and varied fruits.

But Dickinson did climb, As she wrote about 1862, "For largest Woman's heart / Could hold an Arrow—too—" (*P* 309). She could and she did set her own artistic targets. Albert Gelpi has most sensibly argued that "she knew what she was doing and, with the professional self-assurance which underlay her personal insecurity, wrote her poems accordingly."[23] Adrienne Rich puts it similarly: "I have a notion that genius knows itself; that Dickinson chose her seclusion, knowing she was exceptional and knowing what she needed. . . . Given her vocation, she was neither eccentric nor quaint; she was determined to survive, to use her powers, to practice necessary economies."[24] Having grown up in the intellectually thriving community centered around Amherst College, Dickinson must have found it painful to reach maturity and find that in adulthood she was publicly dissuaded from remaining in a world of thought and books. As a child, she had been praised for her wit, but as a young woman she felt the pressure not only to undergo conversion but also to follow the example of most of her girlhood friends and spend her time with households, sewing circles, charitable works.[25] Since she preferred the flowers of Satan, a "wicked" world of acute sensory, intellectual, and artistic expression, she constantly felt the Eye of God upon her:

> I never felt at Home—Below—
> And in the Handsome Skies
> I shall not feel at Home—I know—
> I don't like Paradise—
>
> Because it's Sunday—all the time—
> And Recess—never comes—
> And Eden'll be so lonesome
> Bright Wednesday Afternoons—
>
> If God could make a visit—
> Or ever took a Nap—
> So not to see us—but they say
> Himself—a Telescope
>
> Perennial beholds us—
> Myself would run away
> From Him—and Holy Ghost—and All—
> But there's the "Judgment Day"!   (P 413)

Neither in the world as it is constructed nor in the heaven that this world has constructed will Dickinson fit. Sunday, the day of the Lord, was a day of church services both morning and evening, services attended before and after an enormous noon dinner. Dickinson would have been at least partially responsible for Sunday dinner's preparations and for cleaning up afterward. To this young poet, a paradise composed of Sundays that consisted of obligatory cooking, cleaning, and churchgoing—that necessitated coping with both neighborly small talk and ministerial sermonizing—probably sounded more like a hell than a heaven. "If God could make a visit," wishes Dickinson, "Or ever took a Nap," so he wouldn't be watching her all the time, this paradise might be bearable. But God himself is a "telescope" who "perennial beholds us," and even though the poet would like to escape from His prying eye, "there's the 'Judgment Day'!" She can't get away from the great eye, which sees her for what she is increasingly becoming, a closet cultural revolutionary, and a very frightened one at that.

An additional cause for uneasiness with this sun-as-eye-of-God is that his "view" of her is at odds with her own view of herself, reminding us of Lucy Snowe's complaint in *Villette* that women are not seen in a true light:

> A Solemn thing within the Soul
> To feel itself get ripe—
> And golden hang—while farther up—
> The Maker's Ladders stop—
> And in the Orchard far below—
> You hear a Being—drop—
>
> A Wonderful—to feel the Sun
> Still toiling at the Cheek
> You thought was finished—
> Cool of eye, and critical of Work—
> He shifts the stem—a little
> To give your Core—a look—   (P 483)

Although at first it sounds as though the poet rejoices in the sun's superior judgment, the last three lines of this poem's second stanza seem reminiscent of the subtle shift in tone of Dickinson's earlier letter to Austin in the hot weather. Obviously she had felt a solemn awe at her own soul's maturation, an awe that conflicted with the powerful, cool, critical eye of God that can effortlessly turn her stem around to give her core "a look" that is curiously ambiguous. The pause before this noun contributes to the reader's sense that something is amiss here, that his look may actually be felt, after all, as censoriously penetrating rather than pleasingly affirming.

Trying to avoid penetrating stares from a censorious "Eye of God," moreover, seems impossible:

> The deepest hid is sighted first
> And scant to Him the Crowd—
> What triple Lenses burn upon
> The Escapade from God—   (*P* 894)

This escapade of Dickinson's was in many ways the major event of her life. She could never adopt the conventional pieties. But she carried within her an acute awareness that, just as Austin judged her writing, recommending simpler (and more "feminine") styles, the great eye of God was going to be there, that she would never ultimately get away with her great escapade from the "triple Lenses" of the Father, the Son, and the Holy Ghost. Just as she wrote much later when about forty-six, "The Sun . . . doth as punctual call" on both "Tare" and "conscientious Flower," judging them both, she realizes how difficult it will be to hide her secret, her ambition (*P* 1372). God and the sun will find her out.

Clearly, Dickinson's own life, her intellectual and artistic ambitions and inclinations, had to be submerged, hidden not only from the telescopic eye of God but also from the eyes of prying neighbors and family members; Austin, for instance, even as Mabel Todd was editing the poems after his sister's death, had no idea of his little sister's genius. As Vinnie once said of her brilliant sister, "Emily had to think. She was the only one of us who had that to do."[26] It was eventually Vinnie who guarded Emily from the hostile daylight world of bustle and calling cards. But Vinnie could not protect her sister from the agony of living her most genuine life in secret. To carry one's genius inside, with the constant awareness that the God of one's country considers it a treacherous gift from Satan, must have been frightening and painful:

> To simulate—is stinging work—
> To cover what we are
> From Science—and from Surgery—
> Too Telescopic Eyes
> To bear on us unshaded—   (*P* 443)

Try as she might to simulate, or disguise herself, the "triple Lenses" still burn. That the poet feels "unshaded" is yet another statement that the sun of her imagination was no friend to her, that it was connected with all the prescriptions that told women not to think, but rather, as Dickinson also says in *P* 443, "Life's little duties do."

2 *Dowering and Depriving*
The Mighty Sun and His Yellow Whip

Of this is Day Composed
A morning and a noon
A Revelry unspeakable
And then a gay unknown
Whose Pomps allure and spurn
And dower and deprive
And penury for Glory
Remedilessly leave.   *Emily Dickinson* (P 1675)

I am open then as a palm held out,
open as a sunflower, without
crust, without shelter, without
skin, hideless and unhidden.
How can I let you ride
so far into me and not fear?   *Marge Piercy*[1]

My daughter, at eleven
(almost twelve), is like a garden.

Oh, darling! Born in that sweet
                          birthday suit
and having owned it and known it for so long,
now you must watch high noon enter—   *Anne Sexton*[2]

A ring of gold with the sun in it?
Lies. Lies and a grief.   *Sylvia Plath*[3]

In 1852 Dickinson wrote her closest friend Sue a letter so dra-
matic that nearly every Dickinson critic has observed its significance. Recognized as an unusually extravagant expression of the
poet's ambivalence toward sexual union, the "man of noon" letter
was written in June of 1852 to Susan Gilbert, at the time engaged

to be married to Emily's brother Austin. The letter begins: "They are cleaning house today, Susie, and I've made a flying retreat to my own little chamber, where with affection, and you, I will spend this precious hour." After first declaring her independence from her household's bustle, Dickinson continues by meditating upon the entire issue of female identity as wife:

> You and I have been strangely silent upon this subject, Susie, we have often touched upon it, and as quickly fled away, as children shut their eyes when the sun is too bright for them. . . . How dull our lives must seem to the bride, and the plighted maiden, whose days are fed with gold, and who gathers pearls every evening; but to the *wife*, Susie, sometimes the *wife forgotten*, our lives perhaps seem dearer than all others in the world; you have seen flowers at morning, *satisfied* with the dew, and those same sweet flowers at noon with their heads bowed in anguish before the mighty sun; think you these thirsty blossoms will *now* need naught but—*dew?* No, they will cry for sunlight, and pine for the burning noon, tho' it scorches them, scathes them; they have got through with peace—they know that the man of noon, is *mightier* than the morning and their life is henceforth to him. Oh Susie, it is dangerous, and it is all too dear, these simple trusting spirits, and the spirits mightier, which we cannot resist! It does so rend me, Susie, the thought of it when it comes, that I tremble lest at sometime I, too, am yielded up.   (*L* I, 93)

Although reading the letter variously, critics do agree on the intensity and centrality of the conflict described here. Albert Gelpi reads this letter as an expression of "an ambivalence which characterized not only her emotional temperament but her religious, poetic, and personal life," and of "the dilemma that determined her response to experience on all levels."[4] John Cody reads the passage as an expression of Dickinson's sexual anxiety, emphasizing that it indicates Dickinson's need to live her heterosexual life vicariously through Susan since the "man of noon" is obviously symbol for a "sexually overpowering husband who causes his flower-wife to be 'bowed in anguish.'"[5] Gilbert and Gubar argue that the letter's "searching examination of the meaning of wifehood" reveals "the poet's keen consciousness of her own warring feelings about that solar Nobodaddy who was both censorious "Burglar! Banker— Father," and idealized "Master/Lover." They emphasize Dickinson's "relentlessly elaborated imagery of male power and female powerlessness."[6] Joanne Dobson in her essay, "'Oh, Susie, it is dangerous': Emily Dickinson and the Archetype," reads the passage as suggestive of Dickinson's attempted realization of her own masculine self, her animus that is "struggling for life against deadly odds" (p. 85).[7] Barbara Mossberg uses the same passage to argue the case for Dickinson's insistent renunciation of female maturity, her adoption of a child persona, to release herself from the pressures of being a "woman" or "wife."[8]

Clearly the sun in this letter has become eroticized in such a highly charged fashion that no one can doubt that Dickinson is writing about much more than housework. It is partly her train of associations that I find especially pertinent here: she moves swiftly from her dislike of housewifely chores to her love for Sue to her hopes for Sue and Austin's approaching marriage to her own fears concerning heterosexual union, a union that would of necessity involve responsibility for increased housewifely chores. The associations come full circle. No wonder the entire subject of marriage seems "Too bright" for the poet—it dazzles gloriously, to be sure, but also painfully.

Part of the pain caused by this scorching noon is caused by its independence and unreliability. Although the bride or the fiancée may feel sorry for such girls as twenty-two-year-old Emily with her "dull" life, the reality in the long run, Dickinson suspects, will be that after these young women actually become wives they will be "forgotten." One doesn't have to look very far, in fact, to find model for such fears. Dickinson's father was frequently absent for long periods of time; professionally ambitious, he often left his wife to cope with three children and a large house, apparently leaving precise and insistent instructions as to how she should carry on in his absence. When he was home, he was very much present: his behavior was demanding and judgmental. Dickinson may very well have seen her mother as a "wife forgotten," as indeed she has been, in a sense, even to us, in that we find it difficult to know her at all— she occupies so little space in the biographical material surrounding the poet's life. Furthermore, in describing a wife as forgotten in this letter, Dickinson may also have meant that a wife was necessarily forgotten as *herself*, losing her own name, losing any autonomy she might have had in her parents' home in assuming the duties of running a household with the express purpose of answering to other people's needs.

Yet of course, this letter to Susie also describes the mighty man of noon as seductively attractive. Blossoms, after all, need both dew and sun. However, when blossoms are not consistently nourished by sunlight, but rather are alternately abandoned and scorched, they wither. Dickinson's metaphoric statements indicate that masculine attention, like the sun, is unresponsive to one's own needs, often absent when one wants it most, or, perhaps more difficult, often scorching and scathing with a too-intruding, too-intense attention and penetration. In many ways, this letter to Susie expresses the central conflict for women in the nineteenth century. Elsa Green, for instance, has shown how in America during the poet's lifetime

> Grown women were supposed to switch their attention entirely away from themselves as distinct, historical identities. In fact, they were supposed to break off connections with an ongoing, private self and let their behavior be directed according to the public, class image of patience, cheerfulness, submission and saintliness. . . . As a woman . . . Emily was supposed to give over moral control of her life to the absolute authority of God, father, brother, and husband.[9]

A world dominated by men of noon quite simply did not provide an adequate growing climate for women like Dickinson, women who, for whatever reasons, needed to live in the mind. And of course, the man of noon—of bustle, of business—did reign supreme in Dickinson's culture; Thoreau warned less cryptically of the dangers of commerce, property owning, and railroads. Dickinson could not utter her cultural criticisms so directly: she was after all dependent on actual men of noon as a flower is dependent on the sun. But the light with which such men and such a climate endowed her wasn't the right light. Rather than nourishing, it devoured.

As I shall show, in writing of the sun as culturally associated with masculine, divine, and sexual energies, Dickinson's youthful ambivalence toward sunlight intensifies. For although her sun imagery radiates across a wide spectrum, from images suggesting the white light of divine as well as human love to images suggesting the scorching light of hell, a dominant theme of Dickinson's obsessive use of the sun as metaphor is a recurring sense of loss and exclusion—even betrayal. At times in the poems the sun does appear as a friendly entity, warming and pleasing in the manner of Emerson's and Thoreau's more traditional sun images, but in Dickinson's imagery these moments seldom last. Often to Dickinson the sun appears an abandoning seducer, a strutting figure, swelled with his own self-importance but paradoxically unreliable, incapable of affecting or warming her. At the extreme end of this spectrum of light-as-metaphor, she perceives of the sun as an overpowering foe, an enemy whose light burns and blackens, devours and paralyzes; at such moments she views the same sun that brings life to a planet as a punitive whip.

None of this is to say that Dickinson didn't want the sun to function healthfully. Often she longed for it, literally and figuratively, and often she wrote of its rays as performing their traditional task of warming and comforting. In a letter to Mrs. Samuel Bowles, for instance, the poet writes, "I ask God on my knees to send you much prosperity, few winter days, and long suns" (*L* II, 212). If an abundance of sun was to be wished for a friend, the comforting warmth of sunlight could be metaphor for the warmth of companionship; in a letter to her intimate friend Mrs. Holland (the recipient of the "broad daylight" and "cooking stoves" letter), Dickinson confides that her friend provides "A warmth as near as if the Sun / Were shining in your Hand" (*P* 1568). Similarly, the home of favorite cousins Louise and Frances Norcross is characterized by a cozy, quiet, well-lit ambiance: "I think of your little parlor as the poets once thought of Windemere,—peace, sunshine, and books" (*L* II, 400). Of course the light here is also interior, manageable, shaded by the pleasant walls of the parlor.

Other loved ones are also associated with light. Remembering her father after his death, she thinks of "his firm Light" (*L* II, 432); years later, she awaited publication of Samuel Bowles' posthumous biography as a "Memoir of the Sun" (*L* III, 908). Dickinson also associates her closest friend and sister-in-law Susan Gilbert Dickinson with the sun: before Sue's marriage to Emily's brother Austin, during a period when Sue was away from Amherst, Dickinson writes: "The sun shines warm, dear Susie, but the *sweetest* sunshine's gone" (*L* I, 102). The year before, she had written to Austin that the sunny March weather was "made on purpose for Susie and you and me" (*L* I, 80).

And even as the sun can represent the joys of human love, it also can represent the bright ecstasy of divine love:

> In thy long Paradise of Light
> No moment will there be
> When I shall long for Earthly Play
> And mortal Company—   (*P* 1145)

In fact, at the most positive end of Dickinson's spectrum of light metaphors, paradise is occasionally equated with the time of day most characterized by light—noon. Dickinson writes Mrs. Holland that "Vinnie says you are most illustrious and dwell in Paradise. I have never believed the latter to be a superhuman site. Eden, always eligible, is peculiarly so this noon. It would please you to see how intimate the Meadows are with the Sun" (*L* II, 508).[10] As in her earlier praise of Mrs. Holland's sunny friendship, the paradise she imagines here is not "superhuman," not ruled by a distant eye of God, but simply an inherent part of an ordinary—although beautiful—day. Further, Dickinson's delight in the intimacy of earth and sun suggests a harmony that might indeed characterize an earthly paradise.

Noon can also represent a more abstract kind of paradise, an immortal state of perfection:

> There is a Zone whose even Years
> No Solstice interrupt—
> Whose Sun constructs perpetual Noon
> Whose perfect Seasons wait—
>
> Whose Summer set in Summer, till
> The Centuries of June
> And Centuries of August cease
> And Consciousness—is Noon.   (*P* 1056)

Here, as Richard Sewall has suggested, Dickinson's equation is of noon with a heavenly "ideal world of pure essence."[11]

Noon as the peak of day can be a time of actual fulfillment, at times heavenly, at times earthly, as it is in this letter to Austin in which sister tantalizes brother with a description of the peaches, grapes, and apples the family are enjoying: "the cider is almost done—we shall have some I guess by Saturday, at any rate *Sunday noon!*" (*L* I, 53). In 1874, she writes Higginson, "Would you with the Bee return, what a Firm of Noon!" (*L* II, 405). A "summer's noon" can even transcend "ecstasy" with its "depth—an Azure—a perfume" (*P* 122), "A fashionless Delight" (*P* 297).

And years earlier, in a letter to Abiah Root, Dickinson tells her friend that their friendship must be growing closer than ever, differing as "morning differs from noon—one may be fresher, cheerier, but the other fails not" (*L* I, 91). But just as there is a subtle hint of ambiguity in this last image, so do these blissful "Certainties of Sun" (*P* 646) present the poet with a number of difficulties. We know she feared she had no place in a Christian paradise; her private rebellion against nineteenth-century cultural and religious confines only caused her to feel increasingly unsure of her own place in a paradise composed of light.[12]

She could imagine heaven variously, as having "different Signs," at times thinking "that Noon / Is but a symbol of the Place," and at other times that dawn or "The Rapture of a finished Day" are like "the place / That Men call 'Paradise.'" But either of these images of paradise, like the Edenic noon described to Mrs. Holland, are earthly in their beauty. Dickinson is not convinced, first, whether a Calvinist heaven could be better than a sensual earth, and second, whether she could ever fit in such a place:

> Itself be fairer—we suppose—
> But how Ourself, shall be
> Adorned, for a Superior Grace—
> Not yet, our eyes can see—   (*P* 575)

A similar and equally subtle ambivalence toward the light of human affection is evident in two passages from letters to Sue. About 1882, rejoicing in the imminent return of Susie, Dickinson refers to her old friend and sister-in-law as "an Avalanche of Sun" (*L*

III, 755). "Avalanche" is a curious word choice, with its suggestion of an uncontrollable barrage of rocks or snow; the poet seems to imply that Sue's return will be characterized by an overpowering light that may bury her. A letter of 1852 affords another insight into Dickinson's imaging of sun. Sue is returning in July, and Dickinson can hardly wait: "I view July so differently from what I used to—once it seemed parched, and dry—and I hardly loved it *any* on account of it's heat and dust; but *now* Susie, month of all the year the best; I skip the violets—and the dew, and the early Rose and the Robins; I will exchange them *all* for that angry and hot noonday, when I can count the hours and the *minutes* before you come" (*L* I, 77). The tone of this passage is strangely ambiguous, like the earlier double-edged letter to Austin, and like the man of noon letter. On the one hand, it seems as if Sue's return will mitigate the unpleasant effect of harsh summer sun and heat; but on the other hand, Sue is clearly associated with this very heat. After all, Massachusetts summers do include rainstorms, breezes, cool spells—yet Dickinson, in her youthful mock-heroic manner, agrees to forego the delights of spring in order to immerse herself in anticipation of an "angry" July noon. That both of these images associate Sue with the effects of too much sun suggest that although the poet adored Sue, her adoration was countered by an almost inexpressible degree of fear that is nevertheless expressed, albeit covertly and metaphorically, in these two passages.

As one of the poet's closest friends, Sue was both editor and muse. Like Bowles, Holland, and Higginson, she often commented on the poems, suggested changes, and she also inspired poems. Furthermore, Sue may have provided the poet with a link to the public world of masculine literary tradition, for Sue arduously hosted such contemporary literati as, for example, Ralph Waldo Emerson. Indeed, Dickinson's ambivalence toward Sue is similar to the "dilemma of influence" that Joanne Feit Diehl has argued the poet experienced in regard to both masculine precursor and muse[13] and is in addition similar to Dickinson's ambivalence toward the mighty man of noon himself.

Such intense ambivalence characterizes a number of Dickinson's poems that focus upon images of the sun. Often, the sun and the light of day are attractive, longed-for elements that are not to be trusted. In several poems, for instance, the light of day is a seductive but abandoning figure, as it is in *P* 1675, a verse so crucial that I have used it as an epigraph for this chapter:

> Of this is Day composed
> A morning and a noon
> A Revelry unspeakable
> And then a gay unknown
> Whose Pomps allure and spurn
> And dower and deprive
> And penury for Glory
> Remedilessly leave

Whereas morning brings an "unspeakable" revelry, noon becomes less sure; although it is gay, it is unknown. And although its "Pomps" are alluring in their brilliance, they quickly turn and "spurn" the speaker. Like the noon she once called "the hinge of day," noon opens the door to joy only to close it. The central drama of the poem is also described in terms of a marriage contract, one that is broken: the day is a rescinded dowry that leaves the poet an abandoned bride, in "penury" instead of "Glory." "Had I not seen the Sun" also makes such a statement of loss:

> Had I not seen the Sun
> I could have borne the shade
> But Light a newer Wilderness
> My Wilderness has made—   (*P* 1233)

Similarly, she explained to Sue in a letter of 1858, "We would'nt mind the sun, dear, if it did'nt *set*" (*L* II, 194).

The image of a teasing but rejecting sun is developed more fully in "The *Sun—just touched* the Morning—" (*P* 232), a poem in which the sun's "*haughty—spangled* Hems" first bring ecstacy but ultimately leave the poet deprived. In one sense this is a love poem: the masculine sun gently wakes the feminine morning to an awareness of brilliant possibilities. In the next stanza, the poet feels "Raised—*Ethereal*" because of the sun's attentions, which she imagines will bring her "*Holiday*" from now on. However, she is dropped and abandoned by this solar "wheeling King," again left with "a *new necessity*." Certainly the poem may be about love's loss, but it can also be read as a poem about writing. We have seen how often Dickinson uses images of climbing and height to indicate her literary ambitions; in feeling "*Raised*" and "*supremer*" she may have felt she reached those Empyrean levels of fine philosophy toward which she had struggled in her 1851 letter to Austin. But in being dropped, she is left alone at the end of the poem with her own mind—"Her *unanointed forehead*," which from now on, she writes, will be "Her *only* One!"

Contrary to the popular mythologized view of Dickinson during the earlier years of this century, the poet had not always written—and read—alone. In fact, as an adolescent, she had an eager forum for her developing and determined imagination among her school-mates, teachers, and friends connected with Amherst College. Young men such as Benjamin Franklin Newton, cousin John Graves, Henry Vaughan Emmons, George Gould, and Joseph Lyman invited her thoughts, her "fine philosophy," and in some instances, drafts of poems. Newton was her first "master"; when he died Dickinson grieved that she had lost the first of her "own friends." Among her girlhood friends, Jane Humphrey must have understood the poet's social and spiritual conflicts; and, of course, Susan Gilbert was a prime confidante for years. But almost all of these intellectual friends, at varying times and in varying ways, stopped encouraging Dickinson's literary aspirations. Some, like Jane Humphrey and Joseph Lyman, married and moved away. Others, like Newton, died.[14]

Dickinson's earlier friends were, of course, partially replaced, by the Hollands, the Bowles, Higginson, and Helen Hunt Jackson, but few of these professional literary people ever understood Dickinson's literary worth with the unreserved enthusiasm of such early friends as Newton. Indeed, as Karl Keller has argued, none of these members of Dickinson's mature circle of literary friends even trusted her judgment.[15] One of the subjects of "The *Sun—just touched* the Morning—" may very well be the failure of such friendships, as it may also be the subject of *P* 231:

> God permits industrious Angels—
> Afternoons—to play—

I met one—forgot my Schoolmates—
All—for Him—straightway—

God calls home—the Angels—promptly—
At the Setting Sun—
I missed mine—how *dreary—Marbles—*
After playing *Crown*!

About a year after she wrote this poem, Dickinson wrote another in which she describes her own self-coronation, this time independent of any solar power. She describes herself as "Adequate—Erect," willfully choosing "just a Crown" (*P* 508). Included in Fascicle 17, "I'm ceded—I've stopped being Theirs—" is surrounded by several poems about grief and loss: "I dreaded that first Robin, so" (*P* 348), "If you were coming in the Fall" (*P* 511), and "The Soul has Bandaged moments—" (*P* 512), to name a few.[16] Here in *P* 508 she has found a strategy to write in the face of loss. She can crown herself "Queen of Calvary" (*P* 348), a "woman—white" (*P* 271), and claim her "throne," a word she lists as an alternative to choosing "just a Crown."

However, in *P* 231 that I have quoted in full above, she was grappling still unsuccessfully with a sense of abandonment. By herself, she can play only marbles, a miniaturized (and perhaps, because of its minimized nature, also a feminized) version of a wonderful game of "Crown"—also a game of circles, spheres—she had enjoyed reciprocally with an "angel" playmate. But as the sun leaves the earth to continue its cycles, so too must such perfect friends leave. She fears then that the greater, loftier game of "Crown" that "Angels" can play is simply not for her, just as she fears the game of "fine philosophy," or literary tradition, is not for her, even though it has excited her so much that she feels "as if the top of [her] head were taken off."[17]

Furthermore, since the sun seems associated with lessened support, with an enticing but unreliable light, several poems express her bitterness, even scorn of the sun. If she has been excluded from the sun's sphere, perhaps he simply isn't worth it after all. In 1873 she wrote Mrs. Holland, "The Sun came out when you were gone. I chid him for delay—He said we had not needed him. Oh prying Sun!" (*L* II, 399). Obviously hoping for good weather during Mrs.

Holland's visit, Dickinson scorns a sun insensitive to her needs. Chastizing him for "prying," moreover, she suggests that he is actually interfering, second-guessing, and rather stupid—a bit like a bothersome neighbor, in fact. This passage is of course playful, but the following one is not. In the summer of 1858, her mother's health poor, she writes Joseph Sweetser: "Much has occurred, dear Uncle. . . . Today has been so glad without, and yet so grieved within—so jolly, shone the sun—and now the moon comes stealing, and yet it makes none glad. I cannot always see the light— please tell me if it shines" (*L* II, 190). More treacherous than the prying sun of the letter to Mrs. Holland, the sunlight here seems completely at odds with Dickinson's interior state. Her own worries are so severe that they overpower the sunlight itself—she can hardly see the light, even though it shines. Dickinson's metaphor is similar to that of contemporary American poet Adrienne Rich when she asks, "What kind of sunlight is it / that leaves the rocks so cold?"; like Rich, Dickinson suggests that the star that warms a planet doesn't necessarily warm *her*.[18]

Often, moreover, the sun in Dickinson's poetry seems to make little difference at all; at times it becomes unreliable to the point of impotence:

> The Sunset stopped on Cottages
> Where Sunset hence must be
> For treason not of His, but Life's,
> Gone Westerly, Today—
>
> The Sunset stopped on Cottages
> Where Morning just begun—
> What difference, after all, Thou mak'st
> Thou supercilious Sun?   (*P* 950)

The first stanza parallels the loss of a life to loss of light at day's end, a common enough analogy. The second stanza argues, however, that daylight seems actually to consist of very little daylight at all; the middle hours of day seem never to have existed, or at least to have gone by so fast they might never have existed. Only the borderlines of day seem real—the result of a sort of "treason" or trick played by life. In the end, the poet jibes, this "supercilious" sun swelled with his own importance has very little lasting effect.

Middle hours, perhaps like middle or adult years, are all but non-existent.

Other instances in the poems show a sunlight incapable of relieving the poet's private concerns, a sun that is incapable of bringing back life, as in *P* 999:

> Superfluous were the Sun
> When Excellence be dead

and in *P* 255:

> To die—takes just a little while—
> They say it doesn't hurt—
> It's only fainter—by degrees—
> And then—it's out of sight—
>
> A darker Ribbon—for a Day—
> A Crape upon the Hat—
> And then the pretty sunshine comes—
> And helps us to forget—

In each of these poems the sun seems superficial, the emotions of mourning causing its light to appear inappropriate, in *P* 999 "superfluous" or unnecessary. In *P* 255 the "pretty sunshine" seems actually flippant, silly, and insubstantial in contrast to death. Although of course these lines may be read literally, that the pleasing sunshine *does* mitigate the pain of a death, one also senses the same ironic undercurrent that began in the 1851 letters to Austin. Read in this way, the tone of *P* 255 seems bitingly sarcastic; "pretty sunshine" appears as insubstantial as ribbons on a hat in contrast to the enormity of dying, going "out of sight."

An additional example of Dickinson's denigration of the sun's capabilities occurs in *P* 1455:

> Opinion is a flitting thing,
> But Truth, outlasts the Sun—
> If then we cannot own them both—
> Possess the oldest one—

Flitting opinion is linked with the sun in the first two lines, whereas "Truth," an abstraction once called by the poet "my country," will endure even after the sun has burnt itself out. Since the sun seems as fickle and short-lived as public opinion, Dickinson would rather possess only "Truth."

The poet's underlying sarcasm surfaces at other times in the poems, as it does here:

> If I should die,
> And you should live—
> And time should gurgle on—
> And morn should beam—
> And noon should burn—
> As it has usual done—
> If Birds should build as early
> And Bees as bustling go—
> One might depart at option
> From enterprise below!
> 'Tis sweet to know that stocks will stand
> When we with Daisies lie—
> That Commerce will continue—
> And Trades as briskly fly—
> It makes the parting tranquil
> And keeps the soul serene—
> That gentlemen so sprightly
> Conduct the pleasing scene!   (*P* 54)

In his Freudian analysis of Dickinson's childhood, John Cody suggests that the poet suppressed volcanic anger which, because of her family's New England values, she could only express through her wit.[19] We have also seen how in letters to Austin Dickinson twisted language so that her deadly serious undercurrent was masked by a playful girlishness. Here too, in "If I should die," the poet's apparent and intended meanings may be quite different. For one thing, Dickinson's opinions regarding trade, commerce, and the "sprightly" gentlemen immersed in such economic concerns were in general very low. And for another, that she brightly asserts "'Tis sweet to know" that this business world of sprightly gentlemen will continue whether she is alive or dead reminds the reader that even while very much alive, this poet has no place in a world of commerce and trade, beaming morns and burning noons. The poem may be, in addition, a statement that she wants no part in it.[20]

"If I should die" also exemplifies the ambiguity that Karl Keller sees as one of Dickinson's primary defenses "against authority, against religious tyranny, against mechanistic thinking, against simplicity of social outlook." She keeps herself free, Keller argues, by escaping through irony and equivocation. The following poem, although not masked by sarcasm, is nevertheless an example of the oxymoronic ambiguity Keller describes as one of Dickinson's "main language structures":[21]

> The Sun is gay or stark
> According to our Deed.
> If Merry, He is merrier—
> If eager for the Dead
>
> Or an expended Day
> He helped to make too bright
> His mighty pleasure suits Us not
> It magnifies our Freight   (*P* 878)

If one is in such despair that one is "eager for the Dead" (a despair expressed in numerous other poems), the sun's brilliance only serves to heighten one's "Freight." In addition, the word "Freight" reminds the reader of the "smaller bundles" that in *P* 352 "cram" a basket the poet had wanted to fill with "firmaments," comprised perhaps of "fine philosophy" and poetry. Baggage, burdens, excessive weight, all loom larger in the sometimes "too bright" light of the sun.

Like her contemporary Thoreau sensing that she marched to a different drummer from that of most of the American populace, Dickinson felt that external, literal weather had no relation to her internal weather. When she was cheerful, she notes in "When I hoped, I recollect," not even sleet and frost could "bite" her; her external shawl had nothing to do with the internal optimism that fueled her. But when she was frightened, "Nature froze" although paradoxically "Worlds were lying out to sun"—like laundry that won't dry because something is inherently wrong with the sun and air (*P* 768).

Given all these ambiguities, it is not surprising that to Dickinson, something often did seem wrong with the very light of day. As I have mentioned previously, light may not have worked for the poet as it functions for most people; Martin Wand and Richard Sewall's suggestion that Dickinson may have suffered from exotropia is especially pertinent. For if she did endure severe eye strain, an obsession with sunlight as image would seem a logical poetic expression of such discomfort. Wand and Sewall also show that patients with exotropia (or who are "walleyed") often complain of discomfort from bright light in general and sunlight in particular.[22] But although such an optic deviation might explain the amazing force and painful intensity of so many of Dickinson's images of light, it does not explain the consistent associations of light with actual violence and destruction.

For much of her career Dickinson is obsessed by the destructive effects of too much sun and heat. Even at sixteen, she asks Abiah Root: "do you not think it has been unusually hot the past summer. I have really suffered from the heat. . . . There were over 100 deaths in Boston last week, a great many of them owing to the heat" (*L* I, 13). Granted, unusually hot weather does in fact, unfortunately cause literal physical suffering. But Dickinson so seldom overtly comments upon news events that, clearly, we must pay careful attention to her imagery, especially when it is often repeated.

The poet connected the sun with the deaths of her own friends: "I cannot realize that the friends I have seen pass from my sight in the prime of their days like dew before the sun will not again walk the streets" (*L* I, 10). Such an identification of young girls with dew, small beads of moisture glistening on earth's surface, and the sun with the force that dries them up, thereby destroying them, is a frequent connection in Dickinson's writing, as we have already seen, for example, in the much-quoted man of noon letter.

In a poem dated about 1870, Dickinson writes of a flower actually being devoured while in the sun's light:

> A full fed Rose on meals of Tint
> A Dinner for a Bee
> In process of the Noon became—
> Each bright Mortality
> The Forfeit is of Creature fair

Itself, adored before
Submitting for our unknown sake
To be esteemed no more—   (*P* 1154)

Here the female character of the rose has developed by feeding upon "meals of Tint," perhaps its own colors, perhaps taking color from its surroundings. But as the sun reaches its height of power, in the normal, daily "process of the Noon" the rose forfeits itself, provides "A Dinner for a Bee," becoming as it submits "esteemed no more." No wonder Dickinson so often wrote, then, of preferring hunger and isolation. She feared that in feasting *she* would be the food—she would be the one exploited. As a girl she had developed, fed on the colors of others' "fine philosophy" and her own exalted thoughts, growing her own intellectual petals of glowing reds and pinks. But as a woman she found that all this preparation was in the end for one thing only, to be yielded up to a male, to be forfeited and forgotten. Why become a "full fed Rose" at all, Dickinson must have wondered. Better to remain in a state of prebloom, remain unyielded, keep one's petals tight against the bee's appetite that seems stimulated by sunlight itself.

The extreme difficulty of her strategy is expressed in the last two stanzas of "Bloom—is Result—to meet a Flower":

To pack the Bud—oppose the Worm—
Obtain its right of Dew—
Adjust the Heat—elude the Wind—
Escape the prowling Bee

Great Nature not to disappoint
Awaiting Her that Day—
To be a Flower, is profound
Responsibility—   (*P* 1058)

The worry here is whether the bud has enough dew. No concerns are expressed as to whether it will have enough light or heat, in fact, quite the contrary, for heat, wind, and bee must be guarded against, just as the worm must be, so that she can remain intact as a flower. Earlier in this poem, Dickinson describes the overblown bloom as like a butterfly offered "To the Meridian." Similarly, in another poem she uses a butterfly to represent a female figure struggling with its most "profound Responsibility":

> The Butterfly's Numidian Gown
> With spots of Burnish roasted on
> Is proof against the Sun
> Yet prone to shut its spotted Fan
> And panting on a Clover lean
> As if it were undone—   (*P* 1387)

Choice of the word "prone" in line four suggests not only the meaning "tending to" but also "lying prostrate"; even with its "Numidian Gown," the small winged creature nevertheless is forced to fold its wings and lean on a clover leaf, out of breath in the heat, panting like a summer dog, "undone"—ultimately with no strength to continue flying in the face of the consuming sun.

If we could "Inquire of the closing Rose / Which rapture she preferred," Dickinson confides in *P* 1416, "she will point sighing / To her rescinded Bud." Similarly, in "Angels, in the early morning" the poet connects youthful hopes with the moisture of early morning and mature disappointment with the dry heat of noon:

> Angels, in the early morning
> May be seen the Dews among,
> Stooping—plucking—smiling—flying—
> Do the Buds to them belong?
>
> Angels, when the sun is hottest
> May be seen the sands among,
> Stooping—plucking—sighing—flying—
> Parched the flowers they bear along.   (*P* 94)

Written when the poet was only twenty-nine, this poem offers a grim picture of reality for many women of Dickinson's era. If, as Ellen Moers suggests, such small round items as pebbles, gems, or buds often represent a woman's self, it seems that their own "Buds," or selves, don't even belong to these angels.[23] Able to enjoy themselves only in the morning, they find that at noon, when the sun is hottest, the dews are gone, and they can only sigh wearily while bearing along their own "Parched" flowers, their essences that have been withered by the very light that helped produce them in the beginning. Dickinson at one time, moreover, referred to poems as flowers: if these buds can be read as poems, the implication is, further, that the sun's rays are inimical to creativity itself.[24]

A poem in a similar vein that also treats the anguish Dickinson experienced because of her inability to pursue her creative life openly and consistently is "A Dew sufficed itself—" (P 1437). She writes of "A Dew" sufficing itself, satisfying a leaf with its moisture as well, confidently looking forward to a "vast" destiny in contrast to an ordinary, "trivial" life. But, the poet continues ominously,

> The Sun went out to work—
> The Day went out to play
> And not again that Dew be seen
> By Physiognomy
>
> Whether by Day Abducted
> Or emptied by the Sun
> Into the Sea in passing
> Eternally unknown
>
> Attested to this Day
> That awful Tragedy
> By Transport's instability
> And Doom's celerity.

In this poem whose plot reads like a gothic novel, the sun and the day are jointly locked in a conspiracy to erase the dew, that had originally had high hopes for its future. In the ordinary process of their "work" and "play," the sun and the day doom the dew. The forces that *should* nurture and stimulate growth instead abduct or empty the dew of its ability to sustain itself.

"I held a Jewel in my fingers" relates more specifically how this "awful Tragedy" takes place:

> I held a Jewel in my fingers—
> And went to sleep—
> The day was warm, and winds were prosy—
> I said, "'Twill keep"—
>
> I woke—and chid my honest fingers,
> The Gem was gone—
> And now, an Amethyst remembrance
> Is all I own—   (P 245)

Like buds, jewels are small, compact, round, or ovoid objects; and like buds, jewels appear often in Dickinson's imagery as emblems for the poet's self, or more specifically, for her artistic genius. In an earlier poem, for instance, Dickinson bemoans that she had once "had a guinea golden" but "lost it in the sand" (*P* 23). In *P* 245, the warm day acts as enemy to the poet's jewel, or genius. Instead of encouraging her actively to use and develop her gift, thereby, perhaps, increasing its value, the warm day with its "prosy" winds lulls her to sleep. Dickinson often used "Prose" to suggest the forces of broad daylight that worked against her mind—while she aligned herself, instead, with poetry. Not surprisingly, then, when she wakes from a nap in the prosaic warmth of day, her gem of self has disappeared. Such a loss occurs, moreover, through no fault of her own "honest fingers." As Barbara Mossberg has suggested, since these are the same fingers that also hold the pen, this poem is a direct statement about the forces that work against creativity for Dickinson.[25]

An even more forceful image of the sun's victory over the poet occurs in *P* 1190:

> The Sun and Fog contested
> The Government of Day—
> The Sun took down his Yellow Whip
> And drove the Fog away—

This is how women are defeated, Dickinson tells us in her coded imagery: since he owns a "Yellow Whip," the sun invariably wins the contest that decides which force will rule the day—or perhaps life itself. Dickinson's own father did of course carry a whip (a practical necessity in the days of horse-driven carriages). Vinnie apparently told a story that Emily at one time registered fury and horror, "screaming to the top of her voice," at their father's whipping the family horse.[26]

Furthermore, as I have previously mentioned, the sun has long been associated with the phallus, several religious representations of the sun showing phallic figures emerging from the disk of the sun. The other contestant for the "Government of Day" is the fog, which softens the effects of the sun, affording privacy, moisture, and shadow. Since fog is a female image, an entity composed of individual particles of dew, the sun's lashing represents a cruel act of male power. If sunbeams slice away shadow and moisture in order to govern the day, they rob the poet of what she called the "vail" she needed.[27] At first glance another charming "nature poem," "The Sun and Fog contested" may be, rather, one of Dickinson's most succinct criticisms of patriarchy.

The sun's painful omnipotence is again the subject of the following poem:[28]

> When I have seen the Sun emerge
> From His amazing House—
> And leave a Day at every Door
> A Deed, in every place—
>
> Without the incident of Fame
> Or accident of Noise—
> The Earth has seemed to me a Drum,
> Pursued of little Boys   (*P* 888)

In an earlier poem, "I felt a Funeral, in my Brain" (*P* 280), Dickinson describes her mind-numbing pain at being reduced to "but an Ear." Concurrent with this funeral service, which is being given for the death of her own mind, sounds the unceasing beat of a drum. Here in "When I have seen the Sun emerge," the equation of the sun's rising with drumming is also painful; although this amazing sun can affect everyone effortlessly, without actually making any noise himself, when he begins to leave "a Day at every Door" the feminine earth becomes "pursued" by little boys who seem to be trying to beat her as if she were an instrument on which to make music. Stretched taut to vibrate to others' rhythms, the female earth is mute, unable to speak unless stricken by drum sticks that sound suspiciously like little brothers of the sun's whip. Although the first six lines of the poem read like an awed description of a natural phenomenon, the last two lines undercut the poet's seeming respect and amazement. Her image in these final lines suggests a sense of entrapment in a world that does not allow her an instrument with which to create her own sounds, music, or ideas. As Margaret Homans asserts, the fact that women have traditionally been identified with the earth has not provided helpful model for women poets: Mother Nature is, after all, only "prolific biologically, not linguistically."[29]

The horror of this view that a sun which causes life also causes such silencing is increased when we find that Dickinson also at times pairs the sun in its violence with another force of nature, the frost. In *P* 1624, for instance, sun and frost are co-conspirators against a "happy Flower":

> Apparently with no surprise
> To any happy Flower
> The Frost beheads it at its play—
> In accidental power—
> The blonde Assassin passes on—
> The Sun proceeds ummoved
> To measure off another Day
> For an Approving God.

Whether the frost commits the beheading while it is playing or while the flower is playing is a typical Dickinson ambiguity; nevertheless the tone of this poem is strongly reminiscent of Brontë's in *Shirley* when she remarks upon the thoughtless violence of the Titan boy who hurls one about in the "burning weather" of the nineteenth century. Accidentally, Dickinson's poem tells us, the frost destroys female floral figures, simply by doing what it naturally does. The "blonde Assassin" is moreover an ambiguous reference: it may refer not only to the frost but also to the sun, which after this act of floral cerebral castration, continues calmly measuring out the day, carrying out the orders of God, which clearly do not include stooping to protect such tiny entities as frost bitten flowers.

Again, in "As Frost is best conceived," the effects of the frost are seen as damaging only in the sun's light:

> If when the sun reveal,
> The Garden keep the Gash—
> If as the Days resume
> The wilted countenance
>
> Cannot correct the crease
> Or counteract the stain—
> Presumption is Vitality
> Was somewhere put in twain.   (*P* 951)

Dickinson is suggesting that the two forces of sun and frost work in tandem: the female image of the garden is gashed, torn, knifed; it bears a "wilted countenance," its new "crease" and "stain" cannot be changed, and of most significance, its own energy has been divided against itself.

That the bright white light of day aligns itself with a killing white frost seems further to emphasize Dickinson's sense of helplessness. It is as if at the two ends of her spectrum of sun imagery we find two brilliant lights: one a light of divinity or love that too often dazzles only to abandon, and the other a destructive light that blackens by scorching or freezing. Although viewed for years as essentially a private poet, the artist par excellence of Calvinist introspection, Dickinson nevertheless criticizes her culture as thoroughly as did Thoreau. David Porter's denigrating of Dickinson's poems because they "simply do not look outward" and "have no inherent order of priorities or perception" exemplifies the sort of impatient misreading to which Dickinson has been subjected—often because of an inability to see associative metaphoric patterns which actually exhibit a definite coherence when viewed in a "true light," to refer again to Brontë's phrase.[30] If Emerson defined woman as being "a docile daughter of God with her face heavenward, endeavouring to hear the divine word and convey it" to him, Dickinson's painful internalization of such patronization is clear.[31] What we find in "decoding" her sun imagery is a statement of the poet's awareness that if this daughter described by Emerson is intelligent and ambitious, she will not be able to lift her face heavenward for long, for she will be either disappointed or destroyed. To kindred spirit Joseph Lyman, one of those who did enthusiastically encourage her "fine philosophy" and who in 1858 was living in the American South, she worried, "I am afraid of those Great Suns."[32] Wives forgotten, daisies scathed, flowers blackened and erased by the combination of sun and frost—Dickinson's images of females victimized by a powerful sun not only remind of us of similar images in such nineteenth-century female writers as the Brontës, but also look forward to those of a twentieth-century woman poet like Anne Sexton, for instance, who wrote in 1968: "Daylight is nobody's friend."[33]

3   *Races Nurtured in the Dark*

Bird, bird, bird, bird we cry,
hear, pity us in pain,
hearts break in the sunlight,
hearts break in the daylight rain,
only night heals again,
    only night heals again   *H.D.*[1]

   I think "feminine literature" is an organic, translated writing
. . . translated from blackness, from darkness. Women have been
in darkness for centuries. They don't know themselves. Or only
poorly. And when women write, they translate this darkness.
                                        Marguerite Duras[2]

But oh, the night! oh, bitter sweet! oh,
    sweet!
O dark, O moon and stars, O ecstasy
Of darkness!   *Elizabeth Barrett Browning*[3]

Night is my favorite Day—I love silence
so—I don't mean halt (stop) of sound—
                        Emily Dickinson (L III.843)

Karl Keller has described Dickinson's poetry as "constructing a
politics of refusal,"[4] perhaps rephrasing a comment made a century
earlier, in 1876, by Dickinson's own friend Helen Hunt Jackson
when she accused the poet of "living away from sunlight."[5] Keller's
description applies to the poet's work, Jackson's to the poet's life;
but as Gilbert and Gubar have suggested, Dickinson often wove
together the text of her art and the facts of her life, frequently
enacting metaphors so that life and art fuse to become the poet's

"letter to the world."⁶ By the 1870s the poet was indeed literally living away from sunlight in that her reclusiveness had become a permanent way of life. Her agoraphobia—fear of public and open places—expressed her fear of all the sun and its light had come to represent: constraining expectations and judgments, as well as debilitating seduction, abandonment, and destruction. In this chapter I shall argue that Dickinson's refusal to participate in the world of sunlight leads to—or derives from—her identification with what she calls in *P* 581 "Races—nurtured in the Dark," an identification that provides a metaphoric room of her own allowing her, to rely again upon Virginia Woolf's phrasing, moments of "being" as opposed to moments of "non-being." I shall argue further that Dickinson's metaphoric identification with darkness reveals not only a politics of refusal to engage in a world dominated by a prosaic, patriarchal and prescriptive sun but also a poetics of acceptance, even assertion, of her position as a woman writer.

By embracing the darkness, Dickinson in fact resists the environmental forces that dominate her world in much the same way that, as Richard Poirier has shown, American writers like Cooper, Melville, and James resist these forces: in writing characterized by what Poirier has called "an eccentricity of defiance," she manages to create through metaphors of darkness a place where her own consciousness can be free.⁷ Just as Thoreau plumbed the depths of Walden Pond, just as Mark Twain's Huck Finn rafted down the wide Mississippi, just as Walt Whitman strode America's opening roads, and just as Henry James and his characters discovered the drawing rooms and museums of Western Europe, so too does Dickinson journey to *another place*. That she found freedom of consciousness within the shaded recesses of her father's house is one of the great paradoxes in literary history. But whereas male heroes have traditionally accomplished imaginative mental journeys while traveling through real geographical space (even Thoreau, who in many ways Dickinson most resembles, went *to* Walden Pond, walked to and from the village, his neighbors, and finally, of course, voluntarily walked away *from* the pond)—a woman intent upon her own spiritual journey had to accomplish it within the only borders she could claim as hers, the interior borders of the self. Suzanne Juhasz has recently argued that in her exploration of the self, Dickinson conceived of the mind as an "actual, substantial" place.[8] I am suggesting here that Dickinson was enabled brilliantly to discover and illuminate the "Undiscovered Continent" of the mind precisely because of her literal and metaphoric strategy to remove herself from the glare of the too brightly lit marketplace and church to inhabit what she felt to be *her* space, the dark. Even smaller and darker than the deep center of Walden Pond, Dickinson's own interior mental space could, she found, paradoxically contain infinite space—and, in a sense, immortality.

When Dickinson laments "A loss of something ever felt I" (*P* 959), bemoaning "a Dominion" from which she has been "cast out," she also realizes that she has been "looking oppositely" for her "Kingdom of Heaven," that as an ambitious female poet she will not find happiness in the traditional heaven of light. Indeed, like Mary Coleridge she must have feared that "On either hand there was no place for me."[9] Realizing that if the light of the sun has excluded her from his sphere, she must look elsewhere for a territory of her own, she announces in 1862,

> Good Morning—Midnight—
> I'm coming Home—
> Day—got tired of Me—
> How could I—of him?
>
> Sunshine was a sweet place—
> I liked to stay—
> But Morn—didn't want me—now—
> so—Goodnight—Day!   (*P* 425)

Again exemplifying what Keller has referred to as her frequent use of oxymoronic ambiguity, she decides that although "Some say goodnight—at night," she will "say goodnight by day" (*P* 1739). That the sun "got tired" of the speaker of the poem indeed reminds us of the many references in the poems to Dickinson's sense of the absence of a legitimate and permanent place for her energies, her poetry, her own voice. One thinks of such poems as "Why—do they shut Me out of Heaven?" (*P* 248), for instance, in which the speaker fears that she sings "too loud." If the daylight world is associated with all those "little duties" that the youthful poet wanted to reject because they forced her to be silent, not to sing or to write, then the same daylight world also rejected *her* by not accepting her for herself, not even seeing her, in fact, as an intellectual woman, let alone as an ambitious poet. Furthermore, the poet writes, such a reversal as having to say "Good Morning" to midnight is hardly "natural"; sunsets at dawn reverse "Nature," she observes, causing her to think boldly that "Jehovah's Watch—is wrong" (*P* 415). Because, as she comments in *P* 972,

> Unto Us—the Suns extinguish—
> To our Opposite
> New Horizons—they embellish—
> Fronting Us—with Night

she would fight what she calls in this poem a "Revolution / In Locality." Indeed, she will live her most active life while the inhabitants of the sun's world are most passive, as she implies when she notes

> Rests at Night
> The Sun from shining,
> Nature—and some Men—
> Rest at Noon—some Men—
> While Nature
> And the Sun—go on—   (*P* 714).

This poem, of course, makes an observation that is not original with Dickinson: that there are people of action, who rest at night, and that there are people of poetry, dreamers, mystics, who function oppositely to the "normal" scheme of things, who "Rest at Noon" while the rest of the world, nature, the sun, and other "prosy" folks, "go on." Dickinson's use of the phrase "go on," in fact, implies further that whatever activities these noontime people pursue may be rather trivial, just as some people's chatter goes on, and on—and just as so many Dickinson poems show the sun going on, and on, with either disastrous or useless results. The poet further implies here, albeit again covertly, that those who spend the night asleep, like the sun, may be missing something important, something that happens only at night.

Certainly in terms of the mystical tradition in literature, a "dark night of the soul" has often been necessary for art, whether male or female; but the conflict between the public demands of a sunlit daytime and the private artistic possibilities of a silent nighttime is heightened for a woman writer like Dickinson, for whom the day was specifically associated with specifically gender-related obligations and expectations. Furthermore, in traditional masculine imagery, it is normally the "light at the end of the tunnel" that is longed for, light that will bring release, relief, renewed energy and inspiration. If to a male writer the light meant renewed health, vigor, and sanity, meant agreeable social contact with the "real" world of sunlight, it meant something very different for a woman writer like Dickinson, as we have seen. For Dickinson, as a result of her reversal of traditional light/dark associations, waking "at Midnight" and "Dreaming—of the Dawn—" are "Sweeter" than waking to "a solid Dawn" that leads to "no Day" at all (*P* 450). "I seek the Dark," she insists, and finds a "purer food" than any the sun can offer (*P* 1109).

For Dickinson, such "purer food" was often the fruit of privacy, a luxury she generally associated with absence of sun. In a long, thoughtful letter in which the sixteen-year-old Dickinson expresses her anxiety in relation to God, affirming that "the world holds a predominant place in my affections," that she could not "give up all for Christ," she also comments at length upon the passing of time. Asking a typically Calvinist question of herself, she wonders "Why do we not strive to make a better improvement" of the hours and the swiftly passing seasons?—a question that paraphrases both the New Testament and Carlyle: "Work while the day lasts for the night is coming in the which no man can work" (*L* I, 13). At first glance Dickinson's admonition may seem a warning of death's imminence and the concomitant necessity for working diligently to improve the state of one's soul, a Carlylean incitement to "Be no longer a chaos" and "Produce!"[10] However, since Dickinson so often identifies the work of the day with forces of sun and superficiality, strictures and judgments of God and culture, this comment may be yet another of the poet's many double-edged statements. For to someone who also said "Blessed are they that play, for theirs is the kingdom of heaven" (*L* XIII, 690), an approaching night in which "no man can work" sounds suspiciously delightful.

A few years later, Dickinson uses another image of darkness to suggest privacy and opportunity for intimacy; hoping for a visit from Abiah, she imagines that they will talk inside her room with "shutters *closed*, dear Abiah and the balmiest little breeze stealing in at the window" (*L* I, 50). In a shadowy room, secure against a prying sun, she and her old friend will be able to "talk of what we were, and what we *are* and may be." The suggestions here of privacy from the rest of the world and from the duties of the day are reminiscent of a later comment Dickinson apparently made to her niece while pretending to lock the door of her room: "It's just a turn—and freedom, Matty!"[11]

Such a strong desire for privacy from the prying eyes of others who would interrupt one's "real life," as Dickinson once called it, often appears in the poems as images of invisibility. As an inhabitant of darkness, one has the luxury of not being seen, a characteristic shared by such "Best Things" as pearls and thoughts that "dwell out of Sight" (*P* 998). Indeed, as the twenty-year old Dickinson wrote Abiah, she loved "to buffet the sea" even though she knew that the "shore" upon which the conventional Abby remained was far "safer." In expressing her vague but intense longings in terms of wanting to dive through the waves of the ocean, the poet is of course expressing her desire to dive for the secrets—the pearls— of the deepest waters of the self, of the unconscious mind. "The Battle fought between the Soul" is an essential battle to Dickinson, even though "No News of it is had abroad—" and "Its Bodiless Campaign" remains "Invisible—Unknown" (*P* 594).

And, like the pearl that develops out of sight, the poet knows that her own "slow Riches"—her own poetic gains—although "perceiveless," grow "steady as the Sun / And every Night . . . numbered more / Than the preceding One" (*P* 843). As Barbara Mossberg has intelligently observed, such an observation demonstrates strong confidence in her literary abilities.[12] After all, Dickinson muses, the heavenly angels themselves are not observed by mortal eyes. She believes her own internal struggles to be *"gallanter"* than any witnessed by nations, by the surface, sunlit world:

> To fight aloud, is very brave—
> But *gallanter*, I know
> Who charge within the bosom
> The Cavalry of Woe—
>
> Who win, and nations do not see—
> Who fall—and none observe—
> Whose dying eyes, no Country
> Regards with patriot love—
>
> We trust, in plumed procession
> For such, the Angels go—
> Rank after Rank, with even feet—
> And Uniforms of Snow.   (*P* 126)

In likening her private "Cavalry of Woe" to the existence of angels "with even feet— / And Uniforms of Snow," she lifts her own difficulties with God and culture to a heavenly status.

Sometime during the sixties, Dickinson did in fact begin wearing a uniform of snow, a white dress that became a cryptic emblem for her self-designated royalty. Just as she dressed herself in clothes the color of snow, moreover, she developed in her poems the notion of snow as a veiling, protective entity. For like the night, time of darkness, winter as the season of darkness offers congenial space. Exemplifying Gaston Bachelard's comment that dreamers like a severe winter because "the winter cosmos is a simplified cosmos," [13] Dickinson relished the darkest season of the year for many of the same reasons she relished the darkest hours of the day. Unlike the violent combination of frost and sunlight that we saw in the previous chapter, the combinations of cold and darkness provide a climate for poetry. In late 1869 she wrote her Norcross cousins: "Read Mr. Lowell's *Winter*. One does not often meet anything so perfect" (*L* II, 337). Appearing in the 1870 *Atlantic Almanac*, Lowell's essay argues the case for winter as the superior season since "his dreams are finer than the best reality of his waking rivals . . . a purer current mounts to the brain, courses sparkling through it, and rinses it thoroughly of all dejected stuff."[14] If winter is for dreamers and "purer currents," here in this season of "chilly polish" Dickinson might find a home similar to her metaphoric home in midnight, one from which she could be neither excluded nor expected to "yield" herself as a sexually mature and therefore vulnerable woman.

About twenty years earlier she had written Jane Humphrey, often the recipient of Dickinson's deepest feelings about herself: "The winter was all one dream, and the spring has not yet waked me, I would *always* dream, and it never should turn to morning, so long as night is so blessed" (*L* I, 35). She preferred "steeper Air," she wrote Samuel Bowles (*L* II, 242), and the "bleak simplicity that knew no tutor but the North," she told Higginson (*L* II, 368), for, as she remarks in this couplet, "Winter under cultivation / Is as arable as Spring" (*P* 1707). Indeed, in one four-line poem undated by Johnson, she exclaims about winter:

> These are the days that Reindeer love
> And pranks the Northern star—
> This is the Sun's objective,
> And Finland of the Year. (*P* 1696)

That in this short poem Dickinson describes the season of snow as the "Sun's objective" causes winter to assume a greater value than summer, if "These are the days" the sun has been striving for all along, these days in which the North Star can play its "pranks," these days that seem as if something amazingly frisky, playful, wonderful, might happen. If she could adjust her days so that night would bring her inspiration, she could also adjust the seasons so that winter would allow her a kindly climate for blooming herself, for putting forth her own kinds of petals:

> God made a little Gentian—
> It tried—to be a Rose—
> And failed—and all the Summer laughed—
> But just before the Snows
>
> There rose a Purple Creature—
> That ravished all the Hill—
> And Summer hid her Forehead—
> And Mockery—was still—

The Frosts were her condition—
The Tyrian would not come
Until the North—invoke it—
Creator—Shall I—bloom?   (*P* 442)

We know that Dickinson often preferred buds to full-blown roses, with their reminders of full-grown sexuality and vulnerability. In "God made a little Gentian," Dickinson suggests that she had never been "made" to be a lush, sexually mature rose. Instead, she was really—had been all along—a gentian, a smaller flower than a rose, with petals structured so that, rather than radiating outward from a cluster of stamens, its petals form a dark, miniature tunnel (as D. H. Lawrence, for instance, makes vividly clear in his "Bavarian Gentians"). As a gentian ripens as a flower, its petals do not, in contrast to the rose, open out to the sun. Furthermore, the gentian is usually blue or purple, colors of the virgin or of royalty, rather than the fleshy pinks and brilliant reds and yellows of roses.[15] When the poet has attempted to become an overtly sexual rose, she appears a pitiful, comic figure in the light of all the sun's season of summer has come to represent. However, *her* season for rising and blooming is "just before the Snows" dominate the landscape. In such a climate, altitude, and season she is able to bloom profusely—in fact, dominate and "ravish" the hills with her purple petals. Although Dickinson often wrote of the painful effects of the sun, here the situation is pleasantly reversed for the poet: summer hides *her* forehead seemingly in shamed acceptance of the gentian's dark power.

In another poem also written about 1862, Dickinson again argues her preference for snow:

I think the Hemlock likes to stand
Upon a Marge of Snow—
It suits his own Austerity—
And satisfies an awe

That men, must slake in Wilderness—
And in the Desert—cloy—
An instinct for the Hoar, the Bald—
Lapland's—necessity—

The Hemlock's nature thrives—on cold—
The Gnash of Northern winds

Its sweetest nutriment—to him—
His best Norwegian Wines—

To satin Races—he is nought—
But Children on the Don,
Beneath his Tabernacles, play,
And Dnieper Wrestlers, run.   (*P* 525)

Whether Dickinson identifies with the hemlock, the children, or the
wrestlers, the "Marge of Snow" offers an austerity conducive to the
imagination and to poetry. This landscape that satisfies "an awe"
provides winds like wine, reviving the soul. Indeed, that the poet
thrives on austerity, on cold, reminds us of Barbara Mossberg's
argument that the poet also thrives on another sort of "austerity,"
that her "hunger aesthetics" are in fact a strategy necessary to her
artistic fulfillment.[16]

One of Dickinson's most anthologized poems uses the image of
winter snow to describe a season of icy fruitfulness for this writer:

It sifts from Leaden Sieves—
It powders all the Wood.
It fills with Alabaster Wool
The Wrinkles of the Road—

It makes an Even Face
Of Mountain, and of Plain—
Unbroken Forehead from the East
Unto the East again—

It reaches to the Fence—
It wraps it Rail by Rail
Till it is lost in Fleeces—
It deals Celestial Vail

To Stump, and Stack—and Stem—
A Summer's empty Room—
Acres of Joints, where Harvests were,
Recordless, but for them—

It Ruffles Wrists of Posts
As Ankles of a Queen—
Then stills its Artisans—like Ghosts—
Denying they have been—   (*P* 311)

By evening out discrepancies of nature—mountains and plains,
high places and low places (perhaps even high people and low

people)—the snow transforms the universe into a harmonious, unbroken whole. Indeed, this landscape is characterized by its "Unbroken Forehead," an image that contrasts sharply with the lost gems, crowns, and selves characteristic of poems showing the sun's destructive influences. Here in *P* 311, the snow spreads out over a wide landscape, providing a scope for the imagination and the mind not possible under a blindingly bright summer sky or even a winter sunlight that revealed "gashes" or conspired to behead flowers. Unlike the sun which pierces veils, the snow *provides* a "Celestial Vail," encouraging the poet's mental processes and keeping God's judgmental eye at bay. That the snow's artisans become silent after their work is done is another indication of how friendly this aspect of nature is for Dickinson: rather than dominating noisily like the little boys pursuing with drum sticks, in this poem nature's "Artisans" of snow become silent, allowing Dickinson's own mind and voice free range. The snow provides an ideal working climate, since it has no voice of its own to silence her.

Furthermore, not only does the snow provide an ideal climate and vision for Dickinson's "Forehead" to move in mental or imaginative space, but the phallic fenceposts in the last stanza also become transformed into amazingly powerful female images: the "Ankles of a Queen," a queen such as Dickinson herself tells us in other poems she will be.[17] Whereas in "Over the fence" she had been unable to climb over the fence rails to pick her own berries (even though she knew she could), here she describes a gigantic female figure who becomes mistress of this entire landscape. Here she can live on an Empyrean level, her "fine philosophy" spreading out unchecked, with no hostile forces to insist she should be doing something else. In this winter landscape, the poet can construct a gigantic snow queen, able to assert her full mental power.

Finally, even the snow itself becomes identified with Dickinson's actual creations, her poems, for when she defensively describes "Publication" as "the Auction / Of the Mind of Man—" (*P* 709) she refers to her own poems as "snow," which is, obviously, an unmarketable product, destroyed in fact *as snow* when exposed to too much sun that melts it down, rendering it once again invisible.[18]

Accomplishing a revolution in locality by finding solace, inspiration, and room in the dark—or the dark season—also leads to a concomitant revolution in vision, what Dickinson calls in *P* 627 "Another way—to see." Several poems suggest that lack of vision in the sunlight world only provides a more accurate vision, just as Oedipus and Lear's blindness symbolizes their new abilities to "see" the truth, as in Dickinson's *P* 939: "What I see not, I better see— / . . . Till jealous Daylight interrupt— / And mar thy perfectness—." In this poem her daydream—or night fantasy—of the beloved is more "real" than the bewildering and overwhelming daylight world. Similarly, in *P* 474, she and a lover outwit the forces that separate them, their superior "vision" allowing them to "see" each other even when "far apart." When the pair are summoned to die, they turn "their backs upon the Sun" and by "setting" themselves," or dying, each sees the "Disc" of the other's face. Here the face of the lover actually becomes a sun itself, paradoxically independent of normal sight or even life.

However, blindness was not always a better way for Dickinson; it was, at times, only a terrible alternative.[19] "From Blank to Blank" (*P* 761), for instance, is a poem of exhausted despair; blindness, the poet tells us, is a better alternative only because the reality of sight has been so excruciating:

> From Blank to Blank—
> A Threadless Way
> I pushed Mechanic feet—
> To stop—or perish—or advance—
> Alike indifferent—
>
> If end I gained
> It ends beyond
> Indefinite disclosed—
> I shut my eyes—and groped as well
> 'Twas lighter—to be Blind—

Such blankness is in fact reminiscent of the blank brilliance of a snowy landscape that might indeed be blinding in its whiteness. Dickinson complained at one time during her difficulties with her own eyes that the "snow light offends them."[20] Here in *P* 761 the poet expresses an extreme negative version of her triumphant vision of a snow that "sifts from Leaden Sieves." In this poem life consists of sewing with blank thread upon blank cloth—an endeavor as impossible as one of the labors required of Hercules. But we have no hope that gods will soon be on the way to help the poet accomplish her impossible task. Rather, she has no reason to continue moving, her indifferent feet have no sense of direction or purpose. Since she cannot "see" to what end she is making her way, it becomes easier to shut her eyes to the external void.

At times, moreover, her pain—or "Madness"—is so extreme that to see earth's beauties only causes her mental fragility to appear more obviously precarious:

> Had we our senses
> But perhaps 'tis well they're not at Home
> So intimate with Madness
> He's liable with them
>
> Had we the eyes within our Head—
> How well that we are Blind—
> We could not look upon the Earth—
> So utterly unmoved—   (P 1284)

Just as the sun's light only accentuated her grief, so too do the beauties her eyes show her accentuate her internal battles. In fact, she suggests that to feel earth's joys would send her reeling into total madness; the blindness causes a blessed numbness that allows her respite from reminders of what she cannot have.

One doesn't easily forget that in choosing "Midnight" as home, Dickinson laments that she had really wanted "Day." Her sense of relegation to the darkness, of not being allowed to participate as herself—as an ambitious writer—in the active world of the sun, necessitates courage and determination:

> We grow accustomed to the Dark—
> When Light is put away—
> As when the Neighbor holds the Lamp
> To witness her Goodbye—
>
> A Moment—We uncertain step
> For newness of the night—
> Then—fit our Vision to the Dark—
> And meet the Road—erect—

And so of larger—Darknesses—
Those Evenings of the Brain—
When not a Moon disclose a sign—
Or Star—come out—within—

The Bravest—grope a little—
And sometimes hit a Tree
Directly in the Forehead—
But as they learn to see—

Either the Darkness alters—
Or something in the sight
Adjusts itself to Midnight—
And Life steps almost straight.　　　　　　(*P* 419)

Left alone without light or friend, the poet begins to fit her "Vision to the Dark," meeting the road ahead "erect." At first she may occasionally bump into something, but as she learns to see in the dark she learns "Another way—to see." Denied her own way of seeing reality in a daylight dominated by what Dorothea Brooke called "the monotonous light of an alien world," the poet will learn to develop night vision, another way to see that will allow her *her* vision.[21]

However, one of Dickinson's most startling poems indicates that she did at some time feel her eye had been "put out":

Before I got my eye put out
I liked as well to see—
As other Creatures, that have Eyes
And know no other way—

But were it told to me—Today—
That I might have the sky
For mine—I tell you that my Heart
Would split, for size of me—

The Meadows—mine
The Mountains—mine—
All Forests—Stintless Stars—
As much of Noon as I could take
Between my finite eyes—

The Motions of the Dipping Birds—
The Morning's Amber Road—
For mine—to look at when I liked—
The News would strike me dead—

So safer—guess—with just my soul
Upon the Window pane—
Where other Creatures put their eyes—
Incautious—of the Sun—   (*P* 327)

Whereas in "Renunciation—is a piercing Virtue—" (*P* 745), the
poet renounces an unnamed "Presence" so that her eyes will not be
put out ("Not now— / The putting out of Eyes—"), here she has
been blinded it seems against her will. But although she "liked as
well to see," she also fears that if she were to have her eyes back
again, the sky, the meadows, forests, noon, birds, and even morning would somehow "strike" her "dead." She chooses, therefore, to
remain at the window of life, safely within the shadows of a house,
very much like Hawthorne's observer characters, Miles Coverdale,
for instance, or Clifford Pyncheon. To be "Incautious—of the Sun,"
after all, might result in further blinding.

Of course, if one lives so that one is, in a sense, invisible to the
world and so that one does not see the visible world, one might
begin to feel not just privacy but privation, not just interiority but
entombment. This other "way—to see" could lead to a way of shutting one's "Cheated" eyes "in the Grave." Dramatically and probably ironically expressing her acute sense of exclusion from the daylight world, Dickinson in at least one poem indicates that she has
been so "Cheated" that she might as well as die, as in "'Tis
Sunrise—Little Maid—Hast Thou / No Station in the Day?":

My little Maid—'Tis Night—Alas
That Night should be to thee
Instead of Morning—Had'st thou broached
Thy little Plan to Die
Dissuade thee, if I could not, Sweet,
I might have aided—thee—   (*P* 908)

Although perhaps a parody of the graveyard verse that filled gift
books and magazines of the mid-nineteenth century, "'Tis Sunrise—Little Maid" may also suggest Dickinson's painful awareness
that her culture provided no actual place for little maidens with big
minds, thereby actually encouraging them, in a sense, to die.

The logical extension of a life in the dark is of course death. Dickinson is, in fact, as obsessed with grave, tomb, and death images as she is with sun imagery, perhaps substantiating May Sarton's comment that "people fear death because they haven't had their lives."[22] But Dickinson also implies that the life her culture expected her to live, a life surrounded by "brittle ladies" and "dimity convictions," was in fact death to her. "'Tis not that Dying hurts us so," she asserts in *P* 335, "'Tis living—hurts us more," wishing that she, like the grass, had so little to do she could "dream the Days away" (*P* 333). Death as a dark, private life of dream "behind the door" would be preferable to a kind of living that involved no time for the imagination, no time for poems. In fact, by "dying" metaphorically to the bright, external world, she paradoxically finds her creative energy:

> A Death blow is a Life blow to Some
> Who till they died, did not alive become—
> Who had they lived, had died but when
> They died, Vitality begun.   (*P* 816)

Death could, as in this poem, provide relief, rest, and independence:

> A long—long Sleep—A famous—Sleep—
> That makes no show for Morn—
> By Stretch of Limb—or stir of Lid—
> An independent One—
>
> Was ever idleness like This?
> Upon a Bank of Stone
> To bask the Centuries away—
> Nor once look up—for Noon?   (*P* 654)

Here again, as in "It Sifts from Leaden Sieves," is a sense of dark, eternal spaciousness—no trivial bundles cram the basket of eternity. Indeed, such a long, independent sleep seems much like rebellious late sleeping, ignoring the calls of morning and even noon with their demands and obligations.

What Dickinson felt she had to do in order to survive as an ambitious poet involved one of the most difficult paradoxes imaginable,

a "politics of refusal" that necessitated constantly walking a metaphorical tightrope:

> To die—without the Dying
> And live—without the Life
> This is the hardest Miracle
> Propounded to Belief.   (*P* 1017)

This dark, almost deathlike private life "behind the door" involved
exactly that kind of internal struggle that Dickinson values in *P* 126
as "*gallanter*." By embracing the darkness, by shutting herself away
from the external world of light, the poet confronted her own
"Vitality" in a manner impossible in the external sphere of the sun,
with its familial, social, and religious demands. Dickinson determined, through her "Revolution / In Locality," to develop her own
self. Her politics of refusal, her strategy of dying to light and life,
involve a determination to confront and accept her own identity—a
word she uses in *P* 822:

> Adventure most unto itself
> The Soul condemned to be—
> Attended by a single Hound
> Its own identity.

However, in journeying down to the subterranean, lightless
levels of her soul, she found much to fear. Her own soul's "Hour
with itself" could be frightening:

> What Terror would enthrall the Street
> Could Countenance disclose
>
> The Subterranean Freight
> The Cellars of the Soul—
> Thank God the loudest Place he made
> Is licensed to be still.   (*P* 1225)

Again she writes in paradox: her interior self is actually the "loudest
Place" in creation; but even though God made it, he and her culture
have "licensed" her most vital self to "be still."

In his discussion of the metaphoric significance we attach to the
parts of a house, Gaston Bachelard notes that the cellar is "first and

foremost the *dark entity* of the house, the one that partakes of subterranean forces.[23] Dickinson's discoveries of her dark irrational depths are fraught with terror—she enjoys no easy harmony in identifying her "subterranean forces." For if in the thought patterns of her culture, darkness, evil, and femaleness were somehow linked, the enormous energies that she confronted within the darkness of her own soul seemed terrifying, even satanic.

At times, in fact, the hidden horrors of her dark soul are equal to the more obvious, open violence of the external sun. As she wrote Dr. and Mrs. Holland in 1859, "Don't leave us long, dear friends! You know we're children still, and children fear the dark" (*L* II, 207). Here twenty-nine, Dickinson equates desertion and perhaps her anger at desertion with night; her exclusion from the world of sunlight could cause her both to triumph in darkness and to fear it.[24] She also writes at other times of fearing the "Unknowns" that "Engulf thee in the night" (*P* 1218) and despairing of a heart that becomes "darker than the starless night," a "black Receptacle" in which there "Can be no Bode of Dawn" (*P* 1378). "Midnight's awful Pattern" together with the loneliness it necessitated could result in unbearable fear:

> The Horror not to be surveyed—
> But skirted in the Dark—
> With Consciousness suspended—
> And Being under Lock—
>
> I fear me this—is Loneliness—
> The Maker of the soul
> Its Caverns and its Corridors
> Illuminate—or seal—   (*P* 777)

Unlike her delighted whisper to Mattie about the freedom she can gain after turning the lock to her door, this poem depicts the room alone as a tomb inhabited by a "Horror not to be surveyed." "Being under Lock" could bring with it the fear that such a journey to the depths of the soul might never end; the soul's creator may "Illuminate" the "Caverns" and "Corridors" of the mind, or it may seal one inside.

And of course, in searching the caves and hallways of the self, one might stumble upon monstrosities, horrors "not to be surveyed."

In "The Soul has bandaged moments—" (*P* 512), a "ghastly Fright" like a goblin becomes a bomb that has "moments of Escape" only to be "retaken" like a "Felon." But the vitality within Dickinson's "Cellars of the Soul" might not hold such horror if she could bring it and keep it above ground. Her immense energy has no sanctioned field upon which to play itself out; imprisoned in her mind's dark basement, it comes close to exploding. Suppressed as it must be, her intellectual energy assumes such terrifying proportions that it seems to become a bomb when it finally does burst the doors and emerges—illicitly—into consciousness and culture.

The poet's awareness of her energies and the difficulties of suppressing them becomes subject of several poems. In "Did you ever stand in a Cavern's Mouth—" (*P* 590), for instance, she confronts the cavern of her own subconscious, "Widths out of the Sun," and shudders in "Goblin" fear. In a less-frightening but equally-striking image, she tells the reader that she is never alone, for "Hosts— do visit me," a "Recordless Company" who are "never gone" (*P* 298). These strange creatures who keep her company are "Like Gnomes," little energetic, masculine creatures who seem to appear through the walls of consciousness.[25] Her awareness of her own energies is not always characterized by fear or even ambivalence, however.

In a letter of 1862 to Higginson, she metaphorically traces her intellectual history, using imagery similar to that of *P* 590 and *P* 298: "When much in the Woods as a little Girl, I was told that the Snake would bite me, that I might pick a poisonous flower, or Goblins kidnap me, but I went along and met no one but Angels, who were far shyer of me, than I could be of them, so I hav'nt that confidence in fraud which many exercise" (*L* II, 271). The American moral code which shaped Dickinson's imagination had from the beginning been shaped by a deep fear of the woods and wilderness; these dark, untamed places seemed perfect analogies for the antichristian forces that kept at bay the "sun of righteousness."[26] But in this passage of her letter, Dickinson tells her "preceptor" that she has found no demons in the forests—only angels, who serve, perhaps, as guides to the woods of her own mind. Here (although once again, cryptically) she expresses strong confidence in her own creative energies. Her culture may fear that left alone to explore the dark recesses of the mind she will be "kidnapped," but she knows that the creatures most New Englanders see as "Goblin" are, paradoxically, angels to her.

All of this imagery suggests, of course, that by "looking oppositely" for her kingdom of heaven, this poet finds paradise where her culture found Satan. One of the common images of Dickinson's time was that of the unredeemed human as a "worm"; the serpent had always been image of evil, from the story of Eden. Dickinson's obvious fascination with worms is further evidence of her great difficulty in accepting the New England Protestant view of humanity as depraved until given up to Christ. About 1858 she asked Samuel Bowles, "Our Pastor says we are a 'Worm.' How is that reconciled" (*L* II, 193). Indeed, how could such a metaphoric definition be explained for the poet? At twenty, Dickinson wrote Abiah Root that her own "flowers of speech," that is, her metaphors, are as dangerous as snakebites; however, as she goes on to say in one of her most amazing linguistic dances of paradox, she in fact loves snakes, and, while she warns Abiah of their dangers, she entices her with their fascination (*L* I, 31). As Margaret Homans has argued, Dickinson linked snakes with the power of language, the power she valued most; but she could only see her own poetic power as "bad," since it needed to assert itself away from the sunny world of dress fittings and calling cards [27] Furthermore, since to Dickinson the God of her fathers represented a God whose public worship often caused her to feel a hot tedium that *kept* her from her own Soul, it would follow that because of the dual nature of her culture's thought, she had to identify with supposedly satanic races nurtured in the dark.

An example of the poet's difficulty with this metaphoric dilemma occurs in *P* 1670, a poem often interpreted as an example of the poet's fear of sexuality.[28] But it can also be read as an example of Dickinson's awareness of her own mental energies and her awareness of her culture's attitudes toward those energies.

In Winter in my Room
I came upon a Worm—
Pink, lank and warm—
But as he was a worm
And worms presume
Not quite with him at home—
Secured him by a string
To something neighboring
And went along.

A Trifle afterward
A thing occurred
I'd not believe it if I heard
But state with creeping blood—
A snake with mottles rare
Surveyed my chamber floor
In feature as the worm before
But ringed with power—
The very string with which
I tied him—too
When he was mean and new
That string was there—

I shrank—"How fair you are"!
Propitiation's claw—
"Afraid," he hissed
"Of me"?
"No cordiality"—
He fathomed me—
Then to Rhythm *Slim*
Secreted in his Form
As Patterns swim
Projected him.

That time I flew
Both eyes his way
Lest he pursue
Nor ever ceased to run
Till in a distant Town
Towns on from mine
I set me down
This was a dream.   (*P* 1670)

Although it is no wonder that this poem has been discussed as involving Dickinson's fearful fascination with the penis, I am con-

vinced that what she really confronts in this poem is her own creative literary energy, which in her imagination is linked with evil, the
serpent in God's first garden, with the wormlike nature of depraved
humankind. Since this "fair" worm must be evil, she must make
sure she has it under control; she places it on a leash, as one would
an unruly dog. Then she continues on her way, on her journey
through life as it were, with this worm/energy on a leash, but as
time goes on she realizes to her horror that while within the
confines of her "chamber," perhaps her own mind, this one-time
worm has become a full-sized snake "ringed with power." Because
she has leashed the snake, tied it up so it has not had full room for its
own energies, she has caused it to grow proportionately in the same
manner that the goblin becomes the bomb in *P* 512. Thus she
shrinks in fearful apprehension that something she has been taught
is evil is, instead, quite "fair." Indeed, she fears the snake because
she recognizes its power.

He in turn recognizes her, sees her to her depths: "He fathomed
me." Immediately after each sees the truth of the other, moreover,
Dickinson's lines seem to describe her own poems. For the lines
"Then to a Rhythm *Slim* / Secreted in his Form / As Patterns swim"
apply to her unusual prosody, consisting as it does of slim rhythms,
rather like snake rustlings; in fact, her snake's rhythm is secreted in
his own form, just as the rhythms of her poems are often dependent
on the substance of the poems themselves rather than on external
requirements of meter and rhyme. Her patterns often do swim, do
seem to follow a flowing, watery movement rather than fixed, traditional stanzaic requirements. The snake therefore represents herself,
her poems, her imagination, her energy, but it also, to the mind of a
young woman raised with Calvinist notions of good and evil, represents evil. Finally, then, when the poem's speaker runs away from
her own power, represented by the snake, she does not run to a
member of her family, or even to a place within her own town, but
to a "distant Town," perhaps a place where in the end her snake can
safely and openly join her, so she can live with her strongest energies openly acknowledged.[29]

Other creatures of satanic darkness occupy Dickinson's poems,
creatures normally associated with dread, with dark, "under-

ground" forces. One of Dickinson's earliest poems, *P* 61, for instance, describes the poet's strategy of darkness, asking a heavenly "Papa" to "Reserve within thy kingdom" a "Mansion" for a "Rat" who, "Snug in seraphic Cupboards" is nibbling "all the day," as if eating away the foundations of her own father's house, while "unsuspecting Cycles / Wheel," reminiscent, as Gilbert and Gubar have suggested, of the generations of God-fearing ancestors whose strictures Dickinson was—in her retreat to solitude and to writing—subverting. That she identifies or at least sympathizes with such a subhuman creature as a mouse or rat who nibbles at the foundations of "Papa's" house provides an image of what Dickinson's writing actually was—a secret form of rebellion. For unlike the dog, the rat is no friend to man, bringing plagues, populating unlighted underground networks of pipes, basements, and cellars. This poem expresses how very rebellious Dickinson felt herself to be; asking the traditional figure of God the Father for *room* to eat up the existing foundation of her father's house or perhaps even the structures of society, she couched her meaning in such a childlike metaphor that few readers would suspect the power behind the rodent's teeth.[30]

Civilization has, after all, had little control over the vast populations of underground nocturnal rodents who effectively destroy gardens and baseboards. Written almost fifteen years after "Papa above," *P* 1356 outlines the abilities of these residents of night's country even more clearly:

> The Rat is the concisest Tenant.
> He pays no Rent.
> Repudiates the Obligation—
> On Schemes intent
>
> Balking our Wit
> To sound or circumvent—
> Hate cannot harm
> A Foe so reticent—
> Neither Decree prohibit him—
> Lawful as Equilibrium.   (*P* 1356)

Refusing the usual "Obligation[s]" of normal, external living, the rat confuses the thoughts of the daylight world's inhabitants. None of the surface world's laws can even touch this nocturnal animal, for he is "Lawful as Equilibrium" or, as Dickinson suggests, part of the natural scheme of things, as "legal" as the basic principles of a universe that is composed of darkness as well as light. In identifying with a rat or mouse, Dickinson states emphatically that she too will not participate in the world of the sun, dominated by men of noon and their rents, legal obligations, "Decrees," or normal, rational, logical "wit." By retreating to the darkness, becoming very small—or, as we have seen, at times invisible—she would have powers undreamed of if she were to battle the sunlight world on its territory. Her strategy was one of quiet undermining.

Another creature of darkness that occupies a central space in Dickinson's metaphors suggesting rebellious nighttime creation is the spider. Albert Gelpi, Sandra Gilbert, and Susan Gubar have discussed the spider's significance to Dickinson as an artist; it is Gilbert's and Gubar's argument that the spider who

> . . . holds a Silver Ball
> In unperceived Hands—
> And dancing softly to Himself
> His Yarn of Pearl—unwinds—   (P 605)

is actually practicing secret female art, although the poem does end with the spider's "Tapestries" being destroyed the next day by a "Housewife's Broom." Another poem whose main character is also a spider is P 1138, "A Spider sewed at Night," in which the poet states emphatically that the spider's sewing involved nothing short of a "Strategy" of "Immortality." In this poem it seems not to matter whether by noon some industrious dutiful housewife will sweep away the carefully woven web of night's work; here, the spider's work will last, long after the housewife who obediently follows the admonitions of the daylight world.[31]

Snakes, rats, spiders, and even thieves are sympathetic inhabitants of darkness in Dickinson's poems. "I know some lonely Houses off the Road" (P 289) describes in detail a robbery that occurs at night; the narrative is charming and light—this theft seems merely a grand adventure by the moon. Primarily playful, the poem nevertheless contains several images that again suggest Dickinson's sympathies with darkness and all it connotes. The clock, for instance, can be silenced; whereas by day clock time dominates, and the positions of the sun are constant reminders of the required stations of the day, at night, time becomes less linear and more dreamlike.[32] As the quality of time is friendly here, so too are the animals in the poem: the "Walls—don't tell" because mice, unlike dogs, "won't bark." These little creatures of night's underground are no threat to the robbers. Part of the humor of the poem relies upon the fact that the old couple who rule the house by day have no idea what is going on in their own house by night, just as Dickinson's parents probably had no idea how much she accomplished for herself in the dark.

The nighttime in fact allowed Dickinson to piece together the events of the day, which often caused disintegration. To feel that one was kin to creatures whom one's culture found disgusting, satanic, or at least, illegal, could of course cause one to feel mad. If one danced not only to a different drummer, as Thoreau counseled Americans to do, but to a beat opposed and inaudible to that of the normal world, and if the normal occupants of the normal sunlit world were not only "good" but also sane, then perhaps one was not only "bad" but also mad. Cody, Gilbert and Gubar, and others have discussed Dickinson's probable psychotic breakdown. Significantly, in her poems that seem to trace her awful experiences with madness, she also associates daylight with experiences that drove her mad, and darkness with healing, as in "The first Day's Night had come—" (*P* 410), in which her soul mends itself during the night "Until another Morn" when "a Day as huge / As Yesterdays in pairs, / Unrolled its horror in my face." From our vantage point, of course, it may seem that madness might have been—in some ways—a healthy response to the precarious position in which Dickinson as ambitious poet found herself. Refusing to join in the "normal" religious fervor surrounding her in the Connecticut Valley or to take part in the usual female small-town social rituals of the mid-nineteenth century, she was indeed abnormal. The position of the writer or artist in America has always been problematic; Hawthorne, Melville, Emerson, and Thoreau all had great difficulties with the prevailing "climate" of their time and locale. It was such an acute awareness of her oppositeness to the rest of her world that brought Dickinson to formulate one of her most famous paradoxes, "Much Madness is divinest Sense— / To a discerning Eye— / Much Sense—the starkest Madness— / 'Tis the Majority / In this, as All, prevail— / Assent—and you are sane— / Demur—you're straightway dangerous— / And handled with a Chain—" (*P* 435). Perhaps more than any other, this poem suggests how strong the prevailing sensibility of the "majority" must have seemed to Dickinson; her own "madness," constituted at least partially by intellectual and poetic genius and ambition must have caused great discomfort among Amherst folks, with their "Dimity convictions." That so much of Dickinson's writing is cryptic and covert emphasizes just how unpopular and "mad" she must have felt her own thoughts to be.

But again paradoxically, this same madness could also lead to triumph. In 1862, Dickinson wrote one of her most jubilant poems, defining how forces of darkness—even aligned as they were with forces of evil—could come to represent all the creative power of divinity itself. She writes in "I think I was enchanted" (*P* 593) of a divinity that fires her own creativity, a divine "Lunacy of Light" under which she can grow as heroic in stature as the queen whose ankles are strong as the snow-covered fence posts in "It sifts from Leaden sieves":

> I think I was enchanted
> When first a sombre Girl—
> I read that Foreign Lady—
> The Dark—felt beautiful—
>
> And whether it was noon at night—
> Or only Heaven—at Noon—
> For very Lunacy of Light
> I had not power to tell—
>
> The Bees—became as Butterflies—
> The Butterflies—as Swans—
> Approached—and spurned the narrow Grass—
> And just the meanest Tunes

That Nature murmured to herself
To keep herself in Cheer—
I took for Giants—practising
Titanic Opera—

The Days—to Mighty Metres stept—
The Homeliest—adorned
As if unto a Jubilee
'Twere suddenly confirmed—

I could not have defined the change—
Conversion of the Mind
Like Sanctifying in the Soul—
Is witnessed—not explained—

'Twas a Divine Insanity—
The Danger to be Sane
Should I again experience—
'Tis Antidote to turn—

To Tomes of solid Witchcraft—
Magicians be asleep—
But Magic—has an Element
Like Deity—to keep—

Dickinson's own private and genuine religious conversion began
with reading "that Foreign Lady"—Elizabeth Barrett Browning.
Although John Walsh has written scathingly that Dickinson
"copied" straight from Barrett Browning's *Aurora Leigh*, it is clear
by now that the Amherst Poet was instead deeply moved and
inspired by the example of the British poet.[33] Indeed, Barrett
Browning enabled Dickinson to actually "see the light" differently;
as a kind of "Lunacy of Light" began to prevail, the American poet
began to see her way to her own poetic and imaginative accomplishments. "Lunacy" of course not only suggests madness, the
kind of madness that undoubtedly is also "divinest sense," but it
also suggests lunar light, the moon's light that governs the night
and illuminates the dark, a light unconcerned with day's "little
Mysteries / As harrass us" (*P* 629). In such an enchanting light, a
light opposite from the direct, prosaic, solar light, small bees are
magically transformed into butterflies, which grow even more
majestic and are transformed into swans; the smallest common
sounds begin to seem like an opera of giants, and gradually, the

days begin to step to "Mighty Metres," music now possible only because of a "Conversion of the Mind" that seemed a "Divine Insanity," like witchcraft or magic, providing a new sense of a different deity. This witchcraft, this womancraft—this knowledge of the forces of darkness—becomes as integral to the poet's identity as her "breath" in *P* 1708. In "All overgrown by cunning moss" (*P* 148) and "Her—'last Poems'—" (*P* 312), moreover, Dickinson reveals how much such successful literary women as Elizabeth Barrett Browning and Charlotte Brontë affected and inspired her. Rather than causing any anxiety of influence, they enabled her to find a literary tradition of her own and a deity of her own in the only room of her own she could imagine: the "feminine" darkness. Recognizing her membership in those female "Races—nurtured in the Dark," she defines herself as a poet who must retreat from the hostile world of sunlit business into the spacious, subterranean, divinely insane sphere of the dark.

4 *Dwelling in Possibility*
A Light of One's Own

I, too, shall not shine, unless I
can find a sun.   *Margaret Fuller[1]*

    I saw a pure white light in me, like a bright beautiful Lamp,
and in that light was my Angel . . . the Light being as a sun about
her. . . . O Eternity has in it a large Subject to dip my pen & write
from! And I see my angel of Spirit dip a pen. . . . Sure if my pen's
liquor is to be from Eternity, it cannot be written dry.
                                                     Anne Bathurst[2]

be cocoon, smothered in wool,
be Lamb, mothered again.
        ....

pale as the worm in the grass,
yet I am a spark
        ....

the sun-disk,
the re-born Sun.   *H.D.[3]*

    As Margaret Homans has demonstrated, Dickinson pushed
beyond the limits of dualism by "undermining the whole concept of
oppositeness."[4] Indeed, this female poet subverts the old, impossible polarities of light and dark by metaphorically creating her own
"Blaze" within the dark as if repeatedly and assuredly answering her
own question:

        To Races—nurtured in the Dark—
        How would your own—begin?

Can Blaze be shown in Cochineal—
Or Noon—in Mazarin?   (*P* 581)

Obviously believing that, as Harold Bloom puts it, "imagination is
the faculty of self-preservation," she not only preserves her self
through the imagination, but she also manages to triumph with a
rare ecstasy.[5]

Catherine F. Smith, in a fascinating discussion of Jane Lead as
female mystic, has observed that many similarities exist between
feminist theory and mystic philosophy; furthermore, she suggests
that "connections of ecstasy and feminism (as affirmation of the
female) may be very old."[6] Also calling attention to a poetic tradition of mystical awareness counter to the dominant rational nature
of much recent American poetry, Robert Bly quotes from the
French poet Francis Ponge, who affirms that poets are "the am-
bassadors of the silent world. As such, they stammer, they murmur,
they sink into the darkness of logos—until at last they reach the
level of ROOTS, where things and formulas are one."[7] I am convinced that much of the transformative power of many of Dickinson's seemingly simple "nature" poems derives from such a mystical
union with a silent and female darkness. From early in her writing
determined to find or create "another sunshine," another kind of
light that could illuminate rather than obliterate artistic essence,
Dickinson creates what she called "glory" through a variety of
images of small lights that emerge and grow from the dark. It is as if
she revises the Nicean Creed, insisting that creation, ecstasy,
transcendence, glory, and immortality do not come about as "Light
from Light," but as lights—colors, jewels, blazes, irridescent wings
—that spring from the soil of a nurturing, feminine dark. Indeed,
it is precisely because of the intense, painful ambivalence that characterizes this poet's experience of sunlight that Dickinson's triumphant images of "glory" resonate so brilliantly. Many of her most
ecstatic poems in fact rely upon an empowered darkness joining
with a relaxed, lessened sun, a sun at rest so that its passive glow can
merge with an active darkness, thus creating rather than destroying.
In addition, sunset and dawn, as examples of times when the sun's

power is relaxed, lessened, but not absolutely absent from the earth, both allow the poet room for art, even for visions of a feminine utopia, *another place* or, to use Charlotte Brontë's phrase, "another sort of sky" where she as a poet can triumph.

Dickinson's determination to find or create a different quality of light appears as early as 1851, in *P* 2 according to Johnson's editing:

> There is another sky,
> Ever serene and fair,
> And there is another sunshine,
> Though it be darkness there;
> Never mind faded forests. Austin,
> Never mind silent fields—
> *Here* is a little forest,
> Whose leaf is ever green;
> Here is a brighter garden,
> Where not a frost has been;
> In its unfading flowers
> I hear the bright bee hum;
> Prithee, my brother,
> Into *my* garden come!

Originally written as the prose conclusion of a letter to Austin, the poem as it appears here has been severed from its surrounding syntax, arbitrarily divided into lines, its first letters capitalized.[8] However, in the letter itself, these lines are syntactically linked to others that cause us to read this "poem" differently. For if *P* 2 seems an ambiguous (even sexual)[9] invitation for Austin to enter his sister's lush and inviting "garden," Letter 58 makes it clear that to Emily, such a garden is a creation of her own mind, indeed, a product of the "darkness there." The letter first describes with disappointment the onset of fall: "Everything has changed since my other letter— the doors are shut this morning, and all the kitchen wall is covered with chilly flies who are trying to warm themselves—poor things. . . . You would say t'was a gloomy morning if you were sitting here —the frost has been severe and the few lingering leaves seem anxious to be going and wrap their faded cloaks more closely about them as if to shield them from the chilly northeast wind."

But such literal fall weather will not chill Austin when he returns, the twenty-one year old poet promises. "Don't think that the sky will frown so the day when you come home!" she assures him, as she confidently continues: "even *should* she (the sky) frown upon her child returning, there is *another* sky ever serene and fair, and there is *another* sunshine, tho' it be darkness there—never mind faded forests, Austin, never mind silent fields—*here* is a little forest whose leaf is ever green, here is a *brighter* garden, where not a frost has been, in its unfading flowers I hear the bright bee hum, prithee, my Brother, into *my* garden come!" Even earlier in this letter she had wistfully told Austin how she had tried to "delay the frosts" until after his visit. But as I have shown, the literal weather, the actual sun, seem so seldom to work in conjunction with Dickinson's internal weather that she withdraws, as if asserting that since she can have no control over external forces, she will refuse them. She therefore imaginatively constructs a different quality of light from that of the undependable sun, in which she will not be separated from friends who nourish her. Here in the "brighter garden" of her own mind, foliage will not fade, reminding us again of Anne Finch's description of "such a night" in which, the sun at rest, the grass can "bear itself upright." Dickinson's imaginative garden, more happily than the famous carriage of "Because I could not stop for Death," also contains immortality: it is a garden that grows by her own lights, a garden of art, of poetry.

About eleven years after she wrote Austin to join her in an imaginary garden governed by "another sunshine," Dickinson in *P* 569 made clear her own priorities:

> I reckon—when I count at all—
> First—Poets—Then the Sun—
> Then Summer—Then the Heaven of God—
> And then—the List is done—
>
> But, looking back—the First so seems
> To Comprehend the Whole—
> The Others look a needless Show—
> So I write—Poets—All—
>
> Their Summer—lasts a Solid Year—
> They can afford a Sun
> The East—would deem extravagant—

Poets are even more important than the sun itself, she asserts, in this list that reads like a ranking of cakes at the state fair. Casually placing God's heaven in third place to begin with, the poet in the next stanza affirms that poetry comprises its own sun, summer, and heaven; the ecstasies of poetry and the imagination cause the rest of these items on the list to seem needlessly showy. Furthermore, poetry's glories are reliable, last "a Solid Year," unlike the earthly sun or even a Godly heaven. Through poetry, moreover, she can attain her own kind of immortality, independent of a judgmental Calvinist God.

She turns, therefore, to a "fictitious Country" where her "Shivering Fancy" (*P* 562) can "dwell in Possibility— / A fairer House than Prose—" (*P* 657). Indeed, the possibility of a paradise of poetry is integral to her notion of "Circumference":

> When Bells stop ringing—Church—begins—
> The Positive—of Bells—
> When Cogs—stop—that's Circumference—
> The Ultimate—of Wheels.   (*P* 633)

Her spiritual dimensions can begin to grow when the influences of traditional church stop: *her* bells can ring "When Cogs—stop," when normal, linear, sun time ceases and qualitative, mystical time begins. "That's Circumference"—a vast, circular, imaginative horizon that allows her to become a queen, a prophet, a poet "All."[10]

If Dickinson gloried in her concept of circumference, with its associations of wide possibilities for the eye and the imagination, she does not, like Emerson, assert without qualification that "the health of the eye seems to demand a horizon."[11] Healthy horizons for this poet are very specifically described in terms of light tempered by darkness. In images of evening or sunset, for example, Dickinson writes of a lesser sun and a larger darkness that provide climate for creativity. Twilight has of course traditionally been a time of the imagination, especially for the Romantics, but Dickinson's images of evening are in addition characterized by a sense of reduced solar power enabling specifically feminine possibility. Like Mary Coleridge who writes of a "fairy town" at twilight, "a far, fantastic place,"[12] and like Charlotte Brontë's Shirley who glories in a twilight sky that makes "earth an Eden, life a poem,"[13] Dickinson writes of twilight as a magical time—the light having "another" quality about it—a time unbounded by daylight household obligations on the one hand and the frightening finality of the dark on the other.

In one of her most lushly visual poems about evening, for instance, a "Housewife in the Evening West"—like a sublime "Mama above"—effortlessly, even carelessly, creates glorious sunsets:[14]

> She sweeps with many-colored Brooms—
> And leaves the Shreds behind—
> Oh Housewife in the Evening West—
> Come back, and dust the Pond!
>
> You dropped a Purple Ravelling in—
> You dropped an Amber thread—
> And now you've littered all the East
> With Duds of Emerald!
>
> And still, she plies her spotted Brooms,
> And still the Aprons fly,
> Till Brooms fade softly into stars—
> And then I come away—   (P 219)

Here the brooms the poet had detested when associated with the chores of broad daylight are tools of a higher trade. These "spotted Brooms," like Gerard Manley Hopkins' "dappled things," and like Dickinson's own "freckled human nature," are in their very irregularity capable of creating a spectacular horizon. And with the sun's eye safely over the hill and out of the way, this housewife's brooms are transformed from ordinary implements of housekeeping into triumphant images of art.

Twilight and evening are also associated in Dickinson's poems with a gentleness and unobtrusiveness that allow her a sense of "Vastness." In "The Crickets sang" (P 1104), for instance, at twilight the crickets themselves "set the Sun." Because the light is now less powerful, these little insects are empowered to sing that same light —as if it were an exhausted child—finally to bed. The "low Grass" is "loaded with Dew" in this "polite and new" between-light, in which the sun no longer dominates, so that

> A Vastness, as a Neighbor, came,
> A Wisdom, without Face, or Name,
> A Peace, as Hemispheres at Home
> And so the Night became.

Such neighborly space, such unobtrusive wisdom, usher in a night that will allow genuine rest.

If sunset could provide a friendly sense of vast space and possiblity, it could also provide "vail," or shelter, from the sun's harsh judgments and intrusions that could in turn allow the mind free range:

> Sunset that screens, reveals—
> Enhancing what we see
> By menaces of Amethyst
> And Moats of Mystery.   (*P* 1609)

By frequently spelling the word "vail" with an *a* rather than with an *e*, this poet may have been not only suggesting her need for "veil" as shelter but may also have been implying her need to be respected, for an archaic meaning of "vail" is "to respect." If this sunset that "screens" simultaneously "reveals"—or re-vails, or re-spects, or re-examines—the paradoxical act described in this poem is one of uncovering—or recovering—the truth by *allowing* it cover—or privacy, or respect.[15] In addition sunset here feeds the imagination, encourages possibility, unlike the prosy landscape of the sun that seemed to restrict, to flatten one as if reducing one to an image on a canvas (we think again of Charlotte Brontë and her image of the "fleshy Cleopatra" as a woman flattened on a canvas, distorted because not seen in a "true light"). This sunset light enhances, allowing the eye to see shades, levels, and depths, "menaces of Amethyst" and "Moats of Mystery" that feed the imagination and poetry, that allow one's mind free range.

Dickinson's fascination with sunset imagery has been brilliantly discussed by Barton Levi St. Armand, who has demonstrated the link between the Amherst Poet and Ruskin's aesthetics, his Romantic typology. But although I am absolutely convinced by St. Armand's demonstration of the visual quality of Dickinson's sensibility and, in particular, her close relation to nineteenth-century landscape artists, I am arguing further that through sunset imagery Dickinson covertly asserts that feminine imaginative energy can emerge when masculine solar power has retreated.[16] In *P* 1127 she writes of an evening that has, in fact, its own weapons—rather than, as we saw earlier, showing a sun enacting violence upon a female daisy, here the poet portrays an evening slaughtering suns, and more than one sun at that:

> Soft as the massacre of Suns
> By Evening's Sabres slain

Whereas the mighty noon was composed of one enormous, too-powerful sun that beheaded daisies, here it is evening that seems enormous and powerful. By refering to "suns" as plural, moreover, the poet subtly devalues the sun's importance, as if one evening, all by herself, armed with sabres (like brooms, perhaps?) can slay numerous suns.

Shira Wolosky has emphasized the defiant, martial, even ferocious tenor of Dickinson's poetry.[17] We see an example of war imagery in the following poem, in which the sun's withdrawal is described as "stooping," a gesture of increasing diminution as well as subservience, whereas the dark light of sunset causes the speaker of the poem to feel such energy that it is "martial":

> The Sun kept stooping—stooping—low!
> The Hills to meet him rose!
> On his side, what Transaction!
> On their side, what Repose!
>
> Deeper and deeper grew the stain
> Upon the window pane—
> Thicker and thicker stood the feet
> Until the Tyrian
>
> Was crowded dense with Armies—
> So gay, so Brigadier—
> That *I* felt martial stirrings
> Who once the Cockade wore—

Charged, from my chimney corner—
But Nobody was there!   (*P* 152)

As the sun stoops lower, the feminine hills rise. His actions require
"Transaction," while hers result from a "Repose" impossible during
the day. Indeed, if the sun is stooping in "Transaction," he is, then,
moving across, moving toward the night, moving "down" toward
the hills. In larger terms, the sun as representative of the masculine
principle is, in effect, relinquishing his domination to the feminine.
And as these female hills therefore assume larger proportions, able
to move, to rise higher in the lessened light of oncoming night, and
as they become "crowded dense" with "gay" armies, the poet
begins to feel a corresponding "martial" energy. Indeed, in the
sun's diminishing influence, the poet seems to remember a time
when she too was armed, was powerful, suggesting that at some
time in the past she had lived a masculine "martial" life, since she
implies that she too had once worn a "Cockade," or an emblem of
masculine rank. The final couplet suggests that just as she charges
the "enemy," perhaps the daylight, she finds it already vanished—
conquered already, perhaps, by the the dusk, by darkness.

   In Dickinson's twilight poems, female images of earth consistently rise to triumphant heights, the hills and valleys swelling to
proportions impossible under the sun's glare and emerging as powerful goddesses:[18]

> Sweet Mountains—Ye tell Me no lie—
> Never deny Me—Never fly—
> Those same unvarying Eyes
> Turn on Me—when I fail—or feign,
> Or take the Royal names in vain—
> Their far—slow—Violet Gaze—
>
> My Strong Madonnas—Cherish still—
> The Wayward Nun—beneath the Hill—
> Whose service—is to You—
> Her latest Worship—When the Day
> Fades from the Firmament away—
> To lift Her Brows on You—   (*P* 722)

Unlike the day that promises but rescinds, dowers but deprives, (and unlike Lucy Snowe's light that sees women falsely), these "Sweet Mountains" tell the truth to the poet with unfailing reliability. Furthermore, the "far—slow—Violet Gaze" of these "same unvarying Eyes" suggests a compassion, peace, and radiance similar to that described by Eastern mystics. Twilight becomes a holy time for the poet; in addressing these silent madonnas, moreover, Dickinson's worship is characterized by a completely different tone from that of the masculine Romantic Wordsworth in, for example, "It is a Beauteous Evening." Whereas his holy evening is characterized as a silent nun "Breathless with adoration" at the masculine "mighty Being" whose voice roars like thunder, Dickinson's evening is a time when masculine deity is finally and blessedly silent so that she, as a rebellious nun herself, can commune with her own maternal deities.[19]

At this time and in this light, images of female earth are free in the sun's absence, and the mountains enjoy the kind of vail so necessary for Dickinson's female figures:

> The Mountains stood in Haze—
> The Valleys stopped below
> And went or waited as they liked
> The River and the Sky.
>
> At leisure was the Sun—
> His interests of Fire
> A little from remark withdrawn
> The Twilight spoke the Spire,
>
> So soft upon the Scene
> The Act of evening fell
> We felt how neighborly a Thing
> Was the Invisible.   (P 1278)

Such invisibility has the same kind of comfort it has in connection with darkness, but here it is "neighborly" rather than isolate. Both mountains and valleys, both high and low places on earth, Dickinson suggests, can do as they like, since the sun's fire is withdrawn. We see the twilight "speaking" the "spire" as if this light that is no longer male-dominated now acts upon the tongue of the spire, causing it to speak a new language in a new, different, light—one in fact composed of both light and dark.

In a kindly dark/light, moreover, one can even enjoy both art and love:

> The Mountains—grow unnoticed—
> Their Purple figures rise
> Without attempt—Exhaustion—
> Assistance—or Applause—
>
> In Their Eternal Faces
> The Sun—with just delight
> Looks long—and last—and golden—
> For fellowship—at night—   *(P 757)*

Again we see the mountains rising easily without becoming exhausted—or faded or burned. In this evening light, in fact, their faces seem "Eternal," so reliable that the often-unreliable sun can actually find strength in *them*. As the sun relinquishes control, these "Purple figures" assume the color of royalty, becoming majestic, queenly, even immortal. And, as the mountains "grow unnoticed," perhaps as the poet has developed her art also unnoticed, the sun begins to look at them with longing, seeming to value them as "he" hasn't before.

At times the mountains at sunset provide immortality in the form of specifically artistic visions, as in "How the old Mountains drip with Sunset" (P 291), in which the poet describes "Visions" so glorious they require "the lip of the Flamingo" to describe them, so amazing that even "Titian—never told" them. And, at times, sunset becomes linked to Dickinson's self-designated sense of her own "royalty," her specialness, her artistic rank, as in these lines:

> Morning—is the place for Dew—
> Corn—is made at Noon—
> After dinner light—for flowers—
> Dukes—for Setting Sun!   *(P 197)*

If we recall her letter to Mrs. Holland in which she complained that although the summer heat was good for corn, *she* suffers from the extremities of the sun, we have a further insight into her relative valuing of times of day; she makes it quite clear that early morning and evening are times most propitious for dew and "Dukes" or other royalty. In fact, Dickinsons' poetic descriptions of her own self-coronation occur at twilight:

None suspect me of the crown,
For I wear the "Thorns" till *Sunset*—
Then—my Diadem put on. (*P* 1737)

When the sun's power lessens, her status rises:

. . . when the Day declined
Myself and It, in Majesty
Were equally—adorned— (*P* 356)

At sunset, she sees herself as *equal to* the day, and of course, as these poems show, she also sees herself as "crowned" with her own poetic "Majesty," able to assert her power and privilege like the giant snow queen of "It sifts from Leaden Sieves." Furthermore, as the following poem illustrates, Dickinson even felt a rivalrous superiority to the sun's public world of letters:

I send Two Sunsets—
Day and I—in competition ran—
I finished Two—and several Stars—
While He—was making One—

His own was ampler—but as I
Was saying to a friend—
Mine—is the more convenient
To Carry in the Hand— (*P* 308)

Competing with "Day" in a contest of sorts, the poet—or Night— speaks here with a confident insouciance. In a chatty, over-the-back-fence manner, Dickinson criticizes "Day" for being laboriously slow and ponderous in contrast to her own swiftness; she can make two sunsets and a number of stars in the time it takes him to make only one. And although his may be "amplest," her own are more convenient, more portable, more flexible—and perhaps, if sunsets are poems, more accessible, more intimate, more adaptable to human proportion and need. Indeed, if sunsets are poems, day's larger, longer, ampler verses seem like traditional (and perhaps ponderous) epics and night's, or Dickinson's, verses shorter, more compact, economical lyrics. Like the image of Mrs. Holland whose friendship warms "as if the sun were shining in your hand" (*L* III, 802), these small poems of Dickinson's are miniature sunsets one can hold in the hand and carry anywhere, like little gems, illuminating the dark—and emerging from the dark.

Light from dark. Consistently, Dickinson emphasizes that it is the inner, the darker life that nourishes the act of creation: lightning, for instance, is "The Apparatus of the Dark" (*P* 1173), just as the secret of stars, she insists, exists "in the Lake," or in the dark pool against which small pinpoints of reflected starlight are contrasted. Always, in Dickinson's thinking, "The Outer—from the Inner / Derives its Magnitude—" (*P* 451), for "Growth of Man— like Growth of Nature— / Gravitates within—" (*P* 750). Her underground strategies provide her with a strength she finds impossible to derive from the external world of the sun. When the poet writes "They shut me up in Prose—" (*P* 613), presumably in the same way they had locked her as a child in the closet for not being "still" enough, she asserts gleefully:

> Still! Could themself have peeped—
> And seen my Brain—go round—
> They might as wise have lodged a Bird
> For Treason—in the Pound—
>
> Himself has but to will
> And easy as a Star
> Abolish his Captivity—
> And laugh—No more have I—   (*P* 613)

One of the great ironies of Dickinson's career is that she does enjoy mental and artistic freedom in that no one understands what she is up to. *They* may think she's been locked in prose, locked drearily away from sunshine, but she knows that her intellectual freedom derives from insulation in darkness. Her "captivity" in prosy life is no more imprisonment than that of a bird impounded as a stray; the bird can fly off, just as the poet can fly, through poetry, through art, and transcend a life of "prose." Indeed, they both can escape "easy as a Star," as if in some sense both bird and poet become stars themselves, suns of their own.

Many of Dickinson's images in fact describe tiny suns that she finds deep within earth's dark recesses. These numerous gem images seem consistent metaphors for the self or the seed of genius belonging to a poet who knew that

Reverse cannot befall
That fine Prosperity
Whose Sources are interior—   (*P* 395)

Even if "Adversity" should "overtake" a diamond found in such "Bolivian Ground," the poet knows full well that nothing can mar this brilliant jewel. "*Gem*-Tactics" (*P* 320), the art of forming small brilliants within the darkness, are in fact a major strategy for this poet's life and art. In working for the "Slow Gold" of immortality, Dickinson affirms that it is nevertheless "Everlasting"; her process is "Beyond the Broker's insight," since his deals only with "Money." Hers has to do with "the Mine" (*P* 406), a dark interior space in which the poet finds, shapes, and polishes her gems and practices her gem-tactics, her creation of tiny, perfect lights within darkness, her writing of poetry.

Another poem also about gem-tactics seems ostensibly about visiting the sea; "I started Early—Took my Dog—" (*P* 520) describes the tide's "Silver Heel" that causes the speaker's shoes to "overflow with Pearl," an immersion in gemlike moisture. Actually, this is another poem about the "Flood Subject," immortality, and the workings of the imagination. As she had told her girlhood friend Abiah that she loved "to buffet the sea" (*L* I, 39), here she allows the sea to buffet her, entice her with mermaids and frigates (or frigates like books?),[20] gradually in fact engulfing her. Like Mary Coleridge's "far fantastic place," an undersea world of mermen and mermaids all singing among the rocks, Dickinson's sea is metaphor for *another place* away from sunlight in which a female imagination can develop unimpeded by the difficulties of absolute isolation.[21] Dickinson's tide is composed of female particles of gemlike dew that cover the poet in silver and pearl *until* they meet the "Solid Town," at which point the ocean senses its alien nature and leaves. It's as if when the poet must emerge from the moist world of gems and poems in order to confront the "Solid Town" of real life's dry necessities, the enormous power of the mind withdraws, the way the tide goes out. In many ways this poem seems to be about the comings and goings of the muse, the "floods" and tides of writing fever.[22]

In other instances, the sea to Dickinson remains a dependable creator, protector, and nourisher of her gems. The sea, in fact, develops "Pearl, and Weed"

> But only to Himself—be known
> The Fathoms they abide—   *(P 732)*

Untouched by the sphere of the sun, the vast, dark reaches of the ocean will not lose a woman's "Gold," will not betray her most valuable secret. With similar imagery, in *P* 270 Dickinson acknowledges her awareness of her genius and the risks necessary for its development:

> *One Pearl*—to me—so signal—
> That I would instant dive—
> Although—I *knew*—to *take* it—
> Would *cost* me—*just a life*!
>
> The Sea is full—I know it!
> That—does not blur *my Gem*!
> It burns—distinct from all the row—
> *Intact—in Diadem*!

Much like Rimbaud's succinct expression of the power of the imagination: "Nacre voit" (Mother-of-pearl sees), in this poem Dickinson affirms the durability of her imaginative vision.[23] For this small, glowing circle of interiority, for this pearl of great price, the poet is willing to "spend" her life. Her unblurred gem, burning "distinct" from all others in the sea is her art, and she knows that deep in the dark waters of the ocean, her "pearl" glows safely like a small light of her own, developing as a gem for her literary crown.

Pearls that gleam like "diadems" in dark seas and hues of ruby, gold, and amythest that glow like visions of glory across darkened skies are not the only colorful images of lights radiating in darkness that Dickinson relies upon to express her energy and genius. Fire, for instance, becomes another metaphor for her irrepressible creative power:

> You cannot put a Fire out—
> A Thing that can ignite
> Can go, itself, without a Fan—
> Upon the slowest Night—

You cannot fold a Flood—
And put it in a Drawer—
Because the Winds would find it out—
And tell your Cedar Floor—   (P 530)

The poet knows that even though cultural and familial pressures
may suppress her, her own "fire"—or creative drive—cannot be
extinguished; at night, it will "Go" by itself. In the second stanza,
the force of fire is changed to the power of water, the phrase "You
cannot fold a Flood" evoking rich associations, for the beautiful
irony of this stanza is of course that Dickinson did fold her small
poems, the results of her "Flood," into small packets and she did
place them inside her own bureau drawer. Both images of wind and
wooden floor, moreover, suggest a sense of the poet's triumph, for
to know that the wind—or the spirit—will carry the truth over
the surface of the earth is to know that somehow, someday, one will
be recognized. The image here of "Cedar floor" may even suggest a
further kind of immortality, when one considers the common use of
cedar closets and chests as preservers of family treasures.

Dickinson also wrote several other poems in which she uses fire
as image for her own strength. If, as we saw earlier, she was relegated to the dark or to a world of cold winter which could be
spacious and hospitable as well as entombing and frightening, this
state of freezing darkness paradoxically helped her to develop her
"Vitality," which she expresses here in terms of fire:

The Zeroes—taught us—Phosphorus—
We learned to like the Fire
By playing Glaciers—when a Boy—
And Tinder—guessed—by power
Of Opposite—to balance Odd—
If White—a Red—must be!
Paralysis—our Primer—dumb—
Unto Vitality!   (P 689)

Vitality as fire is also expressed by images of volcanoes, violent
fires seething in darkness, occasionally and mysteriously erupting in
billowing oceans of lava cloaking whole mountainsides with their
blazing:

A still—Volcano—Life—
That flickered in the night—
When it was dark enough to do
Without erasing sight—

A quiet—Earthquake Style—
Too subtle to suspect
By natures this side Naples—
The North cannot detect

The Solemn—Torrid—Symbol—
The lips that never lie—
Whose hissing Corals part—and shut—
And Cities—ooze away—   (P 601)

These "Solemn" yet "Torrid" lips belong, obviously, to the mouth of the mountain, which as we know from P 722, tells the poet "no lie." Dark, interior silence leads to eruptions of truth, the poet affirms. In fact, such a "still—Volcano—Life" can flicker so quietly and subtly that "natures this side Naples" have no idea of the amazing power that resides within this mountainous darkness. As Sandra Gilbert has shown, Italy has long served as sympathetic "matria" for women writers;[24] in this poem Dickinson suggests that whereas "natures" close to Naples would understand her torrid symbols, her fiery words, natures "this side Naples," or those living in northern climates such as New England (or perhaps those inhabiting a logical world of broad daylights), simply have no idea of her enormous verbal and artistic energies. The last stanza provides an image of enormous female power: these "solemn—Torrid" lips tell the truth with "hissing Corals" that "ooze away" whole cities.[25] Whether genital or linguistic, these "lips" hold a power she recognizes and acknowledges as strength derived from darkness, in the same way a volcano is fire emerging from the dark compression of the "female" earth. And this volcano can effortlessly "ooze away" cities—or the constructions of a patriarchal, rather than "another," sunshine.

A volcano's "lips" can indeed open and shut at will; in the second of the letters to her unknown "Master," Dickinson refers to herself as both "Daisy" and volcano in an explanation that is also evasion: "You say I do not tell you all—Daisy confessed—and denied not.

Vesuvius dont talk—Etna—dont— [Thy] one of them— said a syllable—a thousand years ago, and Pompeii heard it, and hid forever—She could'nt look the world in the face, afterward— I suppose—Bashfull Pompeii!" (*L* II, 233). "Daisy," the image this poet so often uses for herself in relation to male figures, confesses that, actually, if she did speak her "syllables," she would overwhelm her listener, in the same way that Mt. Vesuvius overran Pompeii. Her power may erupt just as mysteriously and spontaneously as a volcano, overwhelming a "bashful" listener or reader or perhaps any town- or plains-dweller who attempts to live removed from the enormous power of the mountain. The implication here is that the people of Pompeii, like those with "natures this side Naples" (perhaps folks with "Dimity Convictions," the "Majority" who "prevail" in their "Sense"), are unable to accept the fiery truth. One thinks immediately of the poet's most famous dare: "Dare you see a Soul *at the White Heat?*" (*P* 365). Most people wouldn't dare to witness such creative energy, she implies through the volcanic imagery in this letter, and even if they did, they might, like Pompeii, be buried beneath the mountain's power.

In the following poem, the poet makes it even clearer that such a volcanic, fiery center does not only exist across the Atlantic:

> Volcanoes be in Sicily
> And South America
> I judge from my Geography—
> Volcanos nearer here
> A Lava step at any time
> Am I inclined to climb—
> A Crater I may contemplate
> Vesuvius at Home.   (*P* 1705)

As Adrienne Rich has suggested, this circular crater Dickinson contemplates at "Home" provides the center of her "circumference," the source of her power.[26] The widest ranges, the farthest arcs, develop from this fire at the very heart of her self, this power that she alone recognizes. Even when her volcano is covered with grass, deceiving the "General thought," her enormous fiery strength throbs below:

On my volcano grows the Grass
A meditative spot—
An acre for a Bird to choose
Would be the General thought—

How red the Fire rocks below—
How insecure the sod
Did I disclose
Would populate with awe my solitude.   *(P 1677)*

But Dickinson also fears that if she revealed her fire, it would be dissipated or extinguished. And, of course, she must also have feared the results of its power, as the Daisy/Vesuvius passage partially suggests.[27] But if she can remain a "reticent volcano," keeping that "red Fire" underground, however, she may be able to attain her version of "Immortality":

The reticent volcano keeps
His never slumbering plan—
Confided are his projects pink
To no precarious man.

If nature will not tell the tale
Jehovah told to her
Can human nature not survive
Without a listener?

Admonished by her buckled lips
Let every babbler be
The only secret people keep
Is Immortality.   *(P 1748)*

Perhaps nowhere else is her enormous ambition so clearly outlined; she will keep to herself her "never slumbering plan," never revealing her ambitious "projects." She asks what may be the most important question of her life: "Can human nature not survive / Without a listener?" Her answer is that it can, and in her case it must. *Her* nature, precisely because of its volcanic and fiery power, must remain "buckled." Her artistic power, like that of the volcano, is the result of compression within the dark confines of the mountain's core.

Just as volcanic fire emerges from the dark of the earth, so do bulbs need growing time in the darkness underground in order to push above the surface and bloom in the daylight. Dickinson once wrote to Mrs. Sweetser, thanking her for a gift of bulbs, "I have long been a Lunatic on Bulbs" (*L* III, 823): bulbs were her floral obsession. The poet's images of bulbs describe an ecstasy as colorful and powerful as her images of sunsets, jewels, and fire:

> So from the mould
> Scarlet and Gold
> Many a Bulb will rise—
> Hidden away, cunningly,
> From sagacious eyes.
>
> So from Cocoon
> Many a Worm
> Leap so Highland gay,
> *Peasants* like me,
> Peasants like Thee
> Gaze perplexedly!   *(P 66)*

Although certainly these images of life springing anew from the "mould," or from death, are Christian in character, and although certainly Dickinson was influenced by biblical metaphor, this imagery also reflects her own particular poetic strategy. For here the poet subverts the surface world of the sun and its "sagacious eyes" by gathering strength from the darkness, the bulb compared to the "Worm" that we found earlier represented her energy. In the same way a worm retreats into the darkness of the cocoon to emerge as a butterfly leaping "so Highland gay," a bulb lifts its brilliant petals after a life underground. Although Dickinson may be one of the "Peasants" who wonder at the transformation, she also identifies with the strategy of this bulb that hides away in the dark, away from the judgmental eye of God and community, in order to develop its own colorful petals—like wings.

Similarly, in "Through the Dark Sod—as Education—" (*P* 392), the bulb of the lily slowly stretches her "white foot," secure in the knowledge that the earth like a dark mother will teach her to ring her "Beryl Bell," or sing her own poems, in "Ecstasy—and Dell." After such "sure" preparation, moreover, the poet knows she is finally safe from "Father's Bells," and can sing out her own realized "Bliss" (*P* 112).[28]

Participation without obliteration in the world of light was in

fact possible after long periods of dormancy underground in darkness:

> Longing is like the Seed
> That wrestles in the Ground,
> Believing if it intercede
> It shall at length be found.
>
> The Hour, and the Clime—
> Each Circumstance unknown,
> What Constancy must be achieved
> Before it see the Sun!   *(P 1255)*

If one can wrestle under earth's cover, "intercede"—inter-seed,
intermingle—with the earth, and even perhaps with others like
herself, one may be able then to "see the Sun" without being
blinded or scathed. Indeed, "intercede" here may mean "mediate"
—Dickinson could be suggesting that the poet, like the seedling,
reconciles the differences between dark and light, earth and sky,
"undermining the whole concept of oppositeness," as Homans has
described the poet's accomplishment. The seed, by wrestling in
darkness, eventually reaches to the sun, all the while retaining its
"white foot," or root, in darkness. By inhabiting both the world of
sun and the world of darkness, it also joins them. Like the images of
poetic possibilities at twilight, these images of bulbs and plants suggest metaphoric solutions to the problems posed by a severely
dominant sunlight. In archetypal terms, of course, she is suggesting
that by gaining strength from the feminine she will be able to confront—and enjoy—the masculine:

> If night stands first—*then* noon
> To gird us for the sun,
> What gaze!
>
> When from a thousand skies
> On our *developed* eyes
> Noons blaze!   *(P 63)*

Not only suggesting that an ability to live in the light comes from
long nurturing by the dark, this pattern of imagery also suggests
that language, speech, and poetry are all actually, paradoxically,
products of silence. Bachelard has stressed that poetry "is truly the

first manifestation of silence" in that it "lets the attentive silence, beneath the images, remain alive. It builds the poem on silent time, a time upon which no rhythmic beat, no hastened tempo, no order is imposed. It builds on a time open to all kinds of spirituality and consonant with our spiritual freedom. What a poor thing is living duration compared with the different kinds of duration created in poems!"[29] Sunsets, gems, volcanic fire, and bulbs are all manifestations of such silent time, of duration different from normal sunlit linear time. Whether red plumes at sunset or red lava on a mountain slope or a red tulip petal rising over the mud, each of these images of poetic energy and possibility requires its own silent, mysterious timetable.[30]

These images are also, in a sense, images of gestation. Needing varying amounts of time safely protected by darkness before emerging into the light—at times emerging *as* light—they are similar to Dickinson's many images of cocoons opening out butterflies and eggs breaking out birds. "Circumference," like "Immortality" this poet's primary business, is paradoxically the result of constriction and isolation within the smallest and most universal of all dark interiors, that of the embryo. The poet, like the embryonic butterfly or bird, must relish silent nourishment from the dark circle of interiority until finally ready for flight, winging—and singing, or writing—over earth's horizons in the widest circumference the poet can imagine, freely dwelling in "Possibility."

After life in the darkness of a "Stealthy Cocoon," the butterfly, for instance, perches "gay on every tree," its "ecstasy" defying "imprisonment," able to rise "above receding grass . . . The Universe to know!" (*P* 129). Her own poetic growth is in fact compared to the development of a pupa:

> My Cocoon tightens—Colors tease—
> I'm feeling for the Air—
> A dim capacity for Wings
> Demeans the Dress I wear—
>
> A power of Butterfly must be—
> The Aptitude to fly
> Meadows of Majesty implies
> And easy Sweeps of Sky—

> So I must baffle at the Hint
> And cipher at the Sign
> And make much blunder, if at last
> I take the clue divine—   *(P 1099)*

She too must develop in darkness, with only the vague but "divine" clue that after what she once called "the Egg–life" (*P* 728), she will attain a power of wings, a butterfly's ability to make "easy Sweeps of Sky," of "Circumference."

Birds in particular become images for Dickinson's poetic determination, corroborating Ellen Moers' observation that female writers often use birds as metaphors for their own sex, partly, she conjectures, because they are little and often victims, but also because they are beautiful and exotic and because they sing: "Of all creatures, birds alone can fly all the way to heaven—yet they are caged."[31] Dickinson spoke specifically of her poetic ambitions using bird imagery; as she wrote her cousin Louise Norcross in 1859, "It's a great thing to be 'great,' Loo, and you and I might tug for a life, and never accomplish it, but no one can stop our looking on, and you know some cannot sing, but the orchard is full of birds, and we all can listen. What if we learn, ourselves, some day!" (*L* II, 199). In another letter to Louise Norcross, Dickinson worries, "It is lonely without the birds to-day, for it rains badly, and the little poets have no umbrellas" (*L* II, 340). In 1862 she wrote Dr. and Mrs. Holland her reaction to finding a bird: "*My* business is to *sing*" (*L* II, 269). Feathers, songs, or poems lead to a heaven of one's own, perhaps the kind of paradise Dickinson had in mind when she said "Instead of going to Heaven, at last / —I'm going, all along" (*P* 324).

Language and literature freed the spirit, allowing one to rise like a bird on the wing to those previously impossible heights of fine philosophy, unfettered by family criticisms and unscathed by solar judgments:

> He ate and drank the precious Words—
> His Spirit grew robust—
> He knew no more that he was poor,
> Nor that his frame was Dust—
>
> He danced along the dingy Days

> And this Bequest of Wings
> Was but a Book—What Liberty
> A loosened spirit brings—   *(P 1587)*

Trimphantly reaching the broadest "Circumference," the poet can leave the dark confines of the "Egg–life" and, as in this poem, become launched in skies and oceans of poetry:

> She staked her Feathers—Gained an Arc—
> Debated—Rose again—
> This time—beyond the estimate
> Of Envy, or of Men—
>
> And now, among Circumference—
> Her steady Boat be seen—
> At home—among the Billows—As
> The Bough where she was born—   *(P 798)*

By "staking" her feathers (once used for writing implements, we might note) she is claiming them for herself, even, perhaps, using them as "stakes" in the greatest gamble of her life. Gaining an arc, she gains "Circumference," her now "steady Boat" as easy on the ocean's great "Billows"—riding the flood—as she was on "The Bough where she was born."

With her own "Redbreast" and her "Rhymes," the poet knows she will bring a "fuller tune" to the music of summer (*P* 250). In one of her most lush and colorful poems, moreover, she equates her own gift—of poetry—with jewels, berries, and even a fire of her own in the form of a hummingbird:

> I could bring You Jewels—had I a mind to—
> But You have enough—of those—
> I could bring You Odors from St. Domingo—
> Colors—from Vera Cruz—
>
> Berries of the Bahamas—have I—
> But this little Blaze
> Flickering to itself—in the Meadow—
> Suits Me—more than those—
>
> Never a Fellow matched this Topaz—
> And his Emerald Swing—
> Dower itself—for Bobadilo—
> Better—Could I bring?   *(P 697)*

Itself a collection of jewels sparkling in the shrubbery, the topaz and emerald hummingbird is also a "little Blaze" that has grown within the dark of the poet's immersion in interiority. One of the most beautiful and powerful of all Dickinson's bird images, the hummingbird has often been used in pre-Christian religions as emblem of the sun itself.[32] She could offer no "Better" gift than this "Route of Evanescence / With a revolving Wheel—" (P 1463) that radiates its own little light, bringing to any garden a flash, a verve, a darting and determined energy and style—much like that of Dickinson's own poems. Like the god Mercury, who according to the *Fables* of Hyginus invented the alphabet after watching the flight of cranes, Dickinson associates the flight of birds with linguistic possibilities.[33]

Such images of small radiant winged figures are also linked in this poet's mind with the light that springs from the night, with the radiance of dawn, traditionally a sacred time.[34] "Not knowing when the Dawn will come," the poet wonders if it has "Feathers, like a Bird" (P 1619), and wondering if there will "really be a 'Morning?'" she uses almost the same phrase in conjunction with mountains and lilies, two other images we have seen in this chapter:

> Will there really be a "Morning"?
> Is there such a thing as "Day"?
> Could I see it from the mountains
> If I were as tall as they?
>
> Has it feet like Water lilies?
> Has it feathers like a Bird?   (P 101)

The ideal morning does indeed have iridescent feathers like a bird — when she describes her notion of a utopian "different dawn," this feminine paradise is a "morn by men unseen" where young "maids" can "dance and game, / And gambol" together with "the birds that sought the sun" last winter:

> Ne'er saw I such a wondrous scene—
> Ne'er such a ring on such a green—
> Nor so serene array—
> As if the stars some summer night
> Should swing their cups of Chrysolite—
> And revel till the day—

Like thee to dance—like thee to sing—
People upon the mystic green—
I ask, each new May Morn.
I wait thy far, fantastic bells—
Announcing me in other dells—
Unto the different dawn!   *(P 24)*

This ecstatic scene of unrepressed female energy is described as if occurring "some summer night," with stars swinging their small lights across the dark sky. Such nighttime revelry will lead, moreover, to "other dells," with "far, fantastic bells," all part of a "*different* dawn." These "far, fantastic bells" are most unlike "Father's bells and factories," moreover, for they will announce the poet in her new morning, her new day, her imagined other sunshine. Such a utopia might someday even become real, if prepared for by the dark:

Sleep is supposed to be
By souls of sanity
The shutting of the eye.

Sleep is the station grand
Down which, on either hand
The hosts of witness stand!

Morn is supposed to be
By people of degree
The breaking of the Day.

Morning has not occurred!

That shall Aurora be—
East of Eternity—
One with the banner gay—
One in the red array—
That is the break of Day!   *(P 13)*

"Souls of sanity" (like the "Majority" in *P* 435 who don't see that "Much Madness is divinest Sense—") are too thick-skulled to realize that sleep is far more than a shutting of eyes, an unfortunate physiological necessity.[35] They have no idea that sleep "is the station grand" during which the imagination—or the unconscious mind—has full reign. Similarly, the poet argues, this same insensitive majority doesn't realize that morning can be far more than simply

"The breaking of the Day." For to this poet, "Aurora" has not yet occurred except in the imagination: morning to Dickinson could suggest all the glory and resolution of Barrett Browning's conclusion to *Aurora Leigh*, with poet, lover, friend, and child united in *another country* in which "The sun is silent, but Aurora speaks."[36] Such an auroral light belonging to a different dawn would usher in a new day, a new race—perhaps one of women poets, like Dickinson's "foreign lady," and like Dickinson herself.

Strengthened beyond the understanding of ordinary folks, Dickinson gains from immersion in the dark an ecstatic energy that enables her to rise as high as the sun himself and even, as the following poem shows, begin to push him aside to make room for her vision, her version:

> I taste a liquor never brewed—
> From Tankards scooped in Pearl—
> Not all the Vats upon the Rhine
> Yield such an Alcohol!
>
> Inebriate of Air—am I—
> And Debauchee of Dew—
> Reeling—thro endless summer days—
> From inns of Molten Blue—
>
> When "Landlords" turn the drunken Bee
> Out of the Foxglove's door—
> When Butterflies—renounce their "drams"—
> I shall but drink the more!
>
> Till Seraphs swing their snowy Hats—
> And Saints—to windows run—
> To see the little Tippler
> Leaning against the—Sun—   (*P* 214)

Having drunk herself into a state of rapture from "Tankards scooped in Pearl," the poet has so fueled herself from these huge vats of the dew of her own Selfhood, her own genius, that she—a "little" revolutionary imbiber of femaleness—can join the sun in "Empyrean." Indeed, to lean "against" the sun suggests that the poet may in addition be confronting the sun, standing in contradiction to the sun, rather than leaning "upon" the sun for support.

With the enormous strength she brings from the dark that allowed these "Tankards" of dew to collect, she can even move the sun aside to make room for her.

The "different dawn" can, in fact, lead to a different noon, to a deep, transcendent, experience and expression of divinity far different from any associated with the broad daylights of cooking stoves and Sunday sermons:

> Further in Summer than the Birds
> Pathetic from the Grass
> A minor Nation celebrates
> Its unobtrusive Mass.
>
> No Ordinance be seen
> So gradual the Grace
> A pensive Custom it becomes
> Enlarging Loneliness.
>
> Antiquest felt at Noon
> When August burning low
> Arise this spectral Canticle
> Repose to typify
>
> Remit as yet no Grace
> No Furrow on the Glow
> Yet a Druidic Difference
> Enhances Nature now (*P* 1068)

This is a poem as paradoxical as any of Dickinson's. For although the "Nation" of little crickets may be "minor," like the crickets in *P* 1104 whose singing sets the sun, these creatures too have a power of their own. They may at first seem "Pathetic from the Grass," but we begin to realize as the poem continues that the song of these field crickets, who live underground in burrows or in the dark spaces below stones or piles of boards, is accomplishing nothing less than actually transforming "Nature." But it is an underground operation; the "minor Nation" celebrates its "Mass" so unobtrusively, so invisibly, that one is aware of no visible "Ordinance," or, we might read, no written doctrine—nothing written, that could be castigated, criticized, or destroyed. Much of the power implicit in the crickets' music, the poet here suggests, resides in its hiddenness, its

quiet seeming dailiness, its "littleness" in the grass; but it is a power
that extends even further through the air, through the atmosphere,
than the singing—or winging—of birds.

The music of the crickets in fact causes even "Loneliness" to become larger, the "gradual Grace" as the result of their mass not just
causing a listener to feel lonely but to realize the dignity, the im-
mensity, or, to use Dickinson's own word, the "Awe" of solitude.
This "Loneliness" that is enlarged in the second stanza represents a
further pushing beyond boundary for Dickinson; the crickets' singing pushes beyond the season of summer, pushes beyond the
normal separation of one person from another, pushes beyond the
self, so that what *was* loneliness becomes (again, paradoxically)
actually a *greater* solitude, a state of more significance. We remember in this context Dickinson's attitude toward isolation in a poem
such as "The Soul selects her own Society—" (*P* 303) or "The Soul's
Superior instants / Occur to Her—alone—" (*P* 306). "Further in
Summer than the Birds" is also a poem about a "Superior instant,"
but in this poem the instant seems expanded, the "Druidic Difference" caused by the crickets' singing seeming to be a change on the
landscape that may in fact remain, that will recur season after season. Furthermore, part of the quiet power of "Further in Summer
than the Birds" lies in the fact that its subject is a communal celebration, a music performed by a "nation" of tiny creatures. Like the
many small creatures of night we find in Dickinson's poems—rats,
snakes, spiders—these crickets are also playing their own instru-
ments, making their own music, but here they are making music
together, and they are actually making it at noon. They are, in
effect, at the very height of daylight celebrating an underground
mass that is changing the entire landscape.

It is particularly interesting that this subtly powerful "unobtrusive Mass" is felt most keenly at noon, as the poet tells us in one of
her most powerful yet puzzling lines: "Antiquest felt at Noon." It is
indeed the word "Antiquest" that seems to stop us, to cause us to
read this line (that occurs almost in the middle of the poem) over
and over. Whether the poet made the word up (something we
know her to have done on numerous occasions) or whether "Antiquest" was actually an "antiquer" form of the superlative "most

antique," and therefore used in the nineteenth century, the word "Antiquest" *means* in many ways in this poem; it is, in fact, one of Dickinson's most many-sided puns, going much further than double entendre.

"Antiquest" can mean, quite simply, "most antique," or most antiquated, old-fashioned, out of date. But, as the *OED* tells us, it has also suggested "old" in the sense of "honorable," or "venerable." We know that Dickinson herself in *P* 70 wrote of her own determined old-fashionedness, equating her lack of contemporariness with a spontaneous and legitimate experiencing of nature as opposed to a new-fashioned, logical, and objectifying classification of natural phenomena. In this poem which begins "'Arcturus' is his other name— / I'd rather call him 'Star,'" she refers to herself in the same line as both "Old fashioned" and "naughty." We know also that the poet saw herself as a bad girl, a bad girl who wouldn't "weep" like a good one, but one who wanted to sing songs. If these crickets and their "unobtrusive" music are felt as "Old-fashioned— naughty," but honorable in their antiqueness, then they are like the poet somehow, in her own singing, her own writing, which she associated with immortality.

The word "Antiquest" may, moreover, also cause us to think of an "anti-quest," reminding us in fact of the poet's statement that she was "looking oppositely" for the Kingdom of Heaven. With this association in mind, it seems that at noon, at the peak of the sun's powers, the oppositeness of the crickets' mass is felt most keenly, is experienced most obviously as a kind of celebration different from, and opposite to, the normal religious observances of a traditional Sunday noon. It is, then, at the peak of "broad daylight" that this "minor Nation" is felt to be most antithetical to traditional expressions of traditional patriarchal deity as practiced in a nineteenth-century "modern" Amherst. Indeed, that the ritual described in this poem is a *mass* seems in itself to be anti-Calvinist, although not quite anti-Christ. For the more "antique" iconography of the Catholic Church does at least include the female, as Mary the mother, who of course is erased completely from later Protestant liturgy.

And finally, in addition, the word "Antiquest" also seems—at least in sound—to be linked to the noun "antic," a word used to refer to a playful trick or prank, a caper, or something fantastic, odd, bizarre, or grotesque. "Blessed are they that play," Dickinson said, "for theirs is the kingdom of heaven" (*L* III, 690). These crickets are singing as part of their normal behavior, as they hop and leap among the grasses. This then is a religious service very different from the usual one composed of a profound, serious pastor intoning to a quiet, silent congregation made up of dutiful, charitable, "good" women (one thinks again of Brontë's character Shirley who refuses to enter the church where the curates will drone over their orations). In a playful, fantastic "antic-quest," these crickets are, like the poet herself, searching for—and successfully expressing—a kind of possibility and immortality unimpeded by customary sunlit constraints, and here in this poem, are making their music felt keenly even at the peak of day.

This antique-est celebration, as anti-quest, as antic-quest, is performed by a *community* of crickets who sing from underneath blades of grass, who live in underground burrows, hidden from sight while their song, their own "natural" religious observances begin to effect the landscape. Like a "nation" of "Nobody's" (here there are far more than the "pair of us" the poet gleefully and paradoxically celebrates in *P* 288, "I'm Nobody! Who are you?") the crickets together are causing a "gradual Grace," a state of immense mystical awareness that dominates the August noon, "burning low" like the "unanointed Blaze" of *P* 365. In such a state of rapture devoid of obvious religious "Ordinance," in a noon antithetical to that of the God of broad daylights and cooking stoves, Dickinson expresses a sense of kinship with a "minor nation" that is singing, and singing together, and that through its music is beginning to enhance "Nature" with its own "Difference."

Such a difference might indeed constitute "glory." As Adrienne Rich has said, Dickinson "chose to have it out at last / on [her] own premises."[37] Standing firmly her ground that dwelling in "Possibility," or art or poetry, was in fact possible, this poet confronted head on a dominant cultural metaphoric pattern of assumptions that had enormous implications for women's lives. Refusing to ignore the blinding resonances of light/dark metaphors that occurred and recurred throughout her culture, Emily Dickinson explored these metaphors, revised them, and finally, transformed them, according to her own "premises," her own actual experiences as woman writing. Indeed, by standing firm on her own dark premises, she pushes the constricting circumference of a culture's assumptions—social, artistic, and spiritual—beyond even the "Dip of Bell" to create a literary flood that swells like "New Horizons" before our "developed eyes."[38]

5 *Enacting the Difference*
A Whole New Metaphor
Beginning Here

The People said, "Who shall be the sun?"   *David Wagoner[1]*

We must break through the old roles to
encounter our own meanings in the symbols we
experience in dreams, in songs, in vision, in
meditation.   *Marge Piercy[2]*

Emily Dickinson's poem "Further in Summer than the Birds" has
become in many ways prophetic, for in our own century, a metaphoric "minor nation" of barely visible creatures singing hidden in
the grass grows to a major nation of vocal women writers literally
conscious of the "Difference" they and their art are beginning to
enact. Indeed, Dickinson's use of the term "nation" to describe the
crickets' voices united in their own celebration implies of course
that this is a *group* who sings of shared values and experiences. In
the twentieth century, a heightened awareness of the tradition of
literature by women, of the fact that women writers have indeed
comprised a community, a nation, for centuries, has begun to effect
the entire literary landscape. As Sandra Gilbert and Susan Gubar,
for instance, have affirmed particularly in *Shakespeare's Sisters*,
Shakespeare has had many literary sisters, and it is precisely due to
the brilliant work of such feminist critics as Elaine Showalter, Ellen
Moers, Gilbert and Gubar, Nina Baym, Annette Kolodny, Carolyn
Heilbrun, Alicia Ostriker, and many others, that we have begun to
recognize the enormous wealth and significance of the tradition of
literature by women.

An awareness of female literary ancestors has indeed often provided a common subject for this emerging nation of women
writers; many poems by women treat as their subjects earlier female
writers: one thinks particularly of Adrienne Rich's poem about
Dickinson that I quoted in the preceding chapter, and of Sandra
Gilbert's poems "Emily's Bread" and "The Emily Dickinson Black
Cake Walk," in which Gilbert makes clear how, rather than causing
any "anxiety of influence," the "grains of darkness" comprising
Emily Dickinson's now-famous black cake nourish the contemporary poet, feed her own sentences, support her on "those late night
streets."[3] Gilbert's reliance upon Dickinson as foremother is of
course reminiscent of Dickinson's own reliance upon Barrett
Browning, the "Foreign Lady" who caused the dark to feel beautiful. The difference beginning to be enacted in our time is, moreover, that a minor nation that originally had met covertly, underground, is becoming a legitimate, major nation, with legitimate
heroes, or role models, as the psychologists would say—with a
sense of its own unique tradition, characterized by common subjects, themes, forms, and metaphors. Just as Dickinson herself tells
us that she discovered the worth of her own mother (whom she had
wittily and thoroughly denigrated throughout her youth), as
"Mines in the same Ground meet by tunneling" (*L* III, 792), so have
many twentieth-century women writers—critics, novelists, and
poets—found the rich mine of the writings of their literary mothers
and have begun to realize that their shared experiences as females
within patriarchal culture has resulted in poetry and fiction that has
often relied upon similar, although previously unrecognized and
undervalued literary strategies.

When in 1925, for instance, Amy Lowell recognized a "nation" of
"singing sisters" in her poem "The Sisters," she was in effect expressing her realization that a tradition of women's poetry did in
fact exist. Indeed, Lowell's statement in this poem that as women
writers "we are one family" lends further emphasis to her recognition that women writers did share, because of their many common
experiences as women, many familial resemblances in their art.[4] Perhaps one of the most fascinating of these resemblances shared by
the "family," or "nation," of women writers in the twentieth cen-

tury is the continued reliance upon imagery of light and dark to express a sense of opposition to values and practices of the dominant culture. Just as Dickinson drew upon traditional associations with the sun and its force to express her fears of gender constraints, so do a number of her literary descendents. And just as the nineteenth-century poet wrote of her ability to identify with "Races—nurtured in the Dark," an ability that enabled her to move beyond the old polarities by paradoxically growing her own lights within a feminine darkness, so do several twentieth-century women writers use darkness as a state of feminine inspirational influence. Indeed, it appears that twentieth-century women writers who experience the dominant culture as existing in opposition to themselves and to their art continue to use this pattern of light/dark metaphor to express their sense of gender in relation to culture. What we shall find among these recent writers is a wide range of metaphorical associations all radiating from the traditional ones, all resembling those of earlier women writers such as the Brontës and Barrett Browning and of course Dickinson, but in addition all varying according to the writer's individual attitude toward her relation to the society surrounding and including her. In our own century we shall find the old, constricting, hierarchical polarities still alive, still shaping experience and therefore art, but we shall also find them being actively changed, and at times changed radically. From the knifelike wit of Charlotte Perkins Gilman and the transforming vision of Virginia Woolf to the furious imagery of Sylvia Plath, the controlled determination of Adrienne Rich, and the vitality of Margaret Atwood and Marge Piercy, women's use of sunlight and darkness in the twentieth century reveals not only a pattern of metaphor shared by a family—or a nation—of women writers but in addition, as I shall show, a determination like Dickinson's to have it out on their "own premises," to revise the old premises, transcend the old polarites, relax and refute the old boundaries, even change the gender of the sun itself.

Although I would like, in this final chapter, to focus primarily upon poetry by women, nevertheless I want to call attention to three fictional works which rely upon a metaphorical strategy very similar to the one that shapes the work of Emily Dickinson. It is especially interesting that all three of these works of fiction are at least partly about madness, and madness in the Dickinsonian sense that "Much Madness" is, actually, "Divinest Sense." And most interesting of all, in these works by Gilman, Rhys, and Woolf, images of light serve to underscore a female character's sense of herself as harmed rather than helped by a world of light that is associated with dominating male forces, and of course, by implication, that is also associated with sanity.

Charlotte Perkins Gilman's *The Yellow Wallpaper* traces the journey of a woman to madness—and also, exemplifying Dickinson's paradox, to a knowledge of the truth. Central symbol throughout this nouvelle is of course the wallpaper, itself a text, its message gradually revealing to the main character the truth of her situation—and of the situations of other women as well. The wallpaper is described as a hideous yellow: not the yellow of jonquils or lemons, but the yellow of urine, bile, old sunlight gone rancid. As the story progresses, so does the narrator's determination to "read" the script of the wallpaper: she "*will* follow that pointless pattern to some sort of a conclusion."

But the wallpaper is one thing by day, and another at night; it changes "as the light changes." The narrator's greatest frustration is that the wallpaper's ugly pattern is difficult to decipher. Not only has it been "strangely faded by the slow-turning sunlight," but by daylight it also exhibits "a lack of sequence, a defiance of law, that is a constant irritant to a normal mind." Furthermore, the narrator complains, in the daylight "it turns a back-somersault and . . . . slaps you in the face, knocks you down, and tramples upon you. It is like a bad dream."[5]

However, at night, by moonlight, everything is changed, finally lucid: the narrator is able to see the truth embedded in the wallpaper's encoded language, that the wallpaper is actually composed of bars, and that behind those bars is a woman (like herself—herself?) struggling fiercely to get out. Since by sunlight the woman in the wallpaper is "subdued, quiet," the narrator reasons that it must be the "pattern that keeps her so still." As the narrator's madness increases, moreover, she notices that in "the bright spots" lighted by the sun, the woman/prisoner remains immobile; however, in the "shady spots," she shakes the bars with all her might.

The story's denouement is also emphasized by such imagery, for the night before the narrator and her husband are to leave this surreal house/hospital/prison, as the room begins to fill with moonlight, the narrator runs to release the woman caught behind the wallpaper's bars: "I pulled and she shook, I shook and she pulled, and before morning we had peeled off yards of that paper." But also by morning, she says, "the sun came and that awful pattern began to laugh at me," so that she redoubles her efforts and is able to greet her astounded husband by blurting out over her shoulder, "I've got out at last . . . in spite of you. . . . And I've pulled off most of the paper, so you can't put me back!" She has, of course, become completely mad; at the same time, she is also acting out her fury at the reality of her marital and cultural situation: she has been imprisoned, surrounded by a fetid, faded, yellowing social script; this paper/text has indeed "stained everything it touched."[6] Like the very light itself, it represents the surrounding walls or dicta of a culture that has constrained intelligent, thinking women, often calling them "mad," and even, at times, making them so.

Another account of the making of a madwoman occurs in Jean Rhys' *Wide Sargasso Sea;*[7] and again, the impossible constrictions that ultimately cause insanity are described in metaphors emphasizing the uncomfortable, impossible dualities of light and dark. Main character Antoinette states her awareness of the old entrapping polarities and hierarchies when she reacts to learning the convent prayer "Let perpetual light shine on them": "Everything was brightness, or dark. . . . That was how it was, light and dark, sun and shadow, Heaven and Hell" (pp. 57–58). In Rhys' novel, published over half a century after Gilman's, the metaphoric associations are clear; female characters identify with shadow and nighttime, male characters with sun. In one of her strongest metaphoric implications, for instance, Rhys images her main character's first cruel betrayal in terms of sun by showing a wounded and cheated Antoinette walking home "in the blazing sun" feeling sick, later remembering that her own mother had always "hated a strong light and loved the cool and the shade (p. 78).

But if Antoinette, like her mother, associates sunshine with death (p. 57), her cold, sadistic husband, the Rochester of Brontë's *Jane Eyre,* is uneasy in the shadows of the jungle, comforting himself after their wedding that the dark, rainy weather will pass so that "it will all look very different in the sun" (p. 66). The strongest indication of his identification with the daylight occurs, moreover, when Antoinette begins to tell him the long, tortured story of her family. It is after dinner, and he doesn't want to hear her story at night: "We won't talk about it now," he says, trying to put her off; he wants her to "rest tonight," since he fears the "long dark veranda with the candles burning low and the watching, listening night outside," where the "feeling of something unknown and hostile was very strong." Admitting to his wife, "I feel that this place is my enemy and on your side" (p. 130), he repeats, "Why not tell me tomorrow, in the daylight?" It is as if hearing Antoinette's own, real story at night is too frightening, because, during this female time of darkness, in the absence of a logical (and masculine) sun, he just might believe her; better to wait until daylight, when, as with the yellow wallpaper, her truth is obscured by the light of normative cultural biases. Antoinette ends their argument by retorting, "You go . . . I wish to stay here in the dark . . . where I belong" (p. 136).

Ultimately, as we know, Rochester destroys this young woman, reducing her to "a ghost in the grey daylight." However, the native woman Christophine has warned Rochester that Antoinette is "Creole girl, and she have the sun in her" (p. 171); and even though it is indeed a gray ghost whom Rochester transplants as the Bertha of *Jane Eyre* to his mausoleumlike family estate in England, Antoinette/Bertha cannot remain only a ghost. For, as she becomes the madwoman in Charlotte Brontë's attic of Thornfield, the suppressed "sun in her" emerges as fire, burning the patriarchal mansion to the ground. She may have lost her country, her name, her life, but she nevertheless destroys her oppressor's territory too. Like Dickinson's bomb abroad, she erupts with all the power and fury of repressed energy, destroying the patriarchal architecture that has destroyed her.

If Gilman's and Rhys' novels demonstrate the physically expressed fury of two women who exemplify Virginia Woolf's comment that "as a woman I have no country," there are nevertheless a number of twentieth-century women writers who in fact create their own countries. Gilman, of course, does exactly this with *Herland,* a female utopia which, incidentally, is devoid of images of glaring sunlight—the effect throughout is of muted, pleasant shadows, of softening trees and meadows.[8] But Woolf herself also creates a woman's country, especially in *Mrs. Dalloway,* and that country is one that comes alive at night and is threatened during the day. Running throughout the novel, in fact, is the chant "Fear no more the heat of the sun." Far more than a simple reference to the death song in *Cymbeline,* the phrase serves to underscore exactly what two forces are pitted against each other in Woolf's fictional world, and which side will triumph, however temporarily.

For throughout *Mrs. Dalloway,* sun and heat are associated with the combined forces of government and medicine. It is as if Dickinson's "Burgler! Banker—Father!" in Woolf's account of a similar struggle for feminine creation becomes Prime Minister, Parliament, and Harley Street physician. As other critics have recognized, *Mrs. Dalloway* is also a novel about time: not only does the reader follow the refrain "Fear no more the heat of the sun," but one also finds frequent reference to clocks, physical manifestations of linear time, government time, and business time, as well as the kind of time Clarissa Dalloway is able to transcend in creating one ecstatic moment, at her party.[9] Both Big Ben and the clocks of Harley Street as the sun's representatives strike the time by "shredding and slicing, dividing and subdividing," counseling submission, upholding authority, on the whole diminishing "the mound of time." Furthermore, at "precisely twelve o'clock," both Clarissa and her double, Septimus Smith, are at their most vulnerable; while at high noon Big Ben booms its longest and loudest, Clarissa must retreat upstairs and, following doctor's orders, lie down and rest in her single narrow bed, musing, "There was an emptiness about the heart of life; an attic room. Women must put off their rich apparel. At midday they must disrobe." At the time of day when the sun is most powerful, Clarissa feels weakest, oldest, most useless, while her husband lunches without her at Lady Bruton's, a woman "more interested in politics than in people."[10] And it is also exactly at noon that

Septimus Smith, crazed victim of the war, is made vulnerable to the frightening and powerful mandates of the "priest of science," Sir William Bradshaw. Castigated as a man whose only prescription is to "invoke proportion," a concept Woolf equates with repression of creative energy, Bradshaw feasts "on the wills of the weakly," loving "blood better than brick," feeding "most subtly on the human will." As the heat of the day increases, Septimus ultimately throws himself upon the railings outside his flat rather than permit himself to yield to "the impress of Sir William's" devouring will.[11]

If, as Phyllis Rose posits, Septimus represents the artist who has buried his creative self, his suicide is then a paradoxical victory of sorts;[12] indeed, Clarissa thinks during her party, after her first shock at hearing the news:

Death was defiance. Death was an attempt to communicate; people feeling the impossibility of reaching the centre which, mystically, evaded them. . . . There was an embrace in death. . . . Or there were the poets and thinkers. Suppose he had had that passion, and had gone to Sir William Bradshaw, a great doctor yet to her obscurely evil, without sex or lust, extremely polite to women, but capable of some indescribable outrage—forcing your soul, that was it—if this young man had gone to him, and Sir William had impressed him, like that, with his power, might he not then have said (indeed she felt it now), Life is made intolerable; they make life intolerable, men that?[13]

But "men like that" are not frightening at Clarissa's party; in the release of the sun's hold over the hot summer day, Mrs. Dalloway yokes the disparate elements of past and present, near and far. Linear sun time is replaced by dark spatial time, as Clarissa becomes "a creature floating in its element," her silver green mermaid's dress that during the day "lost its colour"[14] now shimmering as if an emblem of the light within her. During the day she had had to mend her dress with her needle, bringing together bits of torn fabric, (an image that contrasts sharply, incidentally, with that of Peter Walsh who habitually and somewhat menacingly flashes open his pocket knife as if slicing and fragmenting the air, much like the clocks). Clarissa's "weapon" however is one that heals and even, through the creation of her party, forms a moment of harmony, ecstasy, and transcendence in the midst of post WWI chaos. Whereas traditionally, women have been associated (as witches, bacchantes) with forces destructive to orderly male culture, in Woolf's novel men are associated with the fragmenting forces of sun and patriarchy that destroy creativity and compassion.

But as much as Clarissa Dalloway's needle may seem symbol for a similarly silver-tipped pen, bringing together scraps of lives and experiences, sewing them into one shimmering, colorful garment with threads of language, Mrs. Dalloway is still not the woman poet for whom Virginia Woolf looks to the future in *A Room of One's Own*.[15] But even though, like Woolf, Elizabeth Barrett Browning had sorrowfully queried, "Where are the poetesses? . . . I look everywhere for grandmothers, and see none," as recent criticism is beginning to demonstrate, there were grandmothers—not as many as there are now granddaughters, but there *were* foremothers. Amy Lowell may have lamented in 1925 "We are such a little family / Of singing sisters," but she is at least recognizing that this "queer lot / We women who write poetry" are indeed related; in "The Sisters," moreover, she speaks to the younger female poets who will come to her for matrilineal guidance, as she has looked to Sappho, Barrett Browning, and Dickinson:

> No, you have not seemed strange to me, but near,
> Frightfully near, and rather terrifying.
> I understand you all, for in myself—
> Is that presumption? Yet indeed it's true—
> We are one family.[16]

The "singing sister" who might have filled Woolf's notion of a great woman poet was indeed writing during Woolf's own lifetime; but buried beneath the public attention given her literary brother Ezra Pound, Hilda Doolittle's enormous accomplishment is only now beginning to be understood, particularly by such fine scholars as Susan Friedman, Susan Gubar, and Rachel Blau DuPlessis.[17] The limitations of this book make it impossible for me to discuss light/dark imagery in H. D.'s poetry to the extent that I find it functioning in her work. Nevertheless, a few examples will serve to show how H. D.'s metaphors are deployed within the associational framework of a female metaphoric tradition, and how an understanding of these metaphors enriches a reader's sense of her poetic accomplishment.

Like so many women before her, H. D. writes of the sun as foe, although, as we see in this instance, its power is not necessarily masculine:

> O wind, rend open the heat,
> cut apart the heat,
> rend it to tatters.
>
> Fruit cannot drop
> through this thick air—
> fruit cannot fall into heat
> that presses up and blunts
> the points of pears
> and rounds the grapes.
>
> Cut the heat—
> plough through it,
> turning it on either side
> of your path.[18]

Whether or not the sun's force in this seemingly simple, imagist poem is identified with male force, still it is clear that the natural movement of ripening fruit is impeded, even paralyzed, by the sun's heat. In fact, these ovoid softening fruits can be seen as metaphors for female self, like Dickinson's gems and daisies. But although these pears and grapes are not stolen by the sun, or even necessarily scathed, they are kept from falling to and joining the traditionally female earth. Indeed, H. D.'s fruit is much like that of Dickinson in "A Solemn thing within the Soul," a poem in which the Amherst Poet writes of her ambivalence at the sun's "Still toiling at the Cheek / You thought was finished" (*P* 483). Here too it is the force of the sun that decides when the fruit can "drop," rather than the fruit itself having the power to fall naturally, to know when it is ripe.

H. D.'s image of a wind that could cut through the heat like a plough, moreover, is amazingly similar to American novelist Willa Cather's image in *My Antonia* of a magnified setting sun containing within its disk an also magnified black plough: "There it was, heroic in size, a picture writing on the sun." In Cather's novel it is Antonia who ploughs the earth, in fact who is described as the woman of mythic proportions who begins the new American midwestern world of prosperity and vigor because of her understanding and interaction with the earth. It is as if H. D. is asking for a similar sign through her image. For in asking the wind to divide the unified forces of heat, she is asking for room for the fruit to do what it is clearly yearning to do—drop and be useful. However subtle, H. D.'s metaphors in this poem suggest the same kind of association of sun with paralysis of female energy that occurred so frequently in Dickinson.

Another of H. D.'s shorter poems, "Where is the Nightingale," also turns upon such imagery. The moving final stanza of this poem is so pertinent to my entire study that I used it as an epigraph to Chapter 3:

> Bird, bird, bird, bird we cry,
> hear, pity us in pain,
> hearts break in the sunlight,
> hearts break in the daylight rain,
> only night heals again,
>   only night heals again.[20]

Night as healer is a notion even more emphatically emphasized in the long poem "Sagesse," written when H. D. felt herself to be imprisoned as a patient at the hospital Küsnacht on Lake Zurich. Her poem centers on an owl, a night bird who is "a captive and in prison." The poet exhorts the owl to "stare out, glare out, live on," even though "our little worth / is invisible in the day." For, she continues, "when darkness comes, / you will be no more a fool, a clown, / a white-faced Scops, a captive and in prison, / but noble and priest and soldier, scribe and king / will hail you, sacrosanct." As Norman Holmes Pearson suggests, the poem is about H. D.'s "looking at herself," and about "the spirit at night, before dawn and the rising sun."[21] "Sagesse" is a poem about learning to live in the night, in a cage:

> this is our day—the night. . . .

> We should keep vigil, wait alert
> . . . the day is full of petty cares
> and other people's woes and pain, and rain, always
>   the rain. . . .[22]

Even though H. D. adds that the day also brings "little joys," nevertheless it is clear in this poem, as in so many of Dickinson's, that night is the seed time.

However, in H. D.'s poem, metaphor and divinity are linked very differently from the way they are in Dickinson. For in "Sagesse," the "light and dark" that "hold the planets steady in their course" are described as "*Sombre Mère Sterile* and *Brilliante Mère Féconde*"—two mothers control *both* the light of day and the dark of night, mothers who the poet tells us have carefully chosen "one special shell" to give the poet. They hold this chosen shell, image of interiority,[23] a spiral leading to dark center, to the poet's ear, consoling, counseling, and inspiring her: "listen, my child, fear not the ancient lore / . . . this echo is for you, / listen, my child, it is enough, / the echo of the sea, our secret / and our simple mystery, *Grande Mer.* . ." This sea will tell the poet secrets of the Great Mother, secrets that will guard her from the powers of "the ancient" and undoubtedly male "lore" that may even have caused her to feel captured and owl like to begin with. Such a bonding to the female principle enables the poet to end the poem with a joyous greeting to day, placing flowers on the shrine of gods who share the name of the sun, "*Soleil.*" Calling the sun by its French name in the last line of this twenty-six part poem gives the reader a sense of jubilance about this sun; for, rather than the Anglo-Saxon word "sun," with its connections to the Son of God, the French word rhymes with "gay," as well as with "day," its two syllables lighter, more playful than the one-syllable "sun" that also rhymes with "one" and "ton."

What H. D. accomplishes in "Sagesse" is exactly what Denise Levertov refers to when she argues that H. D. "showed a way to penetrate mystery; which means not to flood darkness with light, so that darkness is destroyed, but to *enter into* darkness, mystery, so that it is experienced." By darkness, Levertov explains that she doesn't mean "evil but the Other Side, the Hiddenness before which man must shed his arrogance."[24] It is H. D.'s unique ability to see this other side of things not as fearful Other or representation of hideous suppressed elements of self, but somehow in recognition of the other side as twin to the self, perhaps the first self. Her imagery suggests a homecoming to night and to her own identity. Unlike even Dickinson, who after all really "chose Day," H. D. says a good morning to midnight which seems like the greeting of an emigrant finally returning to the mother country and finding that here, everyone speaks the old familiar language.

"If you take the moon in your hands," H. D. advises, "and turn it round,"

> (heavy, slightly tarnished platter)
> you're there;
>
> if you pull dry sea-weed from the sand
> and turn it round
> and wonder at the underside's bright amber,
> your eyes
>
> look out as they did here,
> (you don't remember)
> when my soul turned round,
>
> perceiving the other-side of everything,
> mullein-leaf, dogwood-leaf, moth-wing
> and dandelion-seed under the ground.[25]

Turning it round is of course exactly what Marguerite Duras identifies as the answer to the gender-related dilemmas of our time when she says: "Reverse everything. Make women the point of departure in judging, make darkness the point of departure in judging what men call light.[26] And turning it round is also exactly what four recent American women poets do as well. Sylvia Plath, Adrienne Rich, Margaret Atwood, and Marge Piercy all, like H. D., reverse everything, examine everthing from its other side. Their successes vary; as I shall show, Atwood's and Piercy's strategies result in a poetry of transcendence involving a new, healthy associative pattern that not only revises but also transforms the old hierarchy of light and dark. Rich is able to remove herself from the old double binds by a willful determination to survive, even if such survival depends upon an attitude like that of a runaway slave: she studies her oppressor, she watches, waits, and runs. But Plath, whose poetry I shall discuss next, can not successfully turn it round and survive but is instead flattened between both worlds of light and dark, in a sense trapped by her own metaphoric associations.

Indeed, more any other twentieth-century American woman poet, Plath seems obsessed with the polarities of light and dark and their metaphorical associations. The tragedy inherent in Plath's poetry is that as the poet sees these two metaphoric extremes, neither works. Indeed, when one examines such imagery in Plath, it becomes clear that in her metaphoric universe there is no way out.

As it does in Dickinson's poems, sun imagery in Plath's poetry often evokes a sense of loss. For like Anne Sexton who wryly comments in "You all know the story of the other woman," "Daylight is nobody's friend,"[27] Plath too equates the light of day with marital betrayal: "A ring of gold with the sun in it? / Lies. Lies and a grief," she writes in "The Couriers."[28] In contrast, however, she wistfully remembers the place called "Lookout Farm," where "Back then, the sun / Didn't go down in such a hurry." In an earlier time, she remembers, "How it / Lit things, that lamp of the Possible!" (*CP*, p. 247). But now, she implies, in adult womanhood, the sun goes down, abandons, as it does in the metaphors of Plath's literary grandmother Dickinson.

Similarly, in "Suicide off Egg Rock," the sun strikes "the water like a damnation," leaving, Wasteland-like, "No pit of shadow to crawl into." Indeed, this sun burns like acid, shrinking everything in its "corrosive / Ray" (*CP*, p. 115). "Parliament Hill Fields" shows a "wan sun" striking "such tin glints / From the linked ponds that my eyes wince." This poem ends on a note of ambivalence, with the poet/speaker returning from a long walk in the fields to "The old dregs, the difficulties" that "take me to wife"; the last line of the poem reads, "I enter the lit house." In the interior, lighted at evening, are the babies, "the doll grip" of a child to whom she returns. Here is none of the sustenance at twilight in which Dickinson gloried; neither sun's glints nor evening's dark seem to offer any sort of hope or help for a weary young mother. But if this enclosed house with maternal "grip" seems somehow ominous, even more so is the atmosphere of "The Jailer," in which the poet asks, "What would the light / Do without eyes to knife, what would he / Do, do, do without me?" (*CP*, pp. 152, 226).

Similarly, in "Lesbos," a world of women in the kitchen is illuminated by a "fluorescent light" that winces "on and off like a terrible

migrane," a light that mixes with "a stink of fat and baby crap . . . /
The smog of cooking, the smog of hell." Here the "sun gives you
ulcers," causing the speaker to be "silent" with "hate / Up to my
neck." "Thick, thick. / I do not speak" she continues (*CP*, p. 227).
The sounds of "thick," connected immediately to the notion of
muteness, obviously parallel the sounds and statements of "Daddy,"
in which the poem's speaker complains, "I never could talk to you. /
The tongue stuck in my jaw. / It stuck in a barb wire snare. / Ich,
ich, ich, ich, / I could hardly speak" (*CP*, p. 222). This Daddy, moreover, speaks "gobbledygoo," a nonsense language that seems even
more nonsensical and frightening in its incomprehensibility when
the poem "Daddy" is compared with "The Colossus." Here the poet
observes of the father, "The sun rises under the pillar of your
tongue." However, in contrast, the speaker's "hours are married to
shadow," perhaps stuck in the dark interior space of her own throat
like the speaker of "Daddy" who can only stutter. This sun that rises
under the father's pillarlike and obviously phallic tongue is linked,
then, with the patriarchal linguistic power that has figuratively kept
women either in the dark, in the shadows of the tongues—or lan-
guages—of the fathers, or contained them within the kitchens of
"Lesbos," buried beneath too-bright fluorescent lights as well as the
stink and smog of messy diapers and burning casseroles.

Even more obviously associating the sun with patriarchal power
is Plath's "The Surgeon at 2 a.m.," a poem indicting the male physician in a way much like that of Gilman and Woolf. Here, in the
doctor's world, "The white light is artificial, and hygienic as heaven.
The microbes cannot survive it." Whereas the fluorescent light in
the kitchen of "Lesbos" contributed to the fetid, stinking, hellish
world of women, babies, food, and feces (in a far more overtly critical image than Dickinson's "Broad daylight, cooking stoves, and
roosters"), here in this male-dominated, science-dominated world
of the hospital where the surgeon reigns like a god, the light destroys all messy, disorderly, "microbes" that might impede his
specialized work. Even more clean and well lighted than a Heming-
way café, this antiseptic world is populated by red night lights flat as
moons "dull with blood," sleepers wrapped like mummies in "gauze
sarcophagi," with "Gray faces, shuttered by drugs," that follow the

surgeon "like flowers" (*CP,* p. 170). Like Dickinson's daisies, these patients revolve around the surgeon, who Plath tells us says of himself, "I am the sun."

If the sun in Plath's metaphoric universe is male, powerful, surgeonlike, Daddylike, the dark is just as clearly female and maternal. But in Plath's darkness, one finds no Elizabeth Barrett Browning just the other side of the Atlantic, delightedly turning the light around for Dickinson so that the "dark feels beautiful." In "Poem for a Birthday," Plath writes, "Drunk as a foetus / I suck" at "paps of darkness" that fail to nurture. Similarly, the "Zoo Keeper's Wife" complains that the "dead lake [of] the dark envelops me, / Blue-black, a spectacular plum fruit." Ripe plums may be succulent to the teeth and tongue, but to be encased by a plummy darkness is rather to suffer sleepless, dreamless nights feeling "Cold as an eel, without eyelids" (*CP,* pp. 136, 154). The harshly lit world of the fathers is intimidating at best, but in Plath the dark world of the mothers is equally frightening.

In short, Plath's metaphors emphasize even more acutely than biographical evidence that she felt she had no adequate female model. In another section of "Poem for a Birthday," titled "Witch Burning," the speaker's comment that "A thicket of shadows is a poor coat" is an indictment of the mother's powerlessness; as the poet herself continues, "It is easy to blame the dark" for being "lost, in the robes of all this light." The dark mother cannot protect her daughter; in fact, according to the metaphoric logic of this poem, the mother can only stand by as one of the shadows in the background as this girl-witch is destroyed by too much light, by fire. The only coat a mother can give is no protection at all against the fiery patriarchy (*CP,* pp. 135–36).

Futhermore, the world of the mothers is often a world of pure nightmare to Plath. In "All the Dead Dears," she worries

> How they grip us through thin and thick,
> These barnacle dead!
> This lady here's no kin
> Of mine, yet kin she is: she'll suck
> Blood and whistle my marrow clean
> To prove it.

And as she muses further about this "antique museum-cased lady," she imagines that from the mirror, "Mother, grandmother, great-grandmother / Reach hag hands to haul me in." All these "long gone darlings . . . / Get back" at us, the poet realizes, until the speaker feels she is lying "Deadlocked with them, taking root as cradles rock." Foremothers here are "hags," witches that reach to drag the poet down into the world of traditional sexual expectations, the roles played out "by wakes, weddings, / Childbirths or a family barbecue." Ultimately, one is deadlocked in a strangle-hold with these hideous female ancestors, one's own tie to them having begun without one's knowledge as one was rocked in the cradle, perhaps as one sucked "the paps of darkness." Gender constraints are inescapable: "They grip us through thin and thick" (*CP*, p. 70).

Another poem, "The Disquieting Muses," is as virulent as "Daddy," but here the poet's fury is directed at the mother's failure to acknowledge reality—and, more specifically, to accept her own dark self, her angry self—so that the speaker of the poem is haunted by this suppressed maternal anger in much the same way Dickinson is haunted by goblins. Although based upon Giorgio di Chirico's painting also titled "The Disquieting Muses," Plath's poem goes far beyond simply representing even Chirico's haunting "metaphysical" landscape that, according to Judith Kroll, is a painting that "attracts and repels, beguiles and frightens," conveying a "warm nostalgic aura" but at the same time suggesting "an impending catastrophe."[29] In Plath's poem the featureless figures become specifically linked to the maternal, in particular to a mother who always tried to sugarcoat very real horrors; her "witches, always, always / Got baked into gingerbread." Her cute nursery chants had no force against the real, terrible forces of nature, of actuality:

> In the hurricane, when father's twelve
> Study windows bellied in
> Like bubbles about to break, you fed
> My brother and me cookies and Ovaltine
> And helped the two of us to choir:
> "Thor is angry: we don't care!";
> But those ladies broke the panes.

These ladies are of course reminiscent of Bertha in *Jane Eyre,* and of

Catherine and Heathcliffe in *Wuthering Heights;* they are like the wind itself, they are absolute energy, and they can not be stopped by this mother's ineffectual denials.

The first denial that occurs in "The Disquieting Muses" is the mother's apparent refusal to invite "an illbred aunt" or "disfigured and unsightly / cousin" to the poet's christening. Like a fairy tale in its first premise, the poem traces the unbearable results for a daughter whose mother has tried to deny the existence of those "hag hands," of that aspect of the female that Robert Bly, for instance, observes has often been labeled as the Tooth Mother.[30] These witches, these hags, these frightening Furies, simply are too forceful and too real to be baked into cookies. Like Dickinson's hosts of gnomes that are "never gone" (*P.* 298), these shadowy, nodding, stonelike ladies "stand their vigil" by night and day,

> Faces blank as the day I was born,
> Their shadows long in the setting sun
> That never brightens or goes down.
> And this is the kingdom you bore me to,
> Mother, mother.

Plath's image of twilight contrasts sharply with Dickinson's images of glorious sunsets; it is a repulsive, shadowy time of female stasis rather than a luminescent time of peace, creativity, and female ascendency. In fact, the mother seems to inhabit a world of phony blue skies and sunshine, for she is described as "Floating above me in bluest air / On a green balloon bright with a million / Flowers and bluebirds that never were / Never, never, found anywhere." In a humorless parody of commercial greeting card imagery, Plath's tone is scathing: the mother may believe she inhabits a comfy world of Ovaltine, cookies, and balloons, but the poet knows the truth, that she as a woman will never be rid of her "travelling companions," these "Mouthless, eyeless" ladies with heads like darning eggs. The great irony and tragedy of this poem is that it has been the mother's desperate attempt to keep these nightmarish muses of shadow away from her daughter that has resulted in their remaining with such force and fury around her head and feet, grotesque parodies of the angels in Brahams' Lullaby (*CP,* pp. 74–75).

Plath's metaphors make it very clear that neither the world of the fathers nor the world of the mothers can help her. In "Tulips," the speaker sees herself caught, "flat, ridiculous, a cut-paper shadow / Between the eye of the sun and the eyes of the tulips." As female an image as Dickinson's daisies, these too-red flowers seem even more strongly metaphors for biological femaleness, with their colors like blood and their shapes like wombs. These tulips remind one, in fact, of Plath's "Heavy Women" who "Settle in their belling dresses," pregnant like "the Dutch bulb / Forming its twenty petals," stepping "among the archetypes" (*CP,* p. 158). Shadowy, insubstantial, unreal, Plath seems to feel herself caught between the bright world of the daddies and the dark, bloody world of the real mothers, the hags and furies who want to pull you in to their smoggy kitchens of female biological and societal necessity.

Such a sense of enmity between mothers and daughters may be hinted at in another poem whose ancestry seems clearly traceable to Dickinson's (as well as Rossetti's, in *Goblin Market*) goblins, Dickinson's and Barrett Browning's snakes, and Dickinson's rats. Plath's "Blue Moles" was written after finding two dead moles on a walk with Ted, who apparently told Sylvia "They fight to the death."[31] The poem's imagery posits an answer to Ted, an explanation as to why these creatures "out of the dark's ragbag" have fought. They are, Plath muses, "Blind twins bitten by bad nature," who have fought at night while now, in contrast, "The sky's far dome is sane and clear" in its masculine orderliness. It's as if she's writing about women's divided selves by focusing upon these blind twins—if they've been "bitten by bad nature," perhaps they've been hurt by the nature of things that has forced them together, split selves, to occupy so little space crammed down in "dark's ragbag," another image suggesting female space. But this pouchlike womb produces no redeeming infant. Whether Plath was aware that "mole" can also refer to a diseased, fleshy mass in the uterus caused by a hemorrhagic dead ovum we can't know, but she was undoubtedly aware of the meaning of "mole" to refer to a blemish.[32] These moles are caught in the ragbag of darkness, fighting for dominance like the cooky-baking angel-in-the-house mother struggling against the haglike witches. And because they are split, and because they are forced into such a small, dark space, neither survives.

Furthermore, when Plath writes "I enter the soft pelt of the mole / Light's death to them: they shrivel in it," her metaphoric statement assumes even more clarity; perhaps, indeed, this poem served as a cryptic answer to Ted's explanation for the moles' deaths: maybe the light killed them. Maybe they died because of the sky's faraway, logical, "sane" masculine dome. Plath may be very cryptically calling attention to the long-standing belief that women are "naturally" cruel to each other, in contrast to our increasing recognition of the depth of female bonding and of the extent to which culture has conspired to keep women from such strong friendships.

The poem's conclusion emphasizes the poet's attempt to understand the nocturnal life of these moles who, in stark contrast to the friendly riverbank creatures of such children's novels as Kenneth Graham's *Wind in the Willows*, have fought to the death in their dark enclosure:

> What happens between us
> Happens in darkness, vanishes
> Easy and often as each breath.   (CP, pp. 126–27)

Moving "through their mute rooms," grubbing "After the fat children of root and rock . . . to be eaten / Over and over," these moles and their enclosed lives within the dark have far more to do with Plath herself than she would like to acknowledge.

As the dark looms as a hideous, nonmothering mother in Plath's imagery, a place of hag hands, disquieting muses with bald, darning-egg heads, and dead moles, so the moon is singularly devoid of inspiration; in this poet's moon imagery, there is no poetic mother, no divine "Lunacy of Light." For instance, in "Moonrise," the poet announces that she'll "go out and sit in white" like the "Grub-white mulberries," commenting that "A body of whiteness / Rots. . . . / Death may whiten in sun or out of it . . . / I can see no color for this whiteness. / White: it is a complexion of the mind." And it is a deadly complexion, resulting in an attitude of fear/fascination:

Lucina, bony mother, laboring
Among the socketed white stars, your face
Of candor pares white flesh to the white bone,

Who drag our ancient father at the heel,
White-bearded, weary. The berries purple
And bleed. The white stomach may ripen yet.   (*CP,* p. 98)

Such ominous potential for ripening suggests that both this
deadening whiteness and purpling ripeness are too extreme, one
too white, too bony, and the other too bloody, much like the extreme dichotomy between the sun's eye and the dark blood-red of
the tulips. Because of this "white stomach" swelling, the berries
bleed; because of the "bony mother's" whine, the "ancient father,"
the sea, is dragged back and forth. These berries are not fruit but
wounds, and this sea is not renewing, but is itself exhausted. The
ascent of moon means only that death will whiten "in the egg and
out of it."

Similarly, "The Moon and the Yew Tree" shows a moon that provides so little inspiration that the poet announces "I simply cannot
see where there is to go to," for "The moon is no door. It is a face in
its own right, / White as a knuckle and terribly upset." And although this moon is identified as her mother, the poet quickly adds,
"She is not sweet like Mary." Her "blue garments unloose small bats
and owls" (and perhaps even blue moles). This moon also controls
the sea in a negative image, dragging it after itself "like a dark
crime." It is mute, offers no secrets like the paired mothers in H.
D.'s "Sagesse," remaining "quiet / With the O-gape of complete
despair" rather than with the agape of divine love. Furthermore, the
speaker tells us that within this gap of despair, this circle of female
emptiness, she lives: "I live here." But the moon is "bald and wild,"
seeing and caring nothing of how far the poet has "fallen." And just
as ominous, the message of the moon's cohort, the yew tree, is only
"blackness—blackness and silence" (*CP,* p. 172).

The moon's indifference to suffering is even clearer in "Edge," in
which a woman is described as "perfected" in death. The ironic
twist to the word "perfected" is turned further as the poet adds,
"The moon has nothing to be sad about," since "She is used to this

sort of thing. / Her blacks crackle and drag" (*CP,* pp. 272–73). Even when the moon tries to help, she is ineffectual, as in the moon of "Barren Woman" who is "Blank-faced and mum as a nurse" (*CP,* p. 157). Unlike even Anne Sexton's moon, who is at least "alive at night," although "dead in the morning,"[33] Plath's moon possesses no nighttime magic, no divine insanity, no exciting, impelling witchcraft. It is antimuse.

But as empty as Plath's lunar light may be, as deadly as the hygienic, scientific, harsh light of surgeons and fathers may be, and as terrifying and degrading as the nightmare hag hands of darkness may be, there are still instances of transcendence in Plath's poetry. At times they occur when the light is muted, modified. In one of Plath's most serene poems, for instance, "Candles," little lights within darkness (as in Dickinson's poems) provide a sense of transcendence that allows one to go beyond the harshness of daylight on the one hand and the horrors of the night on the other. This poem's tone is one of drowsy joy over a recently born child; and like small guardians over this peaceful scene, the candles are "the last romantics," ignoring exteriors "Simply to plumb the deeps of an eye." Whereas "Daylight would be judicious. . . . These little globes of light are sweet as pears. / Kindly with invalids and mawkish women, / They mollify the bald moon." It is interesting to note, however, that these kindly candles are themselves infertile, "Nun-souled," burning to heaven, never marrying. Female in shape, nevertheless they seem to suggest to the poet a femininity unsullied by the demands of biology, an especially fascinating notion here, since the scene of the poem describes new motherhood. Nevertheless, the poem's conclusion emphasizes the holy quality of this christening scene: "Tonight, like a shawl, the mild light enfolds her, / The shadows stoop over the guests." Perhaps Sandra Gilbert's observation that Plath often "escapes" from her sense of imprisonment by disguising herself as a baby is pertinent here: for in this poem about the advent of a new baby, the polarities of light and dark have been modified.[34] The light is "mild," the shadows "stoop" like fond grandmothers bending protectively over their own children as the "guests" at this gathering (*CP,* p. 148). "Candles" seems, on the whole, to make a statement antithetical to that found in "The Disquieting Muses," the small gentle lights and hovering shadows polar opposites to the demonic witches in "Muses."

In other poems focusing upon female experience, there are further instances of transcendence. In "Wintering," Plath like Dickinson finds the cold, dark season to be "the easy time," living finally "At the heart of the house . . . in the room I have never been in." Writing about a bee hive, she comments that now in winter "The bees are all women, / . . . They have got rid of the men, / The blunt, clumsy stumblers, the boors. / Winter is for women." "The bees are flying. They taste the spring," she adds (*CP,* p. 217). Such an image of winter as a dark time of female privacy yet the source of spring's creative energy is also similar to the incipient strength implied in "Mushrooms." Again, like Dickinson, who coyly defends a nocturnal mouse in "Papa above!" Plath also writes of small creatures of darkness (like the bees in winter) gaining power. She shows these small vegetables of darkness "acquiring the air" overnight, "voiceless . . . Bland-mannered . . . Nudgers and shovers" that silently multiply, gaining a "hold on the loam," by morning "inheriting the earth" (*CP,* p. 139). Plath even describes herself specifically as a member of Dickinson's races nurtured in darkness, when she describes neither father's house nor mother's house but one of her own making: "This is a dark house, very big, / I made it myself. . . . / It has so many cellars, / Such eelish delvings!" "Round as an owl," Plath describes herself here, and somehow, paradoxically, in this house of darkness that is hers only, she asserts "I see by my own light" (*CP,* p. 132).

It is Plath's "own light," in fact, that becomes image for her most ecstatic poems of transcendence, as when she becomes "a pure acetylene Virgin" risen to paradise, or a "red comet," a queen ablaze with her own light. But as others have pointed out, many of these images of transcendence are also tied to images of destruction: when in "Ariel," for instance, the speaker describes herself as "the arrow, / The dew that flies / Suicidal, at one with the drive / Into the red / Eye, the cauldron of morning" (*CP,* p. 239), she is in effect saying that making a desperate attempt to fly at the sun will only result, ultimately, in flying into the cauldron, becoming boiled alive.

With the sun as cauldron—as cooking pot—the sun image suddenly becomes both a male and female one. For this cauldron could be an extreme version of Dickinson's cooking stoves of broad daylight, housed in the hellish kitchens of "Lesbos." Perhaps more than any other poem, "Ariel" demonstrates how deep the despair goes in Plath; as marvelous as the energy is in this poem, it results in suicide. Between the eye of the sun and the eye of the tulips, between the harsh white light of fatherly logic and the smoggy hell of hags and baby crap, there are only a few instances where, alone in darkness, one can create one's own light or, like the mushrooms, silently cover some territory, move over the earth. But mushrooms are vegetable, are as finicky about their growing requirements as daisies, need darkness and moisture before they can move into the light, are easily trampled on— and on and on. When Plath writes of flying—triumphant for one split second—into the sun's cauldron, she writes of her own doom. In the end, both sun's eye and hag hands unite in one combined metaphor of destruction that does indeed haul her in.

If Plath's light/dark metaphors serve as clues to her inability to survive, her incapacity to solve the problem of how to be both woman and poet, the metaphors of her contemporary Adrienne Rich show precisely how serious and how successful Rich has been in surviving, for, as Faulkner says of Dilsey in *The Sound and the Fury*, Rich not only survives but endures. Indeed, Rich's survival technique is not unlike that of Dilsey, who has watched the Compson family deteriorate over several generations, understanding them, but remaining separate, keeping company with her own kind. Rich, in fact, perhaps unwittingly describes her own strategy when she hypothesizes that her precursor Emily Dickinson must have been "determined to survive, to use her powers, to practice necessary economies."[35] For the overall sense gained from reading Rich's poetry is one of a deliberate, at times bitter and exhausted, but always determined, ability to understand the "wreck" of our sociosexual condition, "the wreck itself and not the story of the wreck / the thing itself and not the myth."[36] Rich herself becomes like one of the two mothers who whisper the secret and simple mysteries in the ear of the poet H. D., replacing the traditional, patriarchal "lore" with equally old but feminine truths. Rich's concerns, moreover, seem to go beyond Plath's in scope, for whereas Plath's poems are often descriptions of the wreck as it was occurring in one woman's life, almost step-by-step accounts of the wreck, Rich writes, rather, as if she had stumbled upon a mass grave of supposed suicides that she intuitively suspects are in fact actually victims of cultural murder, even genocide. And she reacts with all the outrage, pain, and fear that such a discovery would engender.

Furthermore, as Rich's poetry is characterized by a strong analytical quality not often found in Plath, so are her images of light more distinctly negative and her images of darkness more clearly positive in their associations. Whereas Plath tried to turn first to the light, then to the dark, only to be repulsed, even horrified, by both masculine and feminine elements, finally writing images of transcendence that also combine male light and female dark in one suicidal cauldron, Rich's images of light are clearly male and clearly hostile and her images of darkness are obviously female and obviously nurturing. But Rich also goes beyond simply fearing the sun and the male power it represents; in studying it, she begins to understand how it works, why it works the way it does. And similarly, in fearlessly entering the dark, taking for granted, as if with a cynical shrug of the shoulders, that female inhabitants of the dark have always been seen as hags crowded into ragbags of darkness, she begins to see through the smog in the world of "fat and baby crap," to find a nobility in women's condition that enables her to emerge weary, perhaps, but unbeaten, and still, as she says of Dickinson, determined to have it out on her own premises.

Not only do Rich's many images of light serve as metaphors that enable her to speak of what Betty Friedan famously called "the problem that has no name," but they also strongly echo Dickinson's, associating sun, light, and heat with male power. Like Anne Sexton, who writes in "Waking Alone" that she fears the husband she also loves "as one in the desert fears the sun,"[37] Rich too writes in "Trying to Talk with a Man" that she and he are "Out in this desert . . . testing bombs . . . walking at noon in the ghost town / surrounded by a silence," his "dry heat" feeling "like power."[38]

Here again the light of day and destructive male energy are linked; furthermore, in this poem the prevailing tone is of an impending explosion, of incipient war. Another of Rich's violent light images occurs in "The Mirror in Which Two are Seen As One":

> Late summer night the insects
> fry in the yellowed lightglobe
> your skin burns gold in its light
> In this mirror, who are you?[39]

Battering themselves hopelessly against the light, moths, like women, beat their lives out against the light that they also need for continued life. A similar sense of ominousness characterizes the light imagery in "Living in Sin":

> By evening she was back in love again
> though not so wholly but throughout the night
> she woke sometimes to feel the daylight coming
> like a relentless milkman up the stairs.[40]

Here is a picture of a young woman who dreads the day's arrival—not with the wistfulness of a young lover who regrets the end of a night's pleasure in lovemaking—but with the gnawing fear that with the clanking of the milk bottles, the reality of her tenuous and one-sided affair will be increasingly impossible to deny.

As we found so often in Dickinson's metaphors, the sun for Rich simply doesn't work: "Jerusalem" tells of a dream in which the poet sees her son riding "to a half-dead war" through a wasteland of sun-dried "cactus and thistles / and dried brook-beds," where children "are swaddled in smoke / and their uncut hair smolders / even here, here / where trees have no shade / and rocks have no shadow."[41] But if in these lines we note a resemblance to the imagery found in a twentieth-century male figure such as T. S. Eliot, the idea of children's hair smoldering leads in Rich's poem to very different associations from those of Eliot's wasteland imagery. For unlike the purifying fire of part 3 in "The Wasteland," what happens according to Rich's metaphors is that the burning, destructive sun begins to burn the speaker of the poems—but rather than burning her so that she is passive and helpless, "laid open to sun's blade," or in Dickinson's phrase, "yielded up," its burning begins to burn its energy into her, so that in a paradoxical manner she is empowered by the same sun that seems to be burning her up. Another of Rich's poems, "August," turns upon a similar association:

> If I am flesh sunning on rock
> if I am brain burning in fluorescent light
>
> if I am dream like a wire with fire
> throbbing along it
>
> if I am death to man
> I have to know it
>
> His mind is too simple, I cannot go on
> sharing his nightmares[42]

By continuing her own metaphoric logic, she concludes that if she has been burned by the light of patriarchal values, then she will burn; if man's sun and light have tried to burn her, then, she begins to realize, clearly she must seem frightening to him, must be "death to man." Therefore, she must have her own source of power like Marie Curie, whose "wounds came from the same source as her power."[43] Similar imagery occurs also in "Burning Oneself Out,"[44] a poem in which "The mirror of the fire / of my mind, burning as if it could go on / burning itself, burning down / feeding on everything / till there is nothing in life / that has not fed that fire." Here the poet becomes powerful fire herself, as if she has lain like an oily rag in the cupboard too long, developing "a gift for burning."[45]

The equation of power with injury is one that we have seen in an extreme form in Plath, particularly in "Ariel." The final image of "Ariel," moreover, of the poet's flying into the sun as boiling cauldron, is much like the imagery in Rich's poem "The Knight." For although "The Knight" is most obviously an antiwar poem that questions the entire charade of battle, it may also comprise a covert metaphoric statement about women's struggles. For if the high hopes of the knight as he rides "into the noon" are similar to those of a woman as she tries to fly against the sun and patriarchy, her expectations reflected in "the gaiety" of armor so bright that it seems like "a thousand splintered suns," the end result of such courage is a body whose nerves are torn "to ribbons," whose tattered flesh holds only one living part remaining, an eye, "a lump of bitter jelly / set in a metal mask." Rich's last stanza stresses the need to "unhorse this rider," to "free him from between / the walls of iron, the emblems / crushing his chest with their weight." If the feminine pronoun is substituted for the masculine here, it would seem that Rich could be writing about Sylvia Plath and many other women who tried to battle against the sun only to be crushed by the emblems of traditional gender constraints, their "rags and wounds still hidden / under the great breastplate" or the mask of superficial feminine behavior. And when Rich concludes this poem by asking

> Will they defeat him gently,
> or leave him hurled on the green[?][46]

she is posing, moreover, a question that she answers over and over throughout her own work. She will not leave those fighters on the ground. Her job as she sees it is to go back to the victims, study the defeats, and learn the battle strategy not only for herself but for her sisters. She recognizes precisely how dangerous this business of riding into the sun has always been, but she will not be deterred from her own determination, as she affirms in "Diving into the Wreck," to learn "the damage that was done / and the treasures that prevail."

If Plath became lost in the wreck, one of those left in tatters on the green, Rich in her poetry becomes much like the archetypal hero who leaves the surface world to travel to the underworld of the dead. And in further contrast to Plath, Rich emerges again into the light, is able to escape the terrifying "hag hands" of darkness. Rich survives, endures, and returns to tell of what she has seen and even to help those who are not strong enough to go down into the dark themselves.

Rich's journey into darkness is very different from Plath's; like Dickinson and H. D. in her identification with darkness as source of strength, she finds in the dark not hags and nodding darning-egg-headed horrors but an entire world of women like herself, who are also survivors, and who, like Clarissa Dalloway and the neighbor-woman in the window, are beginning to be seen by each other, to understand. But of course in diving into the wreck to begin with, Rich describes herself as completely alone, as isolate as Dickinson's society of one. Unlike "Cousteau with his / assiduous team / aboard the sun-flooded schooner," Rich crawls down the ladder all by her-self with limited equipment, with no guides. She knows she must learn by herself "to turn my body without force / in the deep element." Unlike the "drowned face always staring / toward the sun," she must "circle silently / about the wreck," gradually becom-ing transformed by this dive for truth into an androgynous mer-maid/merman whose understanding will result in a new sense of vision and energy.[47] Whatever one's views of the concept of andro-gyny, one cannot help but read this passage as a statement affirming the success of such a dive into darkness. In fact, Rich's finding "the thing itself" here, deep under the ocean in darkness, is reminiscent of H. D.'s learning mysteries from the "Grande Mer" in "Sagesse."

One of the most valuable secrets Rich finds in darkness is that of a strong female community whose very presence serves as strength-ening inspiration of influence. For unlike Plath, when Rich writes of the women she finds in darkness she describes them with relief to know they are there, with joy to know they are *still* there, as in "When We Dead Awaken":

> . . . fellow-creature, sister,
> sitting across from me, dark with love,
> working like me to pick apart
> working with me to remake
> this trailing knitted thing, this cloth of darkness,
> this woman's garment, trying to save the skein.[48]

Rather like the strength derived from female community in women's novels that Nina Auerbach has so thoroughly demon-strated, Rich's races nurtured in the dark seem even more aware of and helpful to each other than Dickinson's.[49] For whereas Dickin-son's divinely insane conversion occurred by reading Barrett Browning in print, Rich writes of more physical and immediate sustenance. In "Sibling Mysteries" for instance, sisters' "eyes drink from each other," each sustaining the other because (much the way Dickinson's "Mines in the same Ground meet by tunneling") "our lives were driven down the same dark canal."[50] "White Night" tells of the way women have worked, women like Dickinson, H. D., and Plath. Furthermore, one has a sense that it is the neighborliness that will grow rather than the solitude:

Light at a window. Someone up
at this snail-still hour.
We who work this way have often worked
in solitude. I've had to guess at her
sewing her skin together as I sew mine
though
with a different
stitch.

Dawn after dawn, this neighbor
burns like a candle
dragging her bedspread through the dark house
to her dark bed
her head
full of runes, syllables, refrains,
this accurate dreamer[51]

This "Night-life" feeds "The drive to connect." It nourishes "The dream of a common language"[52] and calls women to their accurate dreams, to themselves, and thus to each other, reminding us again of Dickinson and her "nation" of crickets. As in "Sibling Mysteries," although women had been tortured, treated like cattle under the sun

in the open square when noon
battered our shaven heads
and the flames curled transparent in the sun

nevertheless "in the deep darkness of the caves," women as sisters have still been able to communicate their accurate dreams, their common language by tracing their "signs by torchlight."[53] Night as time of female community serves as an increasingly successful metaphor in Rich's poetry, as when she writes:

the night-meadow exhaling
its darkness calling

child into woman
child into woman
woman [54]

Even more similar to Dickinson's images of races nurtured in darkness and of mines meeting by tunneling is this example:

The core of the stronghill: not understood:
the mulch-heat of the underwood

where unforeseen the forest fire unfurls;
the heat, the privacy of the miners. . . .

Like "the rainbow laboring to extend herself / where neither men nor cattle understand, woman is

the emerald lying against the silver vein
waiting for light to reach it, breathing in pain;

the miner laboring beneath
the ray of the headlamp: a weight like death.

As Rich cautions in this poem "Natural Resources," "The Miner is no metaphor."[55] Woman is both miner and mined. Just as in "The Mirror in Which Two are Seen as One" a woman gives birth to herself, here the woman is (like the diver into the wreck weighed down with her equipment) mining herself—finding her own gems to bring up to the light. This "dark lode weeps for light," the poet tells us, as if reminding readers of all the women's natural resources that still lie buried under the surface crust of sunlit culture.

But if patriarchal eyes have not yet recognized the wealth of women's "ore," if women as themselves are still invisible to the sun's light, that is all the more reason to understand the world of light that has relegated them to darkness. Much of Rich's light imagery reveals her own tenacity and determination to understand what has brought us here. In "Coast to Coast," for instance, she uses the image of "Seeing through the prism," as if by studying the light with all its separate bands of color isolated, one can more clearly learn exactly what composes this light.[56] Earlier, she had written in the poem "In the Woods" that she shifts her body so that she can "fix the sun precisely / behind the pine-trees crest / so light spreads through the needles" while a child nearby sings "We're hiders, hiding from something bad."[57] Women and children, Rich implies, are hiding from the dominant sunlight of predominantly masculine culture; but she, significantly, will not remain in hiding. As the speaker of this poem, she is trying to adjust her perspective so that she can safely, without being blinded, study the sunlight, arranging herself so that the trees' leaves mitigate the harsh effects of the light, so that she can "fix the sun." It is as if she is protecting the other mothers and their children; by fixing the sun she may also be stopping it, her own vision strong enough to lessen its power. She herself is not a hider; "know thine enemies" is key to her survival strategy. And as difficult as it may be, she is determined to see the light without being destroyed.

When she remarks in "From the Prison House," for instance, that "Underneath my lids another eye has opened / it looks nakedly / at the light / that soaks in from the world of pain," she is not only writing similarly to so many women writers who have associated sunlight with pain, but she is also revising this metaphoric pattern by insisting that painful or not, she will stare out at this light of exterior culture in order to understand it. As she emphasizes in the poem, "This eye / is not for weeping / its vision / must be unblurred."[58] Rich is determined to see it all, no matter how ugly and frightening; as difficult as they may be to face, she even wants "to see" all the "drowned things . . , raised dripping and brought into the sun."[59] Whereas for Plath, "All the dead dears" are hideous partly because they have been repressed—kept out of the light—for Rich, it is essential that we unearth our dead, perform autopsies however gruesome and painful, and learn the causes of our foremothers' living deaths.

The urge to understand is paramount in Rich's poetry. In "Toward the Solstice," she emphasizes that in this season of changing light "there is so much here / I still do not understand." She would like to trace the "spider-thread" of history at "twilight / or dawn in the hushed country light . . . in the failing light, in the slowly lucidifying day." Perhaps at either time of muted light, dawn or dusk, she can learn more fully what has happened to bring us to this point—"while we talk yet again / of dark and light, of blackness, whiteness, numbness / rammed through the heart like a stake."[60] Since the polarity of light and dark—and all that these metaphors have represented for women—has been numbing, deathly, she will be best able to survive if she tries to understand the whole history of women's position in culture at the times when light and dark are at their least extreme. As she emphasizes in "Integrity,"

The length of daylight
this far north, in this
forty-ninth year of my life
is critical.
The light is critical: of me. . . . [61]

As it has always been for women, the length and force of metaphoric daylight is crucial; it is even more important to understand
as the poet approaches fifty, not only because the light of her length
of life is shortening, but in addition, because—the poet may be
implying—the position for women during this particular period of
Rich's own life had become critical, urgent. The poem also implies,
moreover, that that same light is critical or judgmental of the poet.
Like Dickinson's sun that judges, this light that criticizes the
middle-aged poet has burned her shoulders, scalded her forearms,
licking them "with pain / in a sun blotted like unspoken anger." But
although this "hot / misblotted sunlight, critical light" has "imper-
ceptibly" scalded skin, that same sunburned skin will also be
"salved"—saved, soothed—by her own hands. Here in "Integrity"
the patriarchy may harm like sun through mist (it's always there,
always powerful, even when it seems harmless, masked by mist) but
the poet will make her own landing from her own boat, she affirms,
steering it into the shadows and the pines, healing herself.

By moving into the shadows of pines, moreover, Rich calls attention to an image she had used in a poem writtten in 1963, "The
Trees." Whereas Dickinson wrote of rebellious rats nibbling away at
foundations and Plath wrote of mushrooms quietly inheriting the
earth, Rich in this poem writes of huge trees that, having been
indoors for too long, are now "moving out into the forest" inhabiting their rightful territory which will be "full of trees by morning."
These trees are, moreover, so powerful that the reader is urged to

Listen. The glass is breaking.
The trees are stumbling forward
into the night. Winds rush to meet them.
The moon is broken like a mirror,
its pieces flash now in the crown
of the tallest oak.[62]

Trees, wind, and moon join forces here; as the trees gain new
ground, the wind—fresh air and new energy—meets them. The
moon, in addition, is now neither the traditional muse of the male
Romantics nor the bald moon, hag mother antimuse of Plath's
imagery. This old moon is now broken, but its pieces are repieced
together, forming a new crown that flashes brilliantly from the
trees, forests that seem to be covering the earth in their strength and
energy.

Throughout her work, it is the "drive to connect" that urges Rich
forward. She will not succumb, she will not be blinded, she will not
be hauled in. She is like the woman in her poem "Mother-Right"
who, with absolute clarity of purpose, escapes all the confines
experienced by women writers from Dickinson to Plath. And in
this poem, she is escaping patriarchal boundaries, not only by herself, but bringing her child, the future, with her:

> Woman and child   running
> in a field   A man planted
> on the horizon
>
> ....
>
> The man is walking boundaries
> measuring   He believes in what is his
> the grass   the waters underneath   the air
>
> the air   through which child and mother
> are running   the boy singing
> the woman   eyes sharpened in the light
> heart stumbling   making for the open [63]

Unlike her grandmothers and mothers and older sisters in poetry,
Rich has not been rendered mute or weakened by the sun; rather,
she has become so "sharpened" by its rays that she knows precisely
both the dangers of her situation and the extent of her own knowledge and strength. Even though her heart "stumbles"—it does *not*
"tremble"—as she makes for open space, Rich and her child are running from their common enemy to establish a new ground for a
new set of images.

Simply remaining in darkness will not be enough according to
Rich's metaphorical politics: "The woman who sits watching, lis-

tening / eyes moving in the darkness / is rehearsing;" perhaps she is
rehearsing to be ready for the moment when, as in "Transcendental
Etude," a woman quietly left

> the argument and jargon in a room
> and sitting down in the kitchen, began turning in her lap
> bits of yarn, calico and velvet scraps
> ....
>
> in the lamplight
> . . . experienced fingers quietly pushing
> dark against bright, silk against roughness,
> pulling the tenets of a life together
> ....
>
> becoming now the sherd of broken glass
> slicing light in a corner, dangerous
> to flesh, now the plentiful, soft leaf
> that . . . soothes the wound;
> and now the stone foundation, rockshelf further
> forming underneath everything that grows.[64]

Margaret Homans has argued that Rich's image of woman as rock
is simply a reversion to the notion of woman as mute mother
nature;[65] I would suggest rather that Rich's poem sketches possibilities that will result from leaving the room of the old dialectic,
the old "arguments" and polarities, and sitting down not in a hellish
kitchen of "fat and baby crap" but in her own space, source of
warmth and nourishment, and by turning over the bits and pieces
from all the fabrics of women's lives, begin to put them together
into a whole. By such silent, peaceful, female activity (nothing new
for a woman, Rich implies—like Clarissa Dalloway, she's been doing it all along, she just didn't have a name for it), "the musing of
mind" is "one with the body." Such a woman can then become
powerful and dangerous as glass shards that can slice light, healing
and kindly as soft bandages, and even strong as a rock foundation
that would provide a firm basis for a new, dependable, supportive
culture. In light of the metaphoric pattern I have been tracing
throughout these chapters, these are powerful images indeed.

Another recent poet whose light/dark imagery appears as persis-
tently as it does in the work of Dickinson, Plath, and Rich is the

Canadian writer Margaret Atwood. And like those of Rich, Atwood's metaphors not only demonstrate an awareness of the polarities of light and dark and their implications for women in culture but also suggest a movement beyond the self, an affirmation of possibilities for wholeness not only for the individual but also for an entire culture.

In Atwood's poems, the sun seems to be everywhere, and it is overbearing and harsh, often reflecting the intensity of the Canadian climate, the vastness of the northern prairie. In "Crow Song," for example, it is an "arid sun" beating over a field "where the corn has rotted and then / dried up," so that even though the crows "flock and squabble"—perhaps arguing like Plath's blue moles—there is "Not much here for you, my people,"[66] the speaker reflects. A sun that should fertilize and feed instead stains the speaker of Atwood's Suzanna Moodie poems "its barbarous color," as it "shrivels" the "green fruit."[67] Furthermore, just as much as it is in Plath and Rich, the sun is associated with outright destruction. Like Rich who writes of insects that "fry in the yellowed lightbulb," Atwood writes

> What can I say
> to you: with the fat moths
> battering themselves on the light[68]

The electric light here seems a nighttime substitute for the sun, and in Atwood as well as in Rich, equally destructive—although, as the sun is in Dickinson, also seductive. In another poem Atwood shows a sun that "doesn't forgive" but only "looks" at destruction and "keeps going,"[69] much the way Dickinson wrote of a sun that seemed to conspire with frost to behead flowers, afterward indifferently continuing on its rounds, keeping going. Atwood in fact specifically warns the reader that "the story " (or the script of this culture) "is ruthless." The sun doesn't care, she shrugs; "sunheat" from the wall is "grating," and "sunheat" nails "you down" like "all the things / after you / that can be after you / with their clamps and poisoned mazes."[70]

In Atwood's world of metaphor the sunlight is clearly associated with outright victimization. When she describes a man returning from his wars "with a moustache and a sunburn," becoming "insufferable,"[71] she equates the effects of war with the effects of sun. When the poet-narrator is "Sleeping in sun- / light," she complains that "you occupy / me so completely . . . digging your claws in."[72] Meanwhile, her own eyes "lift like continents / to the sun and erode slowly."[73] These continents eroding under the sun occupy far greater space than Dickinson's daisies or gems—Atwood's imagery suggests that her concern is not only with the kernel of self but also with an entire "continent," a term even larger in its scope than Dickinson's "nation." In addition, her sequence of animal songs in *You Are Happy* further illustrates her concern with victims of sunlight. The bull in "Bull Song," for instance, stands "dizzied / with sun and anger," its "neck muscle cut, / blood falling from the gouged shoulder."[74] The rat in "Rat Song" accuses its oppressor of getting "the rifle down" and with "the flashlight, aiming for my brain," whenever he hears "me singing"—or perhaps writing poetry.[75] In an equally violent and frightening image, Atwood's Suzanna Moodie—who becomes transformed into the moon—complains that

> I am being
> eaten away by light[76]

Not only is the light of common day destructive in Atwood's imagery, but her poems also contain a determination to understand what she describes as two distinctly different worlds, worlds of light and dark, described in one poem, for instance, as "Two Gardens." One of these gardens has been "measured," carefully and consciously planted in the sun with "fabric- / textured zinnias, asters / the colours of chintz; thick / pot-shaped marigolds, the / sunflowers brilliant as / imitations." These flowers of the sunlit world seem tidily domestic, associated as they are with the fabric of upholstered sitting-room chairs. Even the sunflowers seem only imitations of something wilder, like representational objects d'art on a table. But lurking just outside the "string borders" of this cosy, cultivated brightly lighted garden, a wilder life of darkness raises itself. Here, plants grow "without sunlight, flickering / in the evening forest / certain ferns; fungi / like buried feet / the blue- / flags, ice flames / reflected in the bay / that melt when the / sun hits noon." These "other" plants are rooted, Atwood asserts, "in another land," adding, "they are mist / if you touch them, your / eyes go through them."⁷⁷

These other kinds of plants are also frightening, but learning one's way in a garden of darkness is essential to Atwood's strategy for survival. Seeing through the surface, allowing oneself to move beyond the surface world of sun, is a major strategy in Atwood's method of becoming whole; as Roberta Rubenstein has shown, Atwood's novel *Surfacing* involves at its center a heroic journey, a going down into darkness in order to emerge whole and healthy for the first time.⁷⁸

But of course this other world of darkness that raises itself beyond the string borders of our carefully weeded lives can be as terrifying as it was to Dickinson. Atwood's speaker Suzanna Moodie observes the fragility of the cleared, lined spaces as opposed to the overpowering quality of the dark wilderness when she describes her men folk planting their small field, their "faces and hands, candles / flickering in the wind against the / unbright earth." She fears for them, recognizing their limitations, their clinging to the illusion that they can dominate the earth: "If they let go / of that illusion solid to them as a shovel, / open their eyes even for a moment / to these trees, to this particular sun / they would be surrounded, stormed, broken / in upon by branches, roots, tendrils, the dark / side of light / as I am."⁷⁹ The woman in this poem recognizes the existence of the dark; the men seem unaware both that it is there and that it is powerful.

But just as it is in Dickinson, H. D., and Rich, this "dark side of light" is also source of strength, even spiritual guidance and inspiration. In "For Archeologists," Atwood provides her directive:

> Deep under, far back
> the early horses run
> on rock / the buffalo, the deer
> the other animals (extinct)
> run with spears in their backs
>
> Made with blood, with coloured
> dirt, with smoke, not meant

to be seen but to remain
there hidden, potent
in the dark, the link between
the buried will and the upper
world of sun and green feeding,
chase and the hungry kill

drawn by hand hard
even to imagine

but passed on
in us, part of us now
part of the structure of the bones

existing still in us
as fossil skulls
of the bear, spearheads, bowls and
folded skeletons arranged
in ritual patterns, waiting
for the patient searcher to find them

exist in caves of the earth.[80]

Like Rich's signs lying in caves waiting to be traced by torchlight, Atwood's "hidden, potent" symbols are "part of the structure of the bones" that will reward a "patient searcher" with the link long missing in our culture, the link that joins and makes whole the dark self ("the buried will") and the sunlit self ("the upper world of sun"). Finding such hidden secrets of darkness is necessary for wholeness: as Suzanna Moodie says at one point, "I was not completed; at night / I could not see without lanterns."[81]

Learning to see in the dark "without lanterns" is also in Atwood's metaphors associated with pleasurable and healthy lovemaking for both male and female partners. Again in *Surfacing*, for instance, although the narrator will not allow her lover to enter her at noon in the sunlight, saying then that "he was one of the killers," at night she leads him outside into the forest for lovemaking in the dark. She explains that "There is something outside which I have protection against but he doesn't. . . . He walks as though blind, blundering into the shadow clumps, toes stubbing, he has not yet learned to see in the dark. My tentacled feet and free hand scent out the way. . . I lie down." She knows she is conceiving a child, and the reader knows that she is also, finally, conceiving herself.[82]

One of Atwood's most lush, sensuous poems also describes love-making at night. "Late August" is a poem about "the plum season," its nights "blue and distended, the moon / hazed." During this "season of peaches / with their lush lobed bulbs / that glow in the dusk" plums burst "with a sound like thick syrup" while "flesh moves over / flesh." The poem ends on a tone of sensuous expectancy and luxury: "there is no / hurry."[83] In the absence of linear sun time, such union between male and female is absolutely possible.

But as lush and ecstatic as these images are, Atwood makes it clear that one cannot remain in the dark forever. For one thing, the creatures who inhabit the wild world of darkness, like the "monsters" who threaten classical heroes who descend to the underworld, "are always hungry." From these creatures of darkness "you can learn / wisdom and great power / if you can descend and return safely."[84] Atwood is, of course, in many ways restating traditional advice for heroes who must constantly be on guard in order to return to the surface world of sun. And like the classical hero, Atwood never shirks from the necessity—and never denies the possibility—of returning to the world above in the light. Atwood makes her own choices—she moves below the surface into the dark, she moves up, surfaces, when she's ready.

One has also a sense, in Atwood's poetry, of the enormous energy gained from the submersion underground, a sense of energy garnered and ready for use. Just as Dickinson had written of the lily's sure foot rising from the dark earth to swing her "Beryl Bell," Atwood also writes of a similar sense of victory in rising out of the darkness. In "Song of the Worms," for instance, Atwood writes of these creatures of the dark soil as if she were writing about women:

> We have been underground too long,
> we have done our work,
> we are many and one,
> we remember when we were human
>
> We have lived among roots and stones
> we have sung but no one has listened,
> we come into the open air
> at night only to love
>
> which disgusts the soles of boots,

> their leather strict religion. . . .
> Meanwhile we eat dirt
> and sleep; we are waiting[85]

Far more overt than Dickinson's little rat in "Papa Above!" and just as angry as Plath's speaker in "Daddy," these worms seem as determined to inherit the earth as Plath's mushrooms, as sure of their strength as Rich's trees. Furthermore, the fact that they are both "many and one" suggests that they are part of an army as enormous and pervasive as bedrock, as Rich's rock foundation which will eventually underlie everything—an underground "nation" ready to emerge and takes its rightful and powerful place in the daylight world above ground.

Not only does Atwood write of such a sense of powerful energy derived from darkness using metaphoric associations similar to Dickinson and Rich, but in addition she even more overtly takes the old metaphors and turns them into new ones while telling the reader exactly what she is doing. She transforms images of women by her open statements that she knows she—and we—create our own metaphors and therefore, our own lives. One of the best examples of Atwood's creation of new metaphoric associations occurs in "Tricks with Mirrors." "I wanted to stop this," announces the speaker of the poem, "this life flattened against the wall, / mute and devoid of colour, / built of pure light, / this life of vision only." Atwood is of course referring to a life lived only as visual object flattened by a light that sees only surface. The image of women as existing only in mirrors is not a new one, but Atwood continues, exploding the metaphor, "I confess: this is not a mirror, / it is a door / I am trapped behind." Now we have an image of two women: a surface, flattened one created by light's reflection, and another one, caught behind the mirror which now has become a locked door. Rather than as in Rich's "Mirror in Which Two are Seen as One," Atwood's poem reveals a mirror in which one is seen as two, one character like the woman learning the truth of Gilman's wallpaper, trying to get out, and another on the surface, quietly and obediently combing her well-groomed hair.

But then the fifth section of the poem begins: "You don't like these metaphors. / All right," Atwood concurs, concluding the poem with a change of metaphor that changes entirely the way this woman/ speaker in the poem can think of herself, and by extension, the way a woman/reader can think of herself:

> Perhaps I am not a mirror.
> Perhaps I am a pool.
>
> Think about pools.[86]

Here is one of the best examples in women's literature of a woman writer subverting the old associations of images, giving them new ones that not only release secrets of darkness but that also—with a brilliantly lucid lunacy of light—allow a different train of associations to create a new mental reality. This is the sort of solution Gaston Bachelard describes when he cites the example of a philosopher who was able to imagine the city noises that kept him from sleeping were instead the rhythmic, lulling sounds of the ocean.[87] Of course, in Atwood's imaging, it is not a minor annoyance that is being modified, but an entire metaphoric chain of associations that determine one's sense of self in relation to culture. For if "I" am a pool rather than a mirror, then I am composed of light on the surface but of darkness within, I can grow pond liles, perhaps sunfish, fingerlings, frogs—I am multidimensional. Furthermore, if I am a pool, I am composed of light, air, water, and also earth. I'm made up of many elements—I move with the breeze, my moisture rises into the air, I am part of the entire natural world. I will not only reflect light—the light of predominately patriarchal culture— Atwood affirms: I have my own life within. And, of course, she may also be warning: "I" can drown "you."

The metaphors of this poet break down the old polarities in yet another way: for even when Atwood writes of the sun as hostile masculine energy, she shows it as far more despicable than do any of the other writers we have seen. The result of such extreme negative imaging causes the sun, paradoxically, and of course, by extension, all it represents, to become devalued. When she angrily states "You are the sun / in reverse, all energy / flows into you and is / abolished; you refuse / houses, you smell of / catastrophe. . . . you demand, / you demand," she is overtly stating what Dickinson did more covertly: "Jehovah's Watch" must be "wrong." The "you" of this poem is at once like the sun and not like the sun—it is like everything the sun is supposed *not* to be—but that, as we have seen, women writers have implied over and over it really is. And when Atwood's speaker asks, "How can I stop you"? and then, "Why did I create you"?[88] the reader realizes that here is a completely different message than any we have encountered before. If women as well as men have had a hand in creating and continuing to create a sun that operates in reverse of the way it should, refusing life, or turning it into refuse or garbage, then by implication, women as well as men can have a hand in destroying that same metaphor, even that same principle of victimization in cultural reality.

Atwood quite simply *refuses* to live with the old metaphoric polarities. She tosses them out with the garbage—or rather, to continue her very clear metaphoric logic, she throws them onto the compost heap, where by their own heat, they can rot and decompose to become transformed into food for food. Such ecological healing is described in this section of the "Circe/Mud Poems":

> Here are the holy birds,
> ....
>
> They eat seeds and dirt, live in a shack,
> lay eggs, each bursting
> with a yellow sun, divine
> as lunch, squeeze out,
> there is only one word for it, shit,
> which transforms itself to beets
> or peonies, if you prefer.[89]

Like these holy hens of the backyard, Atwood seems able to take the refuse of her culture and transform it into food, as beets, and art, or peonies, and new suns like fresh eggs, new possibilities for new lives "divine as lunch." Unlike Rich, who studied the enemy, looking carefully at the light to understand it, Atwood instead moves right in, forgetting distances and ignoring boundaries, diving into the wreck and emerging back to the surface ready with her own plans, her own life, her own fire.

Here the fox in "Song of the Fox," for instance, asserts

> I crackle through your pastures
> I make no profit / like the sun

I burn and burn, this tongue
licks through your body also[90]

Strong as the woman who makes for the open in Rich's poem, this
fox can burn pastures, burning like a tongue, a new language,
perhaps running free over Rich's rock foundation, through Rich's
trees. She (or he) makes no profit as the sun always did; and the
phrase "Like the sun " also can be read together with the following
line "I burn and burn," suggesting that this fox/speaker has become
strong as the sun, its tongue capable of touching others, licking
through them like fire, like words that finally can mean what this
female poet wants them to mean.

A final triumphant image portrayed in Atwood's poetry occurs
in "Eating Fire," a poem in which transcendence is not equated
with destruction:

> Eating fire
>
> is your ambition:
> to swallow the flame down
> take it into your mouth
> and shoot it forth, a shout or an incandescent
> tongue, a word
> exploding from you in gold, crimson,
> unrolling in a brilliant scroll
>
> To be lit up from within
> vein by vein
>
> To be the sun[91]

Like the god she finds "in the water / under my shadow" with
"body sheathed / in feathers, his teeth /glinting like nails, fierce god
/ head crested with blue flame" in "Dream: Bluejay or Archeo-
pteryx"[92] here Atwood tells us that she has appropriated divinity—
and language, as tongue, or scroll, for herself. She has learned to
speak fire, she has learned to contain energy herself, and she has
learned to do all this by transforming not only the old metaphors of
the masculine tradition but also the metaphors of her literary foremothers so that there is indeed a "whole new poetry beginning
here."

As Marge Piercy has argued, "We must break through the old roles to encounter our own meanings in the symbols we experience in dreams, in songs, in vision, in meditation." Such breaking out of the old confining dualities is precisely what several of the writers whose imagery I have been examinining are doing. From H. D.'s myths of the Grande Mer to Rich's politics of determination and Atwood's visionary diving and surfacing, healing self and thereby culture as well—these twentieth-century North American women poets show steady movement toward Plath's "country far away as health."

The last poet I shall examine at length is Marge Piercy, who, much like Atwood, takes the metaphoric fragments shored against the ruin of a race, sorts through them, mends some, smashes some, and quilts the ones that fit into a comfortable blanket, into a whole. And although Piercy's metaphors and associations grow out of the old ones, her anger against the old polarities is hard and clean: we find in the imagery of this poet a refusal, like that of Atwood, to accept the old patterns of imagery, as well as an ability to reshape them.

Her poems include many examples of sun imagery similar to Dickinson's; Piercy often describes a woman vulnerable in love as vulnerable to the sun, as when she writes in "Walking into love," that "your face burns my eyes" and "your orange chest scalds me."[93] In an image highly reminiscent of Dickinson, she writes in "I will not be your sickness" that in love she opens "like a marigold / crop of sun and dry soil" (*Circles*, p. 82). Similarly,"Falling out of love" is like light grating "on the eyes" filing "the optic nerve hot and raw" (*Circles*, p. 41). The poem "You ask why sometimes I say stop" bears even more definite similarity to Piercy's foremother Dickinson, and may even lend additional insight into the associational nuances of Dickinson's man of noon letter:

> You ask why sometimes I say stop
> why sometimes I cry no
> while I shake with pleasure.
> ....
> I am open then as a palm held out,
> open as a sunflower, without

crust, without shelter, without
skin, hideless and unhidden.
How can I let you ride
so far into me and not fear?   (*Circles*, p. 212)

Using exactly the same sort of image, Piercy states explicity the extreme ambivalence toward sexual union about which Dickinson so
covertly and cryptically hints.

Piercy also, at times, images the sun as outright destroyer of
females. Like Atwood, however, Piercy's imagery also indicates
that such victimization won't long continue, as in "Noon of the
sunbather":

The sun struts over the asphalt world
arching his gaudy plumes till the streets smoke
and the city sweats oil under his metal feet.
A woman nude on a rooftop lifts her arms:

"Men have swarmed like ants over my thighs,
held their Sunday picnics of gripe and crumb,
the twitch and nip of all their gristle traffic.
When will my brain pitch like a burning tower?
Lion, come down! explode the city of my bones."

The god stands on the steel blue arch and listens.
Then he strides the hills of igniting air,
straight to the roof he hastens, wings outspread.
In his first breath she blackens and curls like paper.
The limp winds of noon disperse her ashes.

But the ashes dance. Each ashfleck leaps at the sun.
                                                  (*Circles*, p. 7)

Unlike Carolyn Kizer, who in 1961 (two years before Piercy's poem
was published) had written of a Hera who, hanging by her "heels
from the sky" is blinded, scorched, burned, groaning and swinging,
having "lost the war of the air" to a sun who hammers "his wrath to
chains / Forged for my lightest bones," so that this goddess is
"Half-strangled in my hair," drowning in fire,[94] Piercy's poem ends
on a note of defiance and determination. Her ashflecks seem to
have a life of their own; they dance and leap at the sun as if charged
with a new energy of their own—charged, in fact, because of their
anger at this strutting sun-god who takes, burns, and abandons.
But unlike Plath who flies, suicidal, into the "cauldron of morning,"

Piercy's determination is described in healthier metaphor. For like William Blake, she writes of "A just anger" that "shines through me," as she becomes transformed into "a burning bush," her rage turning—godlike—into "a cloud of flame" in which she walks "seeking justice." Such righteous anger "storms" between her "and things, / transfiguring."

> A good anger acted upon
> is beautiful as lightning
> and swift with power   (*Circles*, p. 88)

Such imagery is also Dickinsonian—anger like lightning as the "Apparatus of the Dark"—but Piercy's metaphors here suggest that she herself is appropriating the power of Zeus, even Jehovah himself, for her own.

Piercy's metaphors contain a number of other examples in which she is even clearer about openly appropriating light as energy for herself as well as for other women. In "What's that smell in the kitchen?" she describes with revolutionary fury heightened with humor how "All over America women are burning dinners," wryly commenting that "Burning dinner is not incompetence but war" (*Circles*, p. 288). Here she picks up a ray of light imagery not often used by other writers, that of woman as traditional keeper of the fires of home and hearth. And by describing women as using the hearth fire to enact a "politics of refusal" by no longer nourishing masculine domination and oppression like that of the strutting sun god, she reverses the old hierarchal pattern of sun imagery. Woman is using fire for her own purposes. "If she wants to serve him anything / it's a dead rat with a bomb in its belly," she comments in this poem, building upon the moust/rat/volcano/bomb imagery so frequently found in Dickinson's poems. *She* is not a rat or bomb here, but she will use both as clear metaphors for an anger that she will openly turn against her oppressor, not against herself. She will not, like Plath, fly into a cauldron—she'll spill the cauldron all over Plath's men "with a Meinkampf look / And a love of the rack and the screw." Piercy's metaphors seem to suggest, moreover, that health is right around the corner, that anger can explode, the dinner can be burned, the point will be made, and after that, maybe everybody will go out for Chinese food. The anger has surfaced, it is just and right, it explodes, it will be over, and life can step more than "almost straight," it can start clean.

This female image of fire as potential weapon as well as potential healer is emphasized in "A few ashes for Sunday morning" (*Circles*, p. 16), in which although the speaker complains that "My teeth are cinders," she also emphasizes "I'm telling you this body could bake bread, / heat a house, cure rheumatic pains, warm at least a bed." Her own heat, her own energy.

In addition, Piercy's images, like Rich's, demonstrate a determination to survive and succeed. In "A valley where I don't belong" (*Circles*, pp. 8–9), she writes of an affair about to end, so painfully aware of a lover's inattention that her "throat parches." In a metaphor similar to Rich's in "Living in Sin," she interchanges image of a rooster "clearing the throat of morning" with her own desperate realization that this affair is ending. However, unlike Rich, Piercy ends her poem on a note of determined hope: "Still I know no more inexorable fact, / than that thin red leap of bone: I live, I live. / I and my worn symbols see up the sun." Piercy appropriates both symbol of cock and sun for herself: they are worn as symbols, she knows all that, but like the rooster, she too can crow. She will "see up the sun," even come to identify with it.

Such determination is also exhibited in "Cod Summer." Here although "the grass bleaches" in "full summer" while "the sun / stuns" and "Drops on our heads like a stone," Piercy nevertheless insists that "We must actively look," must learn "on foot" (*Circles*, p. 150). She advocates an interaction with landscape and the natural world similar to Dickinson's in its intensity, but unlike Dickinson's in its openness and muscular vitality. For her, physical activity and freedom of movement—even under the sun—result in liberating understanding: "We go in this landscape together learning it / barefoot and studious with our guides in a knapsack (*Circles*, p 151)." It is partly that it is a "We" who move out into this landscape that interests the reader; somehow one doesn't care if this "we" is two, three, or thirty—the point is, it is not just one woman alone any more. Like Dickinson's "nation" of crickets, this is a community. One of Piercy's most positive images of fulfillment for a group of

people occurs in "The love of lettuce," in which "the three of us /
drunk with sunshine" harvest seedlings grown "out of last year's /
composted dinner" (*Circles*, p. 200). Here of course the imagery suggests the same nourishment gained from the dark underground so
significant in the metaphors of Dickinson, H. D., Rich, and
Atwood. In a similar example, "Doing it differently," Piercy shows
trust flourishing "like a potato plant, mostly underground. . . . but
under the mulch as we dig / . . the tubers, egg-shaped and golden
with translucent skin, / tumble from the dirt to feed us / homely and
nourishing" (*Circles*, p. 109).

In contrast to her foremothers, moreover, Piercy's metaphoric
world of light and dark contains few images of horror in the dark.
In fact, it is, rather, as if she will save all the dead dears herself— she
wastes no time fearing or avoiding them. She sees herself as mother
to her mother: "You can't / imagine how I still long to save you."
Like a kind of revisionary heroine, Piercy wants to carry her mother
off, save her from her past which in fact sounds a great deal like
Plath's world of hags and baby crap. Piercy, moreover, laments that
she can't help her mother as much as she would like, for their lives
"pass / in different centuries, under altered suns." The light of day
has indeed changed for this contemporary woman poet. Nevertheless, still she writes of night as time to hide women safely: "In the
land where the moon hides, mothers / and daughters hold each
other tenderly. / There is no male law at five o'clock." Piercy, moreover, finds her mother's life fuel for her own determined energy:
"The life you gave me burns its acetylene / of buried anger, unused
talents, rotted wishes, / the compost of discontent, flaring into
words / strong for other women under your waning moon"
(*Circles*, p. 280–81). The imagery here is much like Atwood's—the
rotting wishes become compost, hot food for new crops, food for
other women that can flare "into words," so that once-terrifying
hag hands become helpful, nurturing hands that carry one toward
health.

Much of the landscape of Piercy's poetry is one of health, of cycli-
cal, fruitful balance very different from the antilife proportion
espoused by Sir William Bradshaw in Woolf's *Mrs. Dalloway*. Perhaps the best example of such balance leading to energy and health

is the poem "The twelve-spoked wheel flashing" in which image of the wheel of months and seasons describes a merging with the cycles of life and death, light and dark, that result in the poet's becoming a sun herself. For as her own "wheel flashing" she turns like a newborn planet, her own energy lighting other worlds as she whirls:

> A turn of the wheel, I thrust
> up with effort pushing, braced and sweating,
> then easy over down into sleep, body idle,
> and the sweet loamy smell of the earth,
> a turn of the twelve-spoked wheel flashing.

The energy is Piercy's own: she pushes with her own strength, then relaxes, as if accepting that she can move in harmony with the rhythms of the spheres. She accepts that with one turn, she must go "Down into the mud of pain," but that with another, she will revolve "Up into the sun / that ripens you like a pear / bronze and golden, the hope that twines / its strands clambering up to the light / and bears fragrant wide blossoms opening / like singing faces." No destructive, abandoning sun here—instead, it is the poet herself whose alternate pushing and bracing leads her down and then up to this sun that ripens a singing face. She has successfully forged her "life whole, / round, integral as the earth spinning." Turning and turning again and again, this gyre is not widening and losing its center. For Piercy goes "rolling on," she reminds us, "pinned to the wheel of my choice and choosing still . . . learning and forgetting and moving / some part of the way toward / a new and better place" (*Circles*, p. 185). The poet has, of course, in this poem, become a sun herself—a "twelve-spoked wheel" flashing through space.

Perhaps one of Piercy's most positive statements appears in "The Sun," a poem in which she envisions a future for her own followers, perhaps the children of races nurtured in darkness:

> Child, where are you heading with arms spread wide
> as a shore, have I been there, have I seen that land shining
> like sun spangles on clean water rippling?

These children of the future "do not forget their birthright of self / or their mane of animal pride / dancing in and out through the gates of the body standing wide." "The sun is rising, feel it," she commands. "The air smells fresh." And when she affirms, because she can clearly see her "own shadow becoming distinct," that "now at last / it is beginning to grow light" (*Circles*, p. 137), we sense that this will indeed be "another sunshine." For if Piercy's shadow is sharply defined, then she knows that this light will not obliterate, but rather, allow her to see her own outline, see clearly her own essence, even make her own mark on the earth—or announce her arrival in a "different dawn."

Perhaps the time has come for women writers to "dwell in Possibility," no longer needing to fear, like their nineteenth-century American foremother, the prosy warmth of a sun that could rob them of their "gem." Certainly we have seen that during the twentieth century, a number of women writers metaphorically begin to change their own position in relation to the sun, indeed, to change the metaphoric significance of the sun itself. Like Atwood and Piercy, other contemporary women poets also write of their own power as the sun; Diane Wakoski's line "I am / also a ruler of the sun"[95] is one of the most overt statements about a woman's sense of her own energy no longer impeded by cultural restraints. Just as affirming is May Sarton's equation in 1948 of the "pure light that brings forth fruit and flower" with "that great sanity, that sun, that feminine power."[96] No cauldron of morning here. This is a healthy, life-giving sun, a sun of sanity, and here, it is a sun comprised of female energy.

If for any writer or artist, whether male or female, whether a Dickinson or a Whitman, a Plath or a Lowell, the demands of "broad daylight" have often conflicted with the desires of art, the demands of a sun that illuminates and dominates a planet have been experienced by many women writers as particularly associated with gender constraints, with anxieties directly concerned with sexual identity. And if male mystics have long written of the necessary journey through "the dark night of the soul" in order to reach the visions of morning, of the divine "light," the very meanings that culture has ascribed to the natural phenomena of light and darkness have caused even the idea of "divine light" to be fraught with a particular complex of associations whose meanings have caused enormous conflicts for a female writer or thinker. We have seen particularly that Emily Dickinson's reliance upon these metaphors of light and dark emphasizes how painfully she felt herself, as a woman writer, to be at odds with the values and practices of nineteenth-century American culture. Because she experienced her position as a female artist in opposition to a world that associated the sun with God, goodness, language, masculine energy, and sexuality, Dickinson's own journey as a poet to the dark night of her soul and her ability to create her own lights from her own darkness were laden with specific gender-related associations that contributed significantly to the particulars of her metaphoric journey, and to the shape of her own poetic *oeuvre*. That Dickinson was able so brilliantly to transform and transcend the normative metaphoric patterning of her culture, creating in effect a metaphor of her own, has much to do with the genius of her art.

Indeed, Emily Dickinson's use of light/dark metaphors as a dominant motif provides a fascinating example of the relationship between one's own actual daily experiences and cultural metaphorical valuings and practices. Furthermore, her ability to construct a poetry that transcends the dualistic constrictions which would have locked her out of the House of Art raises many questions about the very nature of what we consider "reality." And that so many other women writers, both inhabitants of Dickinson's century and of our own, also treat the same gender- and culture-related issues through metaphors of light and dark serves as powerful reminder of Jonathan Culler's warning that nonlinguistic signs are not "natural" but are simply cultural products, products of shared conventions.

Dickinson's metaphoric strategy, echoed in so many works by so many women writers, has enormous literary and cultural implications. If, whether female or male, semiotician or seamstress, pipefitter or poet, we can revise and reconstruct common cultural metaphorical associational patterns, then it follows that we can, in effect, change the *meanings* of our environments, the meanings of cultural values and practices. Indeed, if, like Dickinson, we can use our own experience to reshape our metaphors, our metaphors can in turn reshape our individual experiences, even our collective culture. If a sun whose hot rays had admonished, judged, sliced, beheaded, seduced, raped, and abandoned, instead can nurture like a warm white womb, the "Possibility" in which we may come to dwell may indeed provide our literature and our society itself with a type of Dickinson's imagined and glorious "different dawn."

What if we thought of the sun as an egg? To paraphrase Adrienne Rich, a whole new metaphor might just begin here.

Notes
Index to Dickinson Poems Cited
Index

Notes

Introduction

1. "Extracts from Addresses to the Academy of Fine Ideas," *The Collected Poems of Wallace Stevens* (New York: Alfred A. Knopf, 1954), p. 258.

2. "Sorties," *La jeune née* (The newly born woman) Union Générale d'Editions, 10/18, 1975, trans. and rpt. in *New French Feminisms*, eds. Elaine Marks and Isabelle de Courtivron (Amherst: University of Massachusetts Press, 1980), p. 90.

3. Thomas H. Johnson, ed., *The Letters of Emily Dickinson*, 3 vols. (Cambridge, Mass.: Belknap Press of Harvard University Press, 1958), II, 203. Hereafter cited as *L*, followed by volume and letter numbers.

4. See *A Concordance to the Poems of Emily Dickinson*, ed. S. P. Rosenbaum, (Ithaca, N.Y.: Cornell University Press, 1964), for references to sun, light, day, and variations of these words.

5. "'Eyes Be Blind, Heart Be Still': A New Perspective on Emily Dickinson's Eye Problem," *New England Quarterly* (September 1979), pp. 400–406.

6. See David Porter, *Dickinson: The Modern Idiom* (Cambridge, Mass.: Harvard University Press, 1981), p. 89. Richard Sewall, one of Dickinson's fairest and most open-minded biographical critics, argues that "she was neither systematic nor consistent. She never set up private symbolic structures as Blake or Yeats did" (*The Life of Emily Dickinson*, 2 vols. [New York: Farrar, Straus & Giroux, 1974], I, 209). Louis Untermeyer writes that Dickinson's lines are "not only self-addressed but written in a code," suggesting that because her poems are so private, any code or system is all but impenetrable (*Modern American Poetry, Mid-Century Edition* [New York: Harcourt, Brace, 1950], p. 7). Albert Gelpi, a brilliant critic of Dickinson, contrasts Dickinson to Whitman: "where his poems grow toward a single organic design, her almost 1800 pieces stand as distinct and contradictory statements" (*The Tenth Muse: The Psyche of the American Poet* [Cambridge, Mass.: Harvard University Press, 1975], p. 22). Even John Cody, whose *After Great Pain: The Inner Life of Emily Dickinson* (Cambridge, Mass.: Belknap Press of Harvard University Press, 1971) is a highly perceptive study of Dickinson's by-now obvious psychotic break, still reads this poet

189

as a psychiatric case, as a woman who would not have had to write poetry if she had been "normal." I begin with the premise that to want to write poetry is normal, even laudable, for women as well as men.

7. See *L* I, 10, 31, 33, 45, 46, among others I shall discuss at length in Ch. 1.

8. Barbara Antonina Clarke Mossberg, *Emily Dickinson: When a Writer Is a Daughter* (Bloomington: Indiana University Press, 1982); Barton Levi St. Armand, *Emily Dickinson and Her Culture: The Soul's Society* (Cambridge University Press, 1984); Shira Wolosky, *Emily Dickinson: A Voice of War* (New Haven: Yale University Press, 1984); Sandra M. Gilbert and Susan Gubar, *The Madwoman in the Attic: The Woman Writer and the Nineteenth-Century Literary Imagination* (New Haven: Yale University Press, 1979); Jack Capps, *Emily Dickinson's Reading* (Cambridge, Mass.: Harvard University Press, 1966).

9. "Nature," *Selections from Ralph Waldo Emerson*, ed. Stephen E. Whicher (Cambridge, Mass.: Riverside Press, 1957), p. 32.

10. Jonathan Culler, *Structuralist Poetics: Structuralism, Linguistics, and the Study of Literature* (Ithaca, N. Y.: Cornell University Press, 1975), p. 5.

11. *Symposium*, trans. W. Hamilton (London: Penguin Books, 1951), pp. 59–60.

12. *The Birth of Tragedy*, trans. William A. Haussmann (Edinburgh: T. N. Foulis, 1910), pp. 23–28.

13. Terry Eagleton's comment is pertinent here, that religion is effective as ideological control because it works "less by explicit concepts or formulated doctrines than by image, symbol, habit, ritual and mythology" (*Literary Theory: An Introduction* [Minneapolis: University of Minnesota Press, 1983], p. 23).

14. *The Female Experience and the Nature of the Divine* (Bloomington: Indiana University Press, 1981), p. 14.

15. See Joseph Campbell, *The Masks of God: Occidental Mythology* (New York: Penguin Books, 1976), esp. pp. 26–29, 80, 111, 199–202, 283–90, 332–41, 389.

16. *New French Feminisms*, pp. 91–92.

17. Discussed in Culler, *On Deconstruction: Theory and Criticism after Structuralism* (Ithaca, N. Y.: Cornell University Press, 1982), p. 58.

18. *The Complete Short Stories of D. H. Lawrence*, 3 vols. (New York: Viking Press, 1961), II, 546–81.

19. Sir James George Frazer, *The Golden Bough: A Study in Magic and Religion*, abr. ed. (New York: Macmillan, 1963), p. 698.

20. Frazer, pp. 686–705.

21. George MacDonald, *The Gifts of the Child Christ: Fairy Tales and Stories for the Childlike*, ed. Glenn Edward Sadler, 2 vols. (Grand Rapids, Mich.: William B. Eerdmans, 1973), I, 17.

22. See Judith Fetterley's Preface to *The Resisting Reader: A Feminist Approach to American Fiction* (Bloomington: Indiana University Press, 1977)

in which she describes her book as a "self-defense survival manual for the woman reader lost in the masculine wilderness of the American novel" (p. viii).

23. MacDonald, "The History of Photogen and Nycteris," pp. 63–101.

24. *Paradise Lost and Selected Poetry and Prose*, ed. Northrop Frye (San Francisco: Rinehart Press, 1951), p. 97.

25. Although I do not want to muddy the metaphorical waters of this study by bringing in questions of a collective unconscious, nevertheless it is pertinent here to mention that Jung has emphasized the sun's connection with male sexuality, citing an image, for instance, in the Mithraic liturgy which shows a phallic tube protruding from the sun. He also cites examples of paintings in which the Virgin Mary is impregnated by a "sort of tube or hose-pipe" coming down from heaven. And perhaps most pertinant of all, he observes that cross-culturally images of sun, light, fire, sex, fertility, and growth are all, as symbolic expressions of the libido, closely associated with speech (*Symbols of Transformation: Analysis of the Prelude to a Case of Schizophrenia*, trans. R. F. C. Hull, 2nd ed., Bollingen Series 20 [Princeton, N. J.: Princeton University Press, 1956], pp. 100–101, 165).

26. See Nicolas J. Perella's *Midday in Italian Literature: Variations on an Archetypal Theme* (Princeton, N. J.: Princeton University Press, 1979) in which Perella demonstrates that image of noon as time of crisis has pervaded Italian literature as a dominant metaphor. See also Reinhard Kuhn, *The Demon of Noontide: Ennui in Western Literature* (Princeton, N. J.: Princeton University Press, 1976), for an exploration of the "demon of noontide" that has for centuries been feared as an almost unconquerable state of *ennui* or spiritual aridity.

27. Perella, pp. 4–9.

28. *Young Emerson Speaks*, ed. A. G. McGiffert (Boston: Houghton Mifflin Co., 1938), pp. 207–8.

29. *Nature, Addresses, and Lectures*, rpt. from Vol. 1 of *Collected Works, 1971*, ed. Alfred R. Ferguson (Cambridge, Mass.: The Belknap Press of Harvard University Press, 1979), p. 35.

30. See Sherman Paul, "The Angle of Vision," *Emerson: A Collection of Critical Essays*, ed. Milton Konvitz and Stephen Whicher, Twentieth Century Views (Englewood Cliffs, N.J.: Prentice-Hall, 1962), pp. 158–78.

31. *Selections*, pp. 416–17.

32. *Walden*, ed. Lyndon Shanley (Princeton, N.J.: Princeton University Press, 1971), pp. 10, 41, 44, 82, 166, 187–88, 240, 309.

33. *Boston Evening Transcript*, 28 September 1894; *Brooklyn Eagle*, 28 April 1892.

34. *Leaves of Grass*, ed. Sculley Bradley and Harold W. Blodgett (New York: W. W. Norton, 1973), pp. 30, 45, 424–33.

35. *The House of the Seven Gables* (New York: W. W. Norton, 1967), pp. 12,

21, 32, 40, 43, 46, 58–59, 68–69, 70–81, 91–92, 100–102, 104, 108–9, 128, 129, 137, 143, 169, 214, 218, 223–24, 285, 300, 305. See also *L* I, 62, in which Dickinson compares herself to Hepzibah in her devotion to her brother.

36. *The Marble Faun*, in *Nathaniel Hawthorne: Novels* (New York: Literary Classics of the United States, 1983), p. 855.

37. *The Scarlet Letter* (New York: Modern Library, 1950), pp. 42–43.

38. As with such characters as Clifford in *The House of the Seven Gables*, Miles Coverdale in *The Blithedale Romance*, and the narrator of such tales as "Sunday at Home."

39. *Moby Dick*, ed. Harrison Hayford and Hershel Parker, (New York: W. W. Norton, 1967), p. 354.

40. *Dickinson and the Romantic Imagination* (Princeton, N. J.: Princeton University Press, 1981), pp. 10–15.

41. *The Prelude*, ed. J. C. Maxwell (Baltimore: Penguin Books, 1971), p. 520.

42. Karl Keller's chapter on Dickinson and Hawthorne in *The Only Kangaroo among the Beauty: Dickinson and America* (Baltimore: Johns Hopkins University Press, 1979) is extremely insightful in its argument that "Dickinson's poems are the narration of a Creation of hers. Her resulting world is a coherent body of disparates, sustained mainly by a contrapuntal language, a fusion of simultaneous opposites. Out of the language of separate realities, she created a fantasy; her poems, like Joyce's language, are play passing into earnestness—magic within the prison" (p. 132).

43. Diehl, p. 36.

44. See Sandra M. Gilbert and Susan Gubar's Introduction, *Shakespeare's Sisters: Feminist Essays on Women Poets* (Bloomington: Indiana University Press, 1979), for their discussion of the difficulty for a woman poet in that the lyric poem, partly by definition, relies upon the strength of a "strong and assertive 'I.'" Gilbert and Gubar argue that women poets have traditionally encountered major obstacles in forcefully defining that "I."

45. Diehl argues that in Keats' poems the sexual act "figures the ultimate imaginative intensity and is consequently creative of essential beauty." But although Keats regards with strong ambivalence the female "supreme embodiment of beauty" as image of "dread power and awesome potency," Dickinson cannot separate lover from precursor poet because, as Diehl demonstrates, Dickinson's muse as Other is father, poet, lover, and Christ (pp. 76–82).

46. Keats, *Letters*, letter no. 62, I, 232, 19 February 1818, to Reynolds.

47. Walter Evert, *Aesthetic and Myth in the Poetry of Keats* (Princeton, N.J.: Princeton University Press, 1965), pp. 30–40.

48. *The Poems of John Keats*, ed. Miriam Allott (New York: W. W. Norton, 1970), pp. 14–17, 85–96.

49. Evert, p. 93.

50. Evert, pp. 107–76. *The Poems of John Keats*, pp. 120–51.

51. See Keats' "Ode to a Nightingale," Coleridge's "Kubla Kahn," and Shelley's "Hymn to Intellectual Beauty."

52. Her delight in books is expressed repeatedly, perhaps most famously in "There is no Frigate like a Book" *P*. 1263. (*The Poems of Emily Dickinson*, ed. Thomas H. Johnson, 3 vols. [Cambridge, Mass.: Belknap Press of Harvard University Press, 1955]. All references to the poems of Dickinson will be by number to the Johnson edition [*P*]. Although R. W. Franklin's *The Manuscript Books of Emily Dickinson*, 2 vols. [Cambridge: Belknap Press of Harvard University Press, 1981], is an exceedingly valuable tool for Dickinson scholars, I have decided for the most part to cite the Johnson edition, since on only a few occasions do I call attention to the placement of a poem in the original fascicle.) Furthermore, according to Thomas Higginson, she explained her first reading experiences ecstatically: "This then is a book! And there are more of them!" (*L* II, 342b). Jack Capps even suggests that a contributing cause of her dissatisfaction at Mount Holyoke was the restriction upon her own reading, p. 17.

53. Such pioneering works as Ellen Moers' *Literary Women* (Garden City, N. Y.: Anchor Press/Doubleday, 1977); Elaine Showalter's *A Literature of Their Own* (Princeton, N.J.: Princeton University Press, 1977); and Sandra M. Gilbert and Susan Gubar's *The Madwoman in the Attic: The Woman Writer and the Nineteenth-Century Literary Imagination* all establish a clear and separate literary tradition of women writers, characterized by distinctive images, metaphors, characters, and themes.

54. *Villette* (New York: Dutton, 1957), pp. 175–86; *Shirley* (New York: Penguin Books, 1974), p. 343.

55. *Jane Eyre* (New York: Random House, 1943), p. 312.

56. See Sandra M. Gilbert's "The Wayward Nun beneath the Hill: Emily Dickinson and the Mysteries of Womanhood," in Suzanne Juhasz, ed., *Feminist Critics Read Emily Dickinson* (Bloomington: Indiana University Press, 1983), for a discussion of Dickinson's worship of female deity as "Sweet Mountains"; see also Gilbert's "From *Patria* to *Matria*: Elizabeth Barrett Browning's 'Risorgimento,'" *PMLA* (March 1984) 194–211, for a discussion of Barrett Browning's vision of matriarchy among the Italian hills. Earlier, Ellen Moers in *Literary Women* had emphasized the frequent occurrence of high, hilly, land as female landscape in the works of a number of women novelists (pp. 390–400).

57. *Middlemarch* (Cambridge, Mass.: Riverside Press, 1956), p. 145.

58. *Daniel Deronda* (New York: Penguin Books, 1967), p. 263.

59. *Selected Brontë Poems*, ed. Edward Chitham and Tom Winnifrith (New York: Basil Blackwell Inc., 1985), pp. 165–66.

60. *Middlemarch*, p. 144. Causaubon, of course, is actually associated with absence from daylight, with Dorothea's imprisonment in marriage, as he

buries himself away from light and health in his ponderous, useless research. However, when Dorothea—or Eliot—describes her first realization of his power over her and of his deadening expectations of her, she describes her new awareness in terms of alien light.

61. Capps, p. 92.

62. Martin Dodsworth has emphasized that "North and South are symbolically states of mind with a personal significance for Margaret" in his Introduction to *North and South* (New York: Penguin Books, 1970), p. 26.

63. One of Dickinson's closest friends, for instance, Samuel Bowles, also ranked *Aurora Leigh* with the Bible (see John Walsh, *The Hidden Life of Emily Dickinson* [New York: Simon and Schuster, 1971]).

64. *The Complete Poetical Works of Elizabeth Barrett Browning* (Houghton, Mifflin, 1900; rpt. St. Clair Shores, Mich.: Scholarly Press, Inc., 1977), Book 2, l. 453; Book 1, l. 325 ff.

65. *Daniel Deronda* (New York: Penguin Books, 1967), p. 306.

66. *The World Split Open: Four Centuries of Women Poets in England and America, 1552–1950*, ed. Louise Bernikow (New York: Vintage Books, 1975), pp. 81–83. Although Finch's imagery reminds one also of the images of male poet John Donne, who writes of a meddlesome sun interrupting lovers, there is a significant difference in Finch's poem—and in Dickinson's poems. For here, the absence of sun allows solitude and an individual peace resulting from an isolate, uninterrupted relation to the world. The night is not significant for its climate appropriate to sexual (or even divine) union. It is the *lack* of such union, in fact, that causes such a sense of peace.

67. Mary E. Coleridge, *Poems* (London: Elkin Mathews, 1908), pp. 6–7.

68. Coleridge, *Poems*, p. 26.

69. *Jane Eyre*, p. 318.

70. See also Elizabeth Barrett Browning's use of the words "veil" and "Vail" in "Casa Guidi Windows," *The Complete Poetical Works*, pp. 248, 253.

71. Coleridge, *Poems*, p. 40.

72. *The World Split Open*, pp. 108–11.

73. *The Complete Poetical Works*, pp. 379–410.

74. "Women and the Alphabet," *Atlantic Monthly*, February 1959, rpt. in *Women and the Alphabet: A Series of Essays* (Boston: Houghton, Mifflin, 1881), pp. 1–36.

75. See "Vesuvius at Home," *Shakespeare's Sisters*, p. 100.

76. *Naked and Fiery Forms: Modern American Poetry by Women, A New Tradition* (New York: Harper & Row, 1976), pp. 1–6.

77. See Mossberg, *Emily Dickinson*, p. 18, where this critic observes that Dickinson's own disclaimer "When I state myself, as the Representative of the Verse—" (*L* II, 268) is actually "a function of her ambivalence toward her own identity."

1.   *Broad Daylight, Cooking Stoves, and the Eye of God*

1. *Poems: Selected and New, 1950–1974* (New York: W. W. Norton, 1974), p. 245.

2. *A Room of One's Own* (New York and Burlingame: Harcourt, Brace & World, 1929), p. 54.

3. See esp. John Crowe Ransom, "Emily Dickinson: A Poet Restored," rpt. Richard B. Sewall, ed. *Emily Dickinson: A Collection of Critical Essays* (Englewood Cliffs, N.J.: Prentice-Hall, 1963), p. 92.

4. *Emily Dickinson*; see esp. Part 2, "The Daughter Construct," pp. 33–96.

5. See Elaine Showalter, *A Literature of Their Own: British Women Novelists from Brontë to Lessing* (Princeton, N.J.: Princeton University Press, 1977): "the repression in which the feminine novel was situated also forced women to find innovative and covert ways to dramatize the inner life" (pp. 27–28). Dickinson did just that—only with poetry.

6. One critic who *has* mentioned the poet's association of "real life" with the sun is Mossberg, who emphasizes the difficulties this poet faced during her daily life, noting briefly that for Dickinson, "day and morning take on the symbolic meaning of the time in which the expectations on her as a dutiful daughter are the greatest and her destiny is most threatened" (*Emily Dickinson*, p. 80). Although I agree wholeheartedly with Mossberg's observation about day's associations for the poet, I am of course also arguing that these images of sun and day comprise an extensive and complex metaphoric pattern.

7. See Jean Strouse, *Alice James: A Biography* (Boston: Houghton Mifflin, 1980).

8. George Whicher, *This Was a Poet: A Critical Biography of Emily Dickinson* (New York: Charles Scribner's Sons, 1938), p. 13.

9. "The Introduction," Cora Kaplan, ed., *Salt and Bitter and Good: Three Centuries of English and American Women Poets* (London: Paddington Press, 1975), p. 62. Earlier in the poem, Finch has complained

> Alas! a woman that attempts the pen,
> Such an intruder on the rights of men . . .

Gilbert and Gubar, in their Introduction to *Shakespeare's Sisters: Feminist Essays on Women Poets*, not only use a section of Finch's poem as epigraph but also stress that Finch's question was still being asked by such twentieth-century women writers as Virginia Woolf.

10. Mossberg, *Emily Dickinson*, pp. 53, 71. Even though Richard Sewall, for instance, in his thorough and fair-minded biography, tries to argue that Dickinson would not have been intimidated by her father, he nevertheless also stresses Edward Dickinson's determination to succeed, to live "ration-

ally," and to occupy a "commanding" position as leader in Amherst and the surrounding community (I, 44-73). I find it fascinating that Sewall suggests that the poet might have helped her father more than she did, that if there is "blame" to be attached in this father/daughter relationship, it should fall on the daughter's shoulders. Sewall is of course reacting against such negative interpretations of Edward's effect on his daughter as John Cody's. Cody had argued that the father's ambitions resulted in extreme ambivalence toward his family, causing all three Dickinson children to be emotionally handicapped (pp. 39–103). What biographers and critics do agree on, however, is that Edward Dickinson was ambitious, determined, busy, and forceful.

11. *Female Education: Tenderness of the Principles Embraced and the System Adopted in the Mount Holyoke Female Seminary* (South Hadley, Mass., 1839), p. 13.

12. *Emily Dickinson and the Image of Home* (Amherst: University of Massachusetts Press, 1975), pp. 76–80.

13. Mossberg's notion is a pertinent one to mention here: she posits that Dickinson "uses obedience as a mode of rebellion," that by "obeying him [Edward Dickinson] to extremes, she seems to be showing the world the absurdity of his commands" (p. 75). My own point here is that, obviously, he *did* command, with the result that she, at least physically or superficially, had to comply.

14. *Emily Dickinson*, p. 60.

15. Margaret Homans notes that Dickinson's humor in this letter "almost makes us forget that this letter represents the usual relations between men and women" (*Women Writers and Poetic Identity* (Princeton, N. J.: Princeton University Press, 1980), p. 197). Also, see Sandra M. Gilbert and Susan Gubar, *The Madwoman in the Attic: The Woman Writer and the Nineteenth-Century Literary Imagination*, who discuss the poet's posing as "essential to her poetic self-achievement," her enactment of the part of a child only one of a series of masks that enable the poet to achieve poetry and transcendence. See esp. pp. 584–610.

16. *Naked and Fiery Forms*, pp. 1–7.

17. See Sewall, pp. 24 ff. It is also interesting to note that her Amherst minister in 1866 declared her "rather less in need of spiritual light than any person he knew" (MacGregor Jenkins, *Emily Dickinson, Friend and Neighbor* (Boston, 1930), quoted in Karl Keller, *The Only Kangaroo among the Beauty*, p. 77). See also Albert Gelpi: "for her the personal God was not the humanly compassionate Son but the awesome Father, the Jehovah-Judge who absorbed all the legalism of the Old Testament into the Calvinist creed." Gelpi also argues that "her choice of vocation was nonetheless made against the authority and will of the Calvinist patriarchy" (*The Tenth Muse: The Psyche of the American Poet*). See also St. Armand, *Emily Dickinson and*

Her Culture, for a brilliant discussion of Dickinson's relation to the excesses of Calvinist rigor, and Shira Wolosky, *Emily Dickinson: A Voice of War*, for a perceptive and thorough analysis of the poet's relation to both the Civil War and the changing role of Calvinism in mid-nineteenth-century America.

18.*Women Writers*, pp. 166–71.

19. Homans' chapter on Dickinson is extremely helpful in its discussion of Dickinson's identification with Eve as Satan's accomplice (esp. p. 169). See also Gilbert and Gubar's chapter in *The Madwoman in the Attic* "Milton's Bogey: Patriarchal Poetry and Women Readers," for a fascinating discussion of women's identification with Milton's Satan, pp. 187–212.

20. See Mossberg's discussion of the relation to Dickinson of food with language, *Emily Dickinson*, pp. 135–46.

21. P. 117–18.

22. Louisa May Alcott, *Little Women* (New York: Collier Books, 1962), p. 119.

23. *The Tenth Muse: The Psyche of the American Poet*, (Cambridge, Mass.: Harvard University Press, 1975) p. 221.

24. "Vesuvius at Home: The Power of Emily Dickinson." pp. 100–101.

25. See Sewall, I, 368-99; see also Keller, pp. 222–50.

26. Millicent Todd Bingham, *Emily Dickinson's Home: Letters of Edward Dickinson and His Family* (New York: Harper, 1955), p. 414.

2.   *Dowering and Depriving*

1. "You ask why sometimes I say stop," *The Twelve-Spoked Wheel Flashing* (New York: Alfred A. Knopf, 1978), p. 68.

2. "Little Girl, My String Bean, My Lovely Woman," Laura Chester and Sharon Barba, eds., *Rising Tides: Twentieth Century American Women Poets* (New York: Washington Square Press, 1973), p. 171.

3. "The Couriers," *Ariel* (New York: Harper & Row, 1961), p. 2.

4. *Emily Dickinson: The Mind of the Poet* (New York: W. W. Norton, 1965), pp. 1–6.

5. Cody, p. 120.

6. *The Madwoman in the Attic*, p. 596.

7. *Feminist Critics Read Emily Dickinson*, p. 85.

8. P. 63. See also St. Armand, *Emily Dickinson and Her Culture*, Ch. 3, for a discussion of what St. Armand labels Dickinson's "solar myth," or, "The Romance of Daisy and Phoebus." Although St. Armand wastes no time speculating whom Dickinson's lover might have been, he does discuss the poet's mysterious relationship to a "Master" as evidenced by sun imagery. St. Armand notes the many references to Apollo or Phoebus figures in the letters or poems.

9. Elsa Green, "The Splintered Crown: A Study of Eve and Emily Dickinson," Diss. University of Minnesota 1959, pp. 109–10.

10. See Sharon Cameron's comment in *Lyric Time: Dickinson and the Limits of Genre* (Baltimore: The Johns Hopkins University Press, 1979) that Dickinson "conceives of immortality not as morning but as 'noon,'" p. 1–2.

11. See Sewall, II, 681.

12. Cameron bases her argument that Dickinson associated immortality with noon on brief readings of "If pain for peace prepares" (*P* 63) and "Where bells no more affright the morn—" (*P* 112). A full discussion of these two poems and their position in the metaphoric spectrum, which is my subject in this volume, follows in Ch. 4.

13. *Dickinson and the Romantic Imagination*, p. 15.

14. See Sewall, I, 161–234; also see *L* II, 239.

15. Karl Keller observes, for instance, that even Sue was, "like almost all the others who made up Emily Dickinson's growing circle of 'literary' friends, messily intrusive." He criticizes, moreover, Sue's frequent inability to discern subtleties in Dickinson's verse, *The Only Kangaroo, pp.* 190–92, 198–210. See also Sewall on the subject of Sue as literary friend to the poet (I, 197, 214).

16. R. W. Franklin, ed., *The Manuscript Books of Emily Dickinson*, pp. 353–78.

17. Thomas Higginson quoted Dickinson as saying, "If I feel physically as if the top of my head were taken off, I know *that* is poetry." *L* II, 342a.

18. "Picnic," *Leaflets* (New York: W. W. Norton, 1969), p. 36.

19. See Cody, pp. 78–79, 83, 263, 273.

20. Cody, pp. 95-98; see also Jean Mudge, pp. 40–42.

21. Keller, p. 144.

22. Martin Wand and Richard B. Sewall, "'Eyes Be Blind, Heart Be Still': A New Perspective on Emily Dickinson's Eye Problem," pp. 400–406.

23. *Literary Women*, pp. 371 ff.

24. See *L* I, 119, in which Dickinson quite obviously refers to poems she and Henry Emmons have exchanged as "flowers" and "immortal blossoms."

25. Mossberg notes the connection between the gem the fingers hold and lose and the pen they must have also held (*Emily Dickinson*, p. 172). See also *P* 613 and *L* I, 171, in which the poet calls poems both "flowers" and "gems."

26. Bingham, p. 235.

27. The fog is an image for protection, for instance, in "I tie my Hat—I crease my Shawl—" (*P* 443); in addition, she wrote Susan Gilbert in 1853 that in her absence, "the world looks staringly, and I find I need more vail" (*L* I, 107).

28. See also *P* 475 in which "doom" is "entered from the Sun"; *P* 226 in

which the "doomed" die next to the sun; and *P* 150 in which a female character dies by leaving "for the sun."

29. Homans, p. 13.

30. David Porter, *Dickinson and the Modern Idiom* (Cambridge, Mass.: Harvard University Press, 1981), pp. 4–5.

31. Quoted in Keller, p. 170.

32. Richard B. Sewall, ed., *The Lyman Letters: New Light on Emily Dickinson and Her Family* (Amherst: University of Massachussetts Press, 1965), p. 52.

33. "You All Know the Story of the Other Woman," *Love Poems* (Boston: Houghton Mifflin, 1969), p. 30.

3.   *Races Nurtured in the Dark*

1. "Where is the Nightingale," *Selected Poems of H. D.* (New York: Grove Press, 1957), p. 52.

2. From an interview by Susan Husserl-Kapit in *Signs* (Winter 1975), rpt. in Elaine Marks and Isabelle de Courtivron, eds., *New French Feminisms: An Anthology* (Amherst: University of Massachusetts Press, 1980), p. 171.

3. *Aurora Leigh*, Book 9, ll. 814–16. In the Dickinson's family copy of *Poems of Elizabeth Barrett Browning* (Dodd, Mead) that is preserved at the Houghton Library at Harvard, this page is marked with a white ribbon.

4. *The Only Kangaroo among the Beauty: Emily Dickinson and America*, p. 6.

5. *L* II, 476c.

6. *The Madwoman in the Attic*, pp. 581–650.

7. *A World Elsewhere: The Place of Style in American Literature* (Oxford University Press, 1966), p. 5.

8. *The Undiscovered Continent*.

9. *Poems*, pp. 5–6.

10. See 9 John 4 and *Sartor Resartus*, Ch. 9, "The Everlasting Yea," *The Norton Anthology of English Literature*, Vol. 2 (New York: W. W. Norton & Company, 1968), p. 66.

11. Martha Dickinson Bianchi, *Emily Dickinson, Face to Face* (Boston: Houghton Mifflin, 1932), p. 66.

12. *Emily Dickinson*, p. 183.

13. *The Poetics of Space* (Boston: Beacon Press, 1969), p. 39.

14. Dickinson apparently read Lowell's "A Good Word for Winter" in the 1870 *Atlantic Almanac*; it is also rpt. in *My Study Windows* (Boston: The Riverside Press, 1871).

15. Both Lawrence's "Bavarian Gentians" and Plath's "Tulips" are interesting to consider in terms of such floral/sexual imagery.

16. *Emily Dickinson*, pp. 143–46.

17. See *P* 348 and *P* 373, for instance.

18. That Dickinson associates the snow with art in this poem is especially interesting in light of the fact that her poem is quite similar to Ralph Waldo Emerson's poem of 1835, "The Snow-Storm." Apparently, Dickinson was so enamoured of one line in particular from Emerson's poem, "Tumultuous privacy of storm," that she copied it and included it in a letter to Mrs. Todd of 1884, (see Jack Capps, p. 175). Dickinson's letter was written over twenty years after her own poem, but undoubtedly she had read Emerson's poem earlier. I find it fascinating that, although personified as male, Emerson's snow, like Dickinson's, retires "as he were not" after he is finished with his art work, with "The frolic architecture of the snow."

19. See Cody, esp. Ch. 9, pp. 397–442, for a discussion of the poet's obsession with sight and blindness as related to her painful ambivalence about her father.

20. Jean Strouse refers to a comment Alice James made about her brother William's language: "She loved his original use of language, quoting in her diary a line he had written after a New England snowstorm: 'The light is shrieking away outside' " (p. 257). The connection between painfully loud noise and snow light is especially interesting in that Dickinson may have experienced such light similarly.

21. See Juhasz' discussion of *P* 419 on pp. 23–24; also Mossberg's discussion of Dickinson's renunciation and letting go of sight in *P* 745, p. 184.

22. Remark made in *Worlds of Light: A Portrait of May Sarton*, film shown 29 December 1979, at MLA Annual Convention in San Francisco. See also St. Armand, *Emily Dickinson and Her Culture*, p. 51 ff, for a brilliant discussion of Dickinson's death motif.

23. Bachelard, *The Poetics of Space*, pp. 18–19.

24. Of course this statement could also be highly ambiguous: as a poet, she is an adult, even a brave one, since she has become accustomed to the soul's "Subterranean Freight." Perhaps she may be suggesting here that whereas dutiful children fear the dark, she—a "bad girl" welcomes it.

25. See Jung's *Symbols of Transformation* for his equation of small digital figures (such as Tom Thumb) with phallic energy, p. 124. See also Dickinson, *L* II, 280, in which the poet signs herself to Higginson as "Your Gnome."

26. See in particular Roderick Nash Smith, *Wilderness and the American Mind*, rev. ed., pp. 23–43, for a discussion of America's historic association of woods and wilderness with the antichrist.

27. See Homans, pp. 171,173.

28. Especially by Cody, pp. 180–82, 437–38;also by Clark Griffith, *The Long Shadow: Emily Dickinson's Tragic Poetry* (Princeton, N. J.: Princeton University Press, 1964) pp. 180–81.

29. See also "A narrow Fellow in the Grass (*P* 986), in which the snake causes the poet the same excitement she experiences reading real poetry,

when she feels so cold nothing can warm her (*L* II, 342a)—as if she feels "Zero at the Bone." Dickinson also refers to language as cooling in a letter to Abiah in which she confides that it makes "me feel so cool, and so very much more comfortable!" (*L* I, 36).

30. *The Madwoman in the Attic*, p. 598.

31. *The Madwoman in the Attic*, pp. 634–38. Albert Gelpi, *Emily Dickinson: The Mind of the Poet*, p. 151.

32. See especially Ann Belford Ulanov, *The Feminine in Jungian Psychology and in Christian Theology* (Evanston, Ill.: Northwestern University Press, 1971), pp. 175–77, for a discussion of female awareness of time as "periodic and rhythmic, as waxing and waning. . . . as a series of unique occurrences. . . . very different from the sense of time as a series of equal or similar moments. It is time as *kairos* rather than as *chronos*."

33. *The Hidden Life of Emily Dickinson* (New York: Simon & Schuster, 1971).

4.   *Dwelling in Possibility*

1. Quoted in Bell Gale Chevigny, *The Woman and the Myth: Margaret Fuller's Life and Writings* (Old Westbury, N. Y.: Feminist Press, 1976), p. 61. Fuller in this fantasy letter to Beethoven asks for "the cold and barren moon" to "give me a son of my own," an interesting plea in light of Dickinson's and Fuller's status as nonsons, as daughters, as Gilbert and Gubar have observed in *The Madwoman in the Attic*, p. 606.

2. Unpublished diary, Bodleian mss. Rawlinson D. 1262, p. 130; D. 1338, 24 January 1693 (unpaginated), rpt. in Catherine F. Smith, "Jane Lead: Mysticism and the Woman Cloathed with the Sun," *Shakespeare's Sisters*, pp. 13–14.

3. *Trilogy* (New York: New Directions, 1973), pp. 30-31.

4. Homans, pp. 176–97.

5. "Poetry, Revisionism, Repression," *Critical Inquiry* 2, No. 2 (Winter 1975), 250.

6. "Jane Lead: Mysticism and the Woman Cloathed with the Sun," *Shakespeare's Sisters*, pp. 17–18.

7. *News of the Universe: poems of twofold consciousness* (San Francisco: Sierra Club, 1980), p. 214.

8. See Johnson's note following *P* 2, *The Poems*, I, and *L* I, 58.

9. See Mossberg, pp. 187–88, who describes Dickinson here as "a generous, creative, powerful, and tempting Eve, who possesses the key to immortality, a literal 'Garden'" but who also "bandaged" this poem in prose while boasting of her poetic powers.

10. See Thoreau's *Walden*, particularly "Sounds," for his discussion of the interruptive quality of the "cogs" and noises of the railroad, its "regular"

time-table, as opposed to the sort of interior, introspective time that he values at Walden Pond.

11. "Nature," *Selections*, p. 27.

12. *Poems*, pp. 24–25.

13. *Shirley*, p. 374.

14. Contrast this image, e.g., to *P* 61, "Papa above!"

15. It is interesting to compare Dickinson's use of veils with Hawthorne's, for instance, with the Veiled Lady in *The Blithedale Romance* in particular.

16. See esp. St. Armand's Ch. 8, "The Art of Peace: Dickinson, Sunsets, and the Sublime."

17. See particularly Wolosky's Introduction and Ch. 3, "War as Theodicean Problem."

18. See Sandra M. Gilbert, "The Wayward Nun beneath the Hill: Emily Dickinson and the Mysteries of Womanhood," in Suzanne Juhasz, ed., *Feminist Critics Read Emily Dickinson*, p. 41–42, who reads this poem as a clear matriarchal prayer.

19. *The Norton Anthology of English Literature*, 2, 159.

20. See *P* 1263, in which the poet asserts "There is no Frigate like a Book / To take us Lands away."

21. *Poems*, p. 24–25.

22. I disagree here with Vivian Pollock in *Dickinson: The Anxiety of Gender* (Ithaca, N. Y.: Cornell University Press, 1984), who reads this as a poem about a testing of sexual innocence.

23. Quoted in Bachelard, *The Poetics of Space*, p. 34.

24. "From *Patria* to *Matria*: Elizabeth Barrett Browning's Risorgimento," *PMLA*, 99 (1984), 194–211.

25. Gilbert and Gubar in *The Madwoman in the Attic* describe this poem as "unmistakably female and violently sexual" (p. 611).

26. "Vesuvius at Home: The Power of Emily Dickinson," in *Shakespeare's Sisters*, pp. 99–121.

27. In this connection it is interesting to read *L* II, 610, in which Dickinson writes of her terror at witnessing a fire in Amherst during the night.

28. Gilbert and Gubar in *The Madwoman in the Attic* describe this poem as one imagining "a female Easter, an apocalyptic day of resurrection on which women would rise from the grave of gender in which Victorian society had buried them alive" (p. 646).

29. *On Poetic Imagination and Reverie*, trans. Collete Gaudin, (Indianapolis: Bobbs Merrill, 1971), p. 25.

30. Emerson's differentiation between mechanical and spiritual time is also pertinent here, in his essay "Works and Days," *Selections*, p. 370, as is Ann Belford Ulanov's observation that "For the feminine style of

consciousness, time is qualitative rather than quantitative" in *The Feminine in Jungian Psychology and in Christian Theology*, p. 175.

31. *Literary Women*, pp. 372–80.

32. See Neumann, *The Great Mother*, pp. 184, 199.

33. See Robert Graves, *The White Goddess* (New York: Farrar, Straus and Giroux, 1948), pp. 223–24.

34. See Mircea Eliade, *Myths, Dreams, and Mysteries* (New York: Harper & Row, 1960), p. 23, for instance.

35. See Robert Bly's trans. of Novalis' poem "The Second Hymn to the Night," which reads in part: "Daylight has got limits and hours, but the hegemony of Night penetrates through space and through time" (p. 49).

36. *The Complete Poetical Works*, pp. 392–93.

37. See the *OED*, p. 374, for a thorough listing of meanings for "antique" and "antiquity."

38. "I Am in Danger—Sir—," *Poems*, p. 85.

5.   Enacting the Difference

1. "Who shall be the sun?" *Who Shall Be the Sun?* (Bloomington: Indiana University Press, 1978), p. 29.

2. "Laying down the tower," *Circles on the Water* (New York: Alfred A. Knopf, 1982), p. 118.

3. *Emily's Bread* (New York: W. W. Norton, 1984), pp. 35, 102.

4. Florence Howe and Ellen Bass, eds., *No More Masks! An Anthology of Poems by Women* (Garden City, N. Y.: Anchor Press/Doubleday Anchor Books, 1973), p. 40–44.

5. *The Yellow Wallpaper* (Old Westbury, N. Y.: The Feminist Press, 1973), pp. 13, 25.

6. *The Yellow Wallpaper*, p. 27.

7. *Wide Sargasso Sea* (New York: Popular Library, 1966).

8. *Herland* (New York: Pantheon Books, 1979).

9. *Mrs. Dalloway* (New York: Harcourt, Brace & World, 1925).

10. *Mrs. Dalloway*, pp. 142, 154.

11. *Mrs. Dalloway*, pp. 152, 154.

12. *A Woman of Letters: A Life of Virginia Woolf* (New York: Oxford University Press, 1978), pp. 126–140.

13. *Mrs. Dalloway*, pp. 280–81.

14. *Mrs. Dalloway*, p. 55.

15. *A Room of One's Own* (New York: Harcourt, Brace & World, 1929), p. 98.

16. *No More Masks!*, p. 40.

17. See, for instance, Susan Stanford Friedman, *Psyche Reborn: The*

Emergence of H. D. (Bloomington: Indiana University Press, 1981); Susan Gubar, "The Echoing Spell of H. D.'s *Trilogy*," *Shakespeare's Sisters*, pp. 200–218; and Rachel Blau DuPlessis, "Romantic Thralldom in H. D.," *Contemporary Literature*, 20, No. 2 (Summer 1979), 181.

18. "Heat," *Selected Poems of H. D.* (New York: Grove Press, 1957), p. 17.
19. *My Antonia* (Boston: Houghton Mifflin, 1918), p. 245.
20. *Selected Poems*, p. 52.
21. See Norman Holmes Pearson, Foreword, *Hermetic Definition,* and also pp. 58–59.
22. *Hermetic Definition*, pp. 71–72.
23. *Hermetic Definition*, pp. 75, 84.
24. *The Poet in the World* (New York: New Directions, 1973), p. 246.
25. "The Moon in Your Hands," *Selected Poems*, p. 66.
26. *New French Feminisms*, p. 174–75.
27. *Love Poems* (Boston: Houghton Mifflin, 1967), p. 30.
28. *The Collected Poems* (New York: Harper & Row, 1981), p. 247. Hereafter cited as *CP.*
29. See Judith Kroll, *Chapters in a Mythology: The Poetry of Sylvia Plath* (New York: Harper & Row, 1976), pp. 24–25.
30. See Robert Bly, *Sleepers Joining Hands* (New York: Harper & Row, 1973), p. 42.
31. *The Journals of Sylvia Plath*, ed. Ted Hughes and Frances McCullough (New York: Dial Press, 1982), p. 324.
32. *The Random House Dictionary of the English Language* (New York: Random House, 1967), p. 922.
33. *Love Poems*, p. 31.
34. "A Fine, White Flying Myth: The Life/Work of Sylvia Plath," *Shakespeare's Sisters*, p. 256.
35. *Shakespeare's Sisters*, p. 102.
36. *Diving into the Wreck* (New York: W. W. Norton, 1973), p. 22.
37. *45 Mercy Street* (Boston: Houghton Mifflin, 1976), p. 57.
38. *Diving*, p. 3.
39. *Diving*, p. 14.
40. *Poems: Selected and New, 1950–1974* (New York: W. W. Norton, 1974), p. 19.
41. *Poems*, p. 101.
42. *Diving*, p. 51.
43. *The Dream of a Common Language* (New York: W. W. Norton, 1978), p. 3.
44. *Poems*, pp. 208–9.
45. *Diving*, p. 20.
46. *Poems*, pp. 43–44.
47. *Diving*, p. 22.

48. *Diving*, p. 5.
49. See Nina Auerbach, *Communities of Women: An Idea in Fiction* (Cambridge, Mass.: Harvard University Press, 1978).
50. *Dream*, p. 51.
51. *Poems*, p. 228.
52. *Dream*, p. 7.
53. *Dream*, pp. 47–52.
54. *Dream*, p. 54–55.
55. *Dream*, p. 60.
56. *A Wild Patience Has Taken Me This Far* (New York: W. W. Norton, 1981), p. 6.
57. *Poems*, p. 71.
58. *Diving*,p. 17.
59. *Dream*, p. 29.
60. *Dream*, pp. 68–71; *A Wild Patience*, p. 40.
61. *Wild Patience*, pp. 8–9.
62. *Poems*, p. 74.
63. *Dream*, p. 59.
64. *Dream*, p. 72–77.
65. *Women Writers*, p. 229.
66. *You Are Happy* (New York: Harper & Row, 1974), p. 33.
67. *The Journals of Susanna Moodie* (Toronto: Oxford University Press, 1970), pp. 24, 33.
68. *You Are Happy*, p. 15.
69. *Power Politics*, (New York: Harper & Row, 1971), p. 33.
70. *Power*, p. 43.
71. *Power*, p. 28.
72. *Power*, p. 45.
73. *Procedures for Underground* (Boston: Little, Brown, 1970), p. 59.
74. *You Are Happy*, p. 31.
75. *You Are Happy*, p. 32.
76. *Journals*, p. 48.
77. *Procedures*, pp. 16–17.
78. "*Surfacing*: Margaret Atwood's Journey to the Interior," *Modern Fiction Studies*, 22 (1976), 387–400.
79. *Journals*, pp. 16–17.
80. *Procedures*, p. 72.
81. *Journals*, p. 27.
82. *Surfacing* (New York: Popular Library, 1976), p. 172, 190.
83. *You Are Happy*, p. 93.
84. *Procedures*, p. 24.
84. *You Are Happy*, p. 35.
86. *You Are Happy*, p. 27–28.

87. *The Poetics of Space*, p. 28.

88. *Power*, p. 47.

89. *You Are Happy*, p. 66.

90. *You Are Happy*, p. 40.

91. *You Are Happy*, p. 79.

92. *Procedures*, pp. 8–9

93. *Circles on the Water* (New York: Alfred A. Knopf, 1982), p. 33. Hereafter cited as *Circles*.

94. *No More Masks*, pp. 169–70.

95. "Sun Gods Have Sun Spots," 1973.

96. Gilbert and Gubar, eds., *The Norton Anthology of Literature by Women* (New York: W. W. Norton, 1985), pp. 1772–73.

Index to Dickinson Poems Cited

Index

Wendy Barker is an associate professor of English at the University of Texas at San Antonio. She won the Ithaca House Poetry Series Competition in 1990, and also in the same year published two collections of poems, *Let the Ice Speak* and *Winter Chickens*. Frequently anthologized, her poems have also appeared in many journals including, among others, *Poetry,* the *American Scholar,* the *Bloomsbury Review,* and *Poetry Now*. In 1986, Barker was awarded a creative writing fellowship in poetry by the National Endowment for the Arts. Her critical essays have appeared in such journals as the *New England Quarterly* and the *Iowa Review*.